"HEADACHE?"

INJURY —

NEIGHBORHOOD MISCHIEF...

+ MULTIPLE HOSPITAL VISITS

"ONLY AS HAPPY AS UNHAPPIEST CHILD"

BLOOD

SWEDEN —
STADIUM
FALL
DOCTOR
HOSPITAL / X RAY

ALTAR / CARPORT

MANIFESTATION / LAW OF ATTRACTION

HARPER

"WALK HOME"

DRUMS.
TEETH.
FEEL. (DEFINE)
SPIRITUAL / RELIGION
CATHOLIC SCHOOL
UNDERSTANDING FAITH
SOLD MY SOUL....

SUMMER ___ OHIO — CHICAGO

TRACEY / PUNK ROCK
RECORD COLLECTION ← UNDERGROUND
NAKED RAYGUN
CUBBY BEAR / STRUM
DISCOVERY / INSPO

JOURNEY HOME / NEW BEGINNING

END CREDITS

"WANNA PLAY SOME ZEP / ACDC?"
SCREAM / AUDITION
LOCAL HEROES
LEARNED FROM RECORDS (SCREAM)
CROSSROADS — SCHOOL / HOME / DAD / D.B.
"YOU'D BETTER BE GOOD..."
FIRST TOUR
VAN
TRAVELS NYC - DETROIT - CHICAGO - WEST
BEGINNING

"PRIVACY / 400 ACRES"
OUT OF SEATTLE "GHOSTS"
VIRGINIA
HOUSE HUNTING. TOO MUCH, TOO SOON.
BUILDING STUDIO / OUT OF CONTRACT
TRANS U.S. DRIVE
PANTERA
JIMMY — HOME
KITTEN / MOM
3RD RECORD
DIDN'T HAVE TO BE A BAND

PSYCHIC / SYDNEY
BIG DAYOUT FEST...
UFO'S / GHOSTS / AURA
WA
SEATTLE HOUSE
DREAMS!
DUI
JAIL

LIFE TAKES ITS COURSE

"DO YOU MIND IF WE TAKE A BREAK?"
— TATTOO / FOLGER THING
— OLYMPIA / 400 BUCKS
NIRVANA
REHEARSALS BARN
HISTORY / 5TH DRUMMER
SIGN TO DGC / PRODUCER
TRIP TO L.A. ← OK HOTEL
NOT COMING BACK
"FOLGER THING"

"SEE YOU DOWN THERE, DUDE"
WHITE HOUSE
HOW DID I GET HERE?
KENNEDY CENTER
GIG
SPEECH — WINGED IT
PHOTO WITH W
PAUL / OBAMA
NERVOUS / PRINT
CROSS THE B

TORONTO
RIVOLI —
SOUNDCHECK — POSTERS
IGGY — HISTORY
KICKED OUT.
VAN
"WHO'S THE DRUMMER?"

THE STORYTELLER

The Storyteller

TALES OF LIFE AND MUSIC

Dave Grohl

SIMON &
SCHUSTER

London · New York · Sydney · Toronto · New Delhi

I WOULD LIKE TO THANK THE NUMEROUS PHOTOGRAPHERS WHO
SHARED THEIR WORK WITH US FOR THE CREATION OF THIS
BOOK. THESE IMAGES ENHANCE THE STORIES SO MUCH.

Pages i, 4, 10, 22, 29, 34, 37, 51, 63, 70, 79, 82, 98, 116, 123, 135, 161, 176, 180, 187, 190, 244, 256, 278, and 360: courtesy of the author's personal archives; pages ii, viii, 240, 372, and 378 in Target edition: courtesy of Magdalena Wosinska; page 8: courtesy of Kevin Mazur; page 55: courtesy of the author's personal archives c/o Ruthless Records; pages 76, 101, 102, 105, 106, 109, and 112: courtesy of Virginia Grohl's personal archives; pages 148 and 157: courtesy of Charles Peterson; page 192: courtesy of John Silva/ SAM; pages 206, 210, 229, 231, 232, 270, 297, 301, 315, and 351: courtesy of Danny Clinch; pages 237, 318, 334, and 340: courtesy of Jordyn Blum; page 252: courtesy of Mary McCartney; page 285: courtesy of Ross Halfin; page 322: courtesy of Brantley Guitterrez; page 371: courtesy of Andreas Neumann

━ ━ ━

First published in the United States by Dey Street Books, an imprint of William Morrow, 2021
First published in Great Britain by Simon & Schuster UK Ltd, 2021

Copyright © David Eric Grohl, 2021

1 3 5 7 9 10 8 6 4 2

Simon & Schuster UK Ltd
1st Floor
222 Gray's Inn Road
London WC1X 8HB

www.simonandschuster.co.uk
www.simonandschuster.com.au
www.simonandschuster.co.in

Simon & Schuster Australia, Sydney
Simon & Schuster India, New Delhi

A CIP catalogu

Printed in t

FOR VIRGINIA GROHL.
Without her, my stories would be very different.

FOR JORDYN BLUM.
You made my story so much more exciting and beautiful.

FOR VIOLET, HARPER, AND OPHELIA.
May each of your stories be as unique and as amazing as you are.

CONTENTS

PART FOUR: CRUISING

PART FIVE: LIVING

INTRODUCTION

TURN IT UP

Sometimes I forget that I've aged.

My head and my heart seem to play this cruel trick on me, deceiving me with the false illusion of youth by greeting the world every day through the idealistic, mischievous eyes of a rebellious child finding happiness and appreciation in the most basic, simple things.

Though it only takes one quick look in the mirror to remind me that I am no longer that little boy with a cheap guitar and a stack of records, practicing alone for hours on end in hopes of someday breaking out of the confines and expectations of my suburban Virginia, Wonder Bread existence. No. Now my reflection bares the chipped teeth of a weathered smile, cracked and shortened from years of microphones grinding their delicate enamel away. I see the heavy bags beneath my hooded eyes from decades of jet lag, of sacrificing sleep for another precious hour of life. I see the patches of white within my beard. And I am thankful for all of it.

Years ago, I was asked to perform at the 12-12-12 Hurricane Sandy relief concert in New York City. Held at Madison Square Garden, it featured the Mount Rushmore of rock and roll lineups: McCartney, the Rolling Stones, the Who, Roger Waters, and countless other household names. At one point, I was approached by a promoter who asked if I would join some of these most iconic artists in the greenroom to take photos with some fans who had donated large sums of money to the cause. Honored to be involved, I happily obliged and made my way through the maze of backstage corridors, imagining a room full of rock and roll history, all standing in an elementary school photo formation, nothing but leather jackets and British accents. As I entered, I was surprised to find only two of the performers, standing at opposite ends of the space. One had the shiny appearance of a brand-new luxury car. Perfectly dyed hair, spray tan, and a recently refurbished smile that had the look of a fresh box of Chiclets (an obvious attempt at fending off the aging process, which ultimately had the adverse effect, giving the appearance of an old wall with too many layers of paint). The other had the appearance of a vintage, burned-out hot rod. Wiry gray hair, deep lines carved into a scowl, teeth that could have belonged to George Washington, and a black T-shirt that hugged a barrel-chested frame so tightly, you immediately knew that this was someone who did not give one flying fuck.

Epiphany may seem cliché, but in a flash I saw my future. I decided right then and there that I would become the latter. That I would celebrate the ensuing years by embracing the toll they'd take on me. That I would aspire to become the rusted-out hot rod, no matter how many jump-starts I might require along the way. Not everything needs a shine, after all. If you leave a Pelham Blue Gibson Trini Lopez guitar in the case for fifty years, it will look like it was just delivered from the factory. But if you take it in your hands, show it to the sun, let it breathe, sweat on it, and fucking PLAY it, over time the finish will turn a unique shade. And each instrument ages entirely differently. To me, that is beauty. Not the gleam of prefabricated perfection, but the road-worn beauty of individuality, time, and wisdom.

Miraculously, my memory has remained relatively intact. Since I was a child, I have always measured my life in musical increments rather than months or years. My mind faithfully relies on songs, albums, and bands to remember a particular time and place. From seventies AM radio to every microphone I've stood before, I could tell you who, what, where, and when from the first few notes of any song that has crept from a speaker to my soul. Or from my soul to your speakers. Some people's reminiscence is triggered by taste, some people's by sight or smell. Mine is triggered by sound, playing like an unfinished mixtape waiting to be sent.

Though I have never been one to collect "stuff," I do collect moments. So, in that respect, my life flashes before my eyes and through my ears every single day. In this book, I've captured some of them, as best I can. These memories, from all over my life, are full of music, of course. And they can be loud at times.

TURN IT UP. LISTEN WITH ME.

PART ONE

SETTING THE SCENE

DNA
DOESN'T
LIE

"Dad, I want to learn how to play the drums."

I knew this was coming.

There stood my eight-year-old daughter, Harper, staring at me with her big brown eyes like Cindy Lou Who from *How the Grinch Stole Christmas,* nervously holding a pair of my splintered drumsticks in her tiny little hands. My middle child, my mini-me, my daughter who physically resembles me the most. I had always known that she would someday have an interest in music, but . . . drums? Talk about an end-of-the-trough, entry-level mailroom position!

"Drums?" I replied with eyebrows aloft.

"Yeah!" she squeaked through her toothy grin. I took a moment to think, and as the sentimental lump began to balloon in my throat I asked, "Okay . . . and you want me to teach you?" Shifting in her checkered Vans sneakers, she shyly nodded and said, "Uh-huh," and a wave of fatherly pride instantly washed over me, along with an enormous smile. We hugged and headed hand in hand upstairs to the old drum set in my office. Like a weepy Hallmark moment, the kind those hyperemotional Super Bowl commercials are made of (the ones that would leave even the hardest monster truck enthusiast crying in their buffalo chicken dip), this is a memory that I will cherish forever.

The moment we entered my office, I remembered that I had never taken any formal lessons, and therefore I had no idea how to teach someone to play the drums. The closest I had ever come to any structured music instruction was a few hours with an extraordinary jazz drummer by the name of Lenny Robinson who I used to watch perform every Sunday afternoon at a local Washington, DC, jazz joint called One Step Down. A tiny old club on Pennsylvania Avenue just outside of Georgetown, One Step Down not only was a hotspot for established touring acts but also hosted a jazz workshop every weekend where the house band (led by DC jazz legend Lawrence Wheatley) would perform a few sets to the dark, crowded room and then invite up-and-coming musicians to jam with them onstage. When I was a teenager in the eighties, those workshops

became a Sunday ritual for my mother and me. We would sit at a small table ordering drinks and appetizers while watching these musical masters play for hours, reeling in the gorgeous, improvisational freedom of traditional jazz. You never knew what to expect within those bare brick walls, smoke hanging in the air, songs from the small stage the only sound (talking was strictly forbidden). At the time, I was fifteen years old and deep in the throes of my punk rock obsession, listening to only the fastest, noisiest music I could find, but I somehow connected to the emotional elements of jazz. Unlike the convention of modern pop (which at the time I recoiled from, just like the kid from *The Omen* in church), there was a beauty and dynamic in the chaotic tapestry of jazz composition that I appreciated. Sometimes structured, sometimes not. But, most of all, I loved Lenny Robinson's drumming. This was something I had never seen before at a punk rock show. Thunderous expression with graceful precision; he made it all look so easy (I now know it's not). It was a sort of musical awakening for me. Having taught myself to play the drums by ear on dirty pillows in my bedroom, I'd never had anyone standing over me to tell me what was "right" or "wrong," so my drumming was wild with inconsistency and feral habits. I WAS ANIMAL FROM THE MUPPETS, WITHOUT THE CHOPS. Lenny was obviously somewhat trained, and I was in awe of his feel and control. My "teachers" back then were my punk rock records: fast, dissonant, screaming slabs of noisy vinyl, with drummers who most would not consider *traditional,* but their crude brilliance was undeniable, and I will always owe so much to these unsung heroes of the underground punk rock scene. Drummers like Ivor Hanson, Earl Hudson, Jeff Nelson, Bill Stevenson, Reed Mullin, D. H. Peligro, John Wright . . . (the list is painfully long). To this day you can hear echoes of their work in mine, with their indelible impression making its way into tunes like "Song for the Dead" by Queens of the Stone Age, "Monkey Wrench" by Foo Fighters, or even Nirvana's "Smells Like Teen Spirit" (just to name a few). All those musicians were seemingly worlds away from Lenny's scene, but one thing that they all had in common was that same feeling of beautiful, structured chaos that I loved each Sunday at One Step Down. And that's what I strove to achieve.

One humid summer afternoon, my mother and I decided to celebrate her birthday by taking in another weekly jazz workshop at the club. It had quickly become our "thing," one that I still look back on today with fond memories. None of my other friends actually hung out with their parents, especially not at a fucking jazz club in downtown DC, so it made me think she was intrinsically cool and this was another way of strengthening our bond. In the age of Generation X, of divorce and dysfunction, we were actually friends. Still are! That particular day, after a few baskets of fries and a few sets from Lawrence Wheatley's quartet, my mother turned to me and asked, "David, would you go up and sit in with the band as a birthday present to me?" Now, I don't remember exactly what my initial response was, but I'm pretty sure it was something along the lines of "ARE YOU OUT OF YOUR FUCKING MIND?" I mean, I had only been playing the drums (pillows) for a few years, and having learned from the old, scratched punk rock records in my collection, I wasn't anywhere NEAR ready to step up and play JAZZ with these badasses. This was a fantastically unimaginable request. This was being thrown to the lions. This was a disaster waiting to happen. But . . . this was also my mom, and she had been cool enough to bring me here in the first place. So . . .

Reluctantly, I agreed to do it, and slowly got up from our little table, weaving through the packed room of jazz enthusiasts to the coffee-stained sign-up sheet next to the stage. It had two columns: "Name" and "Instrument." I read through the list of other seemingly accomplished musicians' names on the list and, with pen shaking in hand, quickly scribbled "David Grohl—drums." I felt like I was signing my own death warrant. I stumbled back to our table in a daze, feeling all eyes on me as I sat down and immediately started sweating through my ripped jeans and punk rock T-shirt. What had I just done? Nothing good could come from this! The minutes seemed like hours as musician after amazing musician was called up to entertain those hallowed walls and hardened ears. Every one of them could hang with those jazz cats just fine. I became less and less confident with each moment. My stomach was in knots, my palms sweating, my heart racing, as I sat and tried my best to follow the band's mind-bending time signatures, wondering how on earth I could possibly keep up with the skill of the incredible instrumentalists who graced this stage every week. *Please don't let me be next,* I thought. *Please, god . . .*

Before long, Lawrence Wheatley's deep baritone drawl came booming over the PA speakers and announced the dreaded words that still haunt me to this day: "Ladies and gentlemen, please welcome . . . on the drums . . . David Grohl."

I tentatively stood to a smattering of applause, which quickly dissipated once the people saw that I was clearly not a seasoned jazz legend, but rather a skinny suburban punk with funny hair, dirty Converse Chucks, and a T-shirt that read KILLING JOKE. The horror in the band's faces as I walked to the stage made it look as if the Grim Reaper himself were approaching. I stepped onstage, the great Lenny Robinson handed me his sticks as I reluctantly sat on his throne, and for the first time I saw the room from his perspective. No longer sheltered behind the safety of my mother's table full of snacks, I was now literally in the hot seat, frozen under the stage lights with the eyes of every audience member bearing down on me as if to say, "Okay, kid . . . show us what you've got." With a simple count, the band kicked into something I had never played before (i.e., any jazz song ever), and I did my best to just keep time without fainting in a pool of my own vomit. No solo, no flash, just hold down the tempo and don't fuck it up. Thankfully, it went by in a flash (sans vomit) and without incident. Unlike most of the other musicians who had performed that day, I had a song that was surprisingly short (though certainly not unintentionally). Imagine that! Done and dusted, I walked away with the relief one feels at the end of root canal surgery. I stood and thanked the band, mouth dry, with a nervous smile, and took an awkward bow. If the band had only known my intention, they would have understood such a desperate act of foolishness. With every ounce of charity in these poor musicians' hearts, they had unknowingly allowed me to give my mother a birthday gift that she would never forget (to the dismay of about seventy-five paying customers), which meant more to me than any standing ovation I could have wished for. Humbled, I walked back to our little table of hors d'oeuvres in shame, thinking that I had a long, long way to go before I could ever consider myself a real drummer.

That fateful afternoon lit a fire in me. Inspired by failure, I decided that I needed to learn how to play the drums from someone who actually knew what they were doing, rather than stubbornly trying to figure it out all by myself on my bedroom floor. And in my mind, there was only one person to show me how: the great Lenny Robinson.

A few Sundays later, my mother and I returned to One Step Down, and with my naive courage barely summoned, I cornered Lenny on his way to the bathroom. "Umm . . . excuse me, sir. Do you give lessons?" I asked in my best *Brady Bunch* mumble. "Sure, man. Thirty dollars an hour," he said. I thought, *Thirty dollars an hour? That's six lawns I'd have to mow in the suffocating Virginia heat! That's a weekend's pay at Shakey's pizza! That's an eighth of an ounce of weed I'd have to not smoke this week. DEAL.* We exchanged phone numbers and set a date. I was well on my way to becoming the next Gene Krupa! Or so I hoped . . .

Our thirteen-hundred-square-foot house in Springfield was nowhere near big enough for a full drum set (hence the ad hoc, makeshift pillow practice set in my tiny bedroom), but for this special occasion I brought in the bottom-of-the-line five-piece Tama kit from my band Dain Bramage's practice space, nowhere near Lenny's caliber of gear. I awkwardly placed the dirty drums in front of the living room stereo and shined them up with some Windex I found under the kitchen sink as I anxiously awaited his arrival, hoping that soon all the neighbors would hear him ripping it to shreds . . . and think that it was me!

"He's here! He's here!" I exclaimed as if Santa Claus had just pulled into our driveway. Barely containing myself, I greeted him at the door and invited him into our little living room, where the drums sat shining, still reeking of barely dry glass cleaner. He sat down on the stool, surveyed the instrument, and proceeded to blaze those same impossible riffs that I had seen so many Sundays at the jazz club, a blur of hands and sticks delivering machine gun drumrolls in perfect time. Mouth agape, I couldn't believe this was happening on the same stretch of carpet where I had spent my life dreaming of becoming a world-class drummer someday. It was finally real. This was my destiny. I was soon to become the next Lenny Robinson, as his riffs would soon become mine.

"Okay," he said when he finished. "Let's see what you can do."

With every ounce of courage I could muster, I launched into my "greatest hits" montage of riffs and tricks that I had stolen from all of my punk rock heroes, crashing and smashing that cheap drum set like a hyperactive child having a full-blown tantrum in an explosion of raw, rhythmless glory. Lenny watched closely and with a stern look quickly realized the amount of work that was going to be required in this gig. After a few cacophonous minutes of disastrous soloing, he stopped me and said, "Okay . . . first of all . . . you're holding your sticks backward." Lesson one. Embarrassed, I quickly flipped them around to their proper direction and apologized for such a rookie move. I had always held them backward because I thought the fat end of the stick would produce a much bigger sound when it hit the drums, which proved effective in my brand of Neanderthal pummeling. I didn't realize it was practically the antithesis of proper jazz drumming. Silly me. He then showed me a traditional grip, taking the stick in my left hand and placing it through my thumb and middle finger, just like all the true drumming greats had done before him, and definitely before me. This simple adjustment completely erased everything I had thought I knew about drumming up until that point, rendering me debilitated behind the kit, as if I were learning to walk all over again after a decade-long coma. As I struggled to keep hold of the stick in this impossible new fashion, he started showing me simple, single-stroke rolls on a practice pad. Right-left-right-left. Slowly hitting the pad to find a consistent balance, over and over again. Right-left-right-left. Again. Right-left-right-left. Before I knew it, the lesson was over, and it was then that I realized at thirty dollars an hour, it was probably cheaper for me to go to Johns Hopkins and become a fucking brain surgeon than to learn how to play drums like Lenny Robinson. I handed him the money, thanked him for his time, and that was that. My only drum lesson.

"Okay . . . ummm . . . so, this is the kick drum. Your foot goes there," I said as Harper's tiny sneaker rested on the bass pedal. "This is your hi-hat; your other foot goes there." She settled into her seat, sticks in hand, ready to whale. Not knowing what the hell

I was doing, I fast-forwarded past all of the confusing right-left-right-left bullshit that Lenny Robinson had shown me (all respect, Lenny) and went straight to teaching her a beat. "Ummm . . . okay . . . here's a simple kick-snare pattern . . ." After a few frustrating attempts, I stopped her and said, "Wait. I'll be right back," as I ran out of the room. I knew what she needed. It wasn't me. It was AC/DC's *Back in Black*.

I put on the title track and told her to listen. "Hear that?" I asked. "That's the kick drum. And that's the hi-hat. And that's the snare drum." She listened closely and started to play. Her timing was incredibly solid, which any drummer knows is more than half the battle. She had a natural, built-in meter, and once she settled into the coordination of her movements, she started playing with tremendous feel. I jumped and cheered as my heart swelled with pride, headbanging and singing along with the lyrics as Harper played. Then something curious struck me: her posture. Her broad back arched forward slightly, angular arms and skinny elbows positioned out a bit, chin raised above the snare . . . and I saw it. SHE WAS A MIRROR IMAGE OF ME PLAYING THE DRUMS AT HER AGE. I felt as if I were time-traveling and having an out-of-body experience all at once. Not only that, but here was my mini-me, my grinning twin, learning to play the drums exactly as I had thirty-five years before: by listening to music with her parent. I wasn't necessarily surprised, though. Like I said, I always knew this was coming.

As I offered in the foreword to my mother's book, *From Cradle to Stage*, I believe that these musical impulses aren't so much a mystery as they are perhaps predetermined, residing somewhere deep within the DNA strand, just waiting to be unlocked.

I wrote, "DNA is a miraculous thing. We all carry traits of people we have never met somewhere deep within our chemistry.

I'm no scientist, but I believe that my musical abilities are proof of this. There is no divine intervention here. This is flesh and blood. This is something that comes from the inside out. The day that I picked up a guitar and played Deep Purple's 'Smoke on the Water' by ear, I knew that all I needed was that DNA and a whole lot of patience (something that my mother clearly had an abundance of). These ears and this heart and mind were born of someone. Someone who shared that same love of music and song. I was blessed with a genetic symphony, waiting to perform. All it took was that spark."

In Harper's case, that "spark" had just come the day before as she sat in her seat at the Roxy nightclub on Sunset Boulevard, watching her older sister, Violet, play her first show at the ripe old age of eleven.

Yes, I knew that one was coming, too.

Violet was an intensely verbal child. By the age of three, she was already speaking with the clarity and vocabulary of a much older kid, often stunning unsuspecting waiters at restaurants from her booster seat with fully enunciated requests like "Excuse me, sir? Could I please have some more butter for my bread?" (I practically pissed my pants laughing every time, watching people do a double take as if we were a twisted ventriloquist act.) Once, while she was having a tantrum over something at the dinner table at home, I tried to calm her by saying, "Look, it's okay, everyone gets angry sometimes. Even I get angry!" to which she responded, "I'm not angry! I'm just FRUSTRATED!" (I *still* don't know the difference, but Violet does.) I eventually realized that she had a strong aural memory and an advanced sense of pattern recognition, which made it easy for her to imitate or repeat things perfectly by ear. That soon led to doing accents by request, where she would run through spot-on imitations of an Irish person, a Scottish person, an English person, an Italian person, and so on, all before she was even out of her smoothie-stained car seat.

Before long, Violet's love of music attuned her ear to pitch, key, and tone. As she sang from the back seat, I began to hear her zeroing in on the subtle movements of each of her favorite singers' voices. The harmonies of the Beatles, the vibrato of Freddie Mercury, the soul of Amy Winehouse (perhaps the most memorable, as there's nothing like hearing your five-year-old daughter sing "Rehab" word for word while wearing *Yo Gabba Gabba!* pajamas). It was clear that she had the gift. Now it was only a matter of time before she found the spark.

That spark eventually became a wildfire, and music became her life's divining rod, until in time she formed a rock band with her classmates. She became stronger and more confident with every performance, with a voracious and wonderfully diverse ear for music, singing along to everything from Aretha Franklin to the Ramones, widening her range as she set forth on a path of discovery and inspiration. Her genetic symphony was in concert, and all we could do was sit back and listen. After all, this is something that comes from the inside out.

That day of Violet's performance at the Roxy on Sunset Boulevard, the first "official" show with her band, I sat with my family in the audience as she sang her set. "Don't Stop Believin'" by Journey, "Hit Me with Your Best Shot" by Pat Benatar, and "Sweet Child O' Mine" by Guns N' Roses were my personal faves, but during the performance, I had to stop and take in the moment. To my left, Harper's eyes were filled with dreams of becoming a musician someday; to my right, my mother was proudly witnessing another generation of her family baring their soul to a room full of strangers. It was a profound experience, best summed up in a text my mother sent the next day that read, "Now YOU know what it's like to nervously sit in an audience as YOUR child steps onstage for the first time to follow their life passion with a funny haircut, dressed in jeans and a t-shirt." She was right. THIS WASN'T DIVINE INTERVENTION. THIS WAS FLESH AND BLOOD.

Since then, I have performed with both of my children in front of thousands of people around the world, and each time I am filled with a feeling much like my mother's pride on that humid summer afternoon at One Step Down so many years ago. It is my life's greatest gift to see the passion and courage of my own children as they take that leap, and I hope that someday *their* children will somehow feel the same joy and echo the final words that I wrote for my mother's book years ago:

"But, beyond any biological information, there is love. Something that defies all science and reason. And that I am most fortunate to have been given. It's maybe the most defining factor in anyone's life. Surely an artist's greatest muse. And there is no love like a mother's love. It is life's greatest song. We are all indebted to the women who have given us life. For without them, there would be no music."

THE
HEARTBREAK
OF SANDI

Her name was Sandi.

And she was my first heartbreak.

It was 1982, and as a gangly thirteen-year-old entering seventh grade, I was overwhelmed with the nervous excitement of meeting all the new, unfamiliar faces at Holmes Intermediate School. Life up until that point had been confined to my quaint little North Springfield neighborhood, surrounded by the same kids I had grown up with since kindergarten in our suburban maze of rolling hills and crowded cul-de-sacs. Just twelve miles south of Washington, DC, North Springfield was nothing more than a rural crossroads until it was eventually subdivided in the late 1950s and early '60s and developed into winding streets lined with small, cookie-cutter brick homes. The American dream. There were only three types of houses where I'm from: the one-level econo-model, the split-level *Brady Bunch* model, and the two-story mac-daddy party crib (all under 1,700 square feet), planted on tiny lots, yard after yard. Take a wild guess which one I lived in. That's right, econo all the way, baby. With three bedrooms and one bath, it was just enough space for my mother to comfortably raise two children on her meager Fairfax County Public Schools salary. We never had much, but we always had enough. North Springfield was a tight community of mostly young families; there were no real strangers there. It was a community where everyone knew your name, which street you lived on, and which church you attended after your juicy divorce. In turn, each block hosted its own gang of scruffy hoodlums who terrorized the otherwise friendly sidewalks (mine included), and I spent my childhood climbing trees, chewing tobacco, playing hooky, lighting firecrackers, searching the creeks for crawfish, and spray-painting walls with the best of them. A faded Kodachrome portrait come to life, this was true seventies Americana shit. Banana-seat bikes and BB guns. A life somewhere between Rob Reiner's *Stand by Me* and Tim Hunter's classic *River's Edge*.

The prospect of moving on to another school filled with kids from different, outlying neighborhoods seemed practically international to me. I had been walking the single block to my elementary school around the corner my entire life. I had carefully prepared for this next step, though. With a few new shirts purchased at the discount fashion outlets off the Pennsylvania Turnpike and a fresh bottle of Old Spice, I looked forward to branching out and finally finding my niche. Maybe even meeting my suburban soul mate beneath the fluorescent lights of the locker-lined hallways at my new school. I had never been in love, but I knew she was out there, somewhere.

With a big plastic comb tucked into the back pocket of my corduroy pants and dirty Nike sneakers, I boarded that bus every day in hopes that I'd make it to the final bell without either getting my ass kicked or getting expelled. I was a fucking horrible student, and I was already in the early stages of my punk rock chrysalis, having discovered the B-52s and Devo on *Saturday Night Live,* somehow connecting to the subversive, radical aesthetic of their music, so I was taking baby steps in the shadows. AS MUCH AS I WANTED TO FIT IN AND BE ACCEPTED WITHIN MY CIRCLE OF FRIENDS, DEEP DOWN I FELT DIFFERENT. It would be years before I found the courage to embrace my individuality, but at the time I was almost closeted, hiding my love of alternative culture for fear that I would be ostracized by the cooler kids. I *played along,* I suppose, but knew that I wasn't necessarily cut out for the Key Club or the football team. I was a bit of a misfit, longing to feel understood, waiting for someone to accept the real me.

And then, I saw her.

Sandi was the most beautiful girl I had ever seen. Ice-blue eyes, feathered blond hair, and a smile so blinding it could have charged every Tesla from Brentwood to Beijing, had Teslas existed in 1982. Farrah Fawcett had nothing on her. Cheryl Tiegs, eat your heart out. Bo Derek? Christie Brinkley? Not even close. My knees went weak the moment our eyes met from across the crowded hallway, and I felt what could only be described as love at first sight. Like I'd had the wind knocked out of me with a sledgehammer, I was crippled by her beauty. Like a deer in headlights, I was paralyzed by her stare. Some people find angels in burnt tortillas. I found an angel in lip gloss and Jordache jeans.

I was no Casanova, by any means. My giant horse teeth and knobby knees were no help in my quest to find a girlfriend, and I was painfully shy around the ladies, so if anything I was shown a bit of sympathy or charity by the opposite sex, as they certainly didn't see me as a candidate for best hickey at the homecoming dance. Sure, I had played my share of spin the bottle at basement parties all over North Springfield, but George Clooney, I was not. More like Barney Fife with a skateboard.

Nevertheless, I had met my match, and I could not rest until

I made Sandi mine. I would race home from school every day, slam my bedroom door, and write her poems and songs on my Sears Silvertone guitar, spilling my heart out to her in god-awful melodies for no one's ears but hers. She had become my muse, my beacon, and every waking moment was devoted to daydreaming of our perfect, inevitable communion. I was hopelessly in love, and my skinny little heart surely could not survive another day without even just a sliver of her reciprocation. I rehearsed my proposal to her over and over in my mind every day, and after what seemed like a never-ending period of painfully awkward courtship (handwritten notes passed between classes, phone calls after school . . . I laid it on pretty thick), I somehow seized the opportunity and managed to turn on enough charm (and Old Spice) to ask her to go steady with me. To my amazement, she said yes (again, charity came into play), and we soon took that grand leap from just walking side by side between classes to walking hand in sweaty hand between classes. I felt like a king. A nerd god. I, DAVID ERIC GROHL, WAS NOW FORMALLY COMMITTED IN A MUTUAL RELATIONSHIP WITH THE MOST BEAUTIFUL GIRL IN THE WORLD . . . OR AT LEAST IN OUR GRADE. I had finally found my suburban soul mate, the love of my life, the person I would grow old with someday, surrounded by litters of loving grandchildren. I had found my other half. And she had found hers.

Or so I thought.

To be honest, I'm not even sure it lasted a week. I don't really know what happened. From my perspective, things were going great! We were young, happy, and free! Like Burt Reynolds and Loni Anderson, David Copperfield and Claudia Schiffer, Siegfried and Roy, a power couple of epic proportions and infinite possibilities! The world was our middle school oyster, and we had a lifetime of devotion to look forward to. And then, out of the blue, she dropped the MOAB (mother of all bombs) on my ass . . .

"You know . . . I'm new here . . . and I don't really want to get tied down."

Completely blindsided, I was frozen in my tracks by such devastating sacrilege. Time stood still. My mind went blank. My throat clenched and I could not breathe. My entire universe was suddenly ripped out from beneath my feet, and with those words like a poison scythe slicing through my heart, I was struck down and reduced to a puddle of agony. I agreed and shrugged it off with a smile, of course, but I was officially dead inside. Annihilated.

Forlorn, I returned home to my volumes of nauseatingly romantic scribblings, gathered them all, and burned them in a ceremonious ritual at the altar that I had of course built for Sandi in the carport. Okay, maybe I just threw them in the fucking trash can outside, but I did purge my pages of puppy-love poetry so as to cut the proverbial cord and try to get on with my boring preteen life. I should have known she would never love me. After all, I was just a skinny weirdo who listened to strange music while wearing torn Toughskins who no one would ever understand.

That night I had a dream. I was on a giant stage, drowned in colored lights as I played a triumphant guitar solo to a sold-out arena of adoring fans, blazing the fretboard with a proficiency never delivered before by a mortal man. The rapturous response from the audience was so deafening, it practically drowned out the sound of the mind-bending riffs I was laying down on those motherfuckers. Looking out at the thousands of screaming faces as I tore through my lead, I suddenly noticed Sandi in the front row, arms outstretched to touch me, sobbing uncontrollably, clearly consumed with regret that she had dumped me, the world's greatest rock star superhero, earlier that day (though we were still thirteen in my dream). I woke with a start, and that hopeless feeling of sorrow and dejection had disappeared, now replaced with a sense of inspired empowerment. AS I LAY THERE STARING AT THE CEILING, IT DAWNED ON ME THAT MAYBE MY GUITAR WAS THE LOVE OF MY LIFE AFTER ALL. Maybe I didn't need Sandi. Maybe my Silvertone could help me heal my wounded heart. Maybe I could write my way out of this mess. I was more determined than ever to make this rock and roll dream come true.

This is perhaps the impetus behind every song that I have ever written. Not to exact revenge on Sandi, of course, but to guard my most vulnerable corners by using heartbreak as fuel. What could be more inspiring than the exposed nerves of a wounded heart? In a way, I cherish my numerous heartbreaks almost more than the actual love that preceded them, because the heartbreak has always proven to me that I can feel. Trust me, the sweet sting of a love refused is powerful enough to send any scribe scrambling for pen and paper, aching to find beauty in the pain of being eighty-sixed by another. And more often than not, the result is good, because it's real, and it fucking hurts so bad.

Over the years, Sandi and I drifted our separate ways. Different friends, different schools, different paths in life, eventually losing touch and becoming just childhood memories for one another. I bumped into her once at a bar in our twenties, and we laughed together in a crowded room for a while, but that was all. The magic was gone. Again, we drifted our separate ways, returning to adulthood and the people that we eventually became. Bygones, you know.

Until one day on the Foo Fighters' 2011 "Wasting Light" tour, a mutual friend called and asked if I could put him on the guest list for our Washington, DC, show at the Verizon Center downtown.

It was our first sold-out arena in my hometown, and my guest list was a virtual high school reunion, with over a hundred old friends all coming to the concert to celebrate and spend one night reliving our distant past. It was almost like I was going to finally experience the homecoming dance I had never been invited to! My friend kindly asked if he could get a plus-one, adding in, "Guess who's coming with me? Sandi!" Holy shit. I couldn't believe it. It had been almost thirty years since she and I had met and I had given her my heart, only for her to smash it into a thousand bloody pieces on the ground before me (please laugh), so I was more than happy to have her come hang out with me and all of our old friends from the neighborhood. This was shaping up to be a night to remember.

I must say, I was a bit nervous. Not for the show, of course (that's the easy part), but to see Sandi. It had been so long I couldn't

imagine that we would even recognize each other after all of the twists and turns our lives had taken over the years. What would she look like? What would she sound like? What would she wear? What would I wear? Hopefully someone would politely reintroduce us, and we would carry on with ridiculous nostalgia all night long until the houselights came up and we were forced to pour out the champagne and go our separate ways again, back to the people we had eventually become. Suffocating in childish anticipation, I scanned the crowded backstage hallways every few minutes to see if I could see her before she saw me, but she was nowhere to be found. My teenage insecurity began to rear its ugly head again after so many years. What if she declined the invitation? What if she didn't want to see me? I didn't think my heart could handle another heartbreak from Sandi. Even the oldest wounds can reopen, you know.

And then, I saw her.

I looked up as she stepped into the dressing room and shot up from my chair. It was like seeing a ghost. I gasped. I couldn't believe it—she looked exactly the fucking same (without the Jordache jeans and feathered hair, of course). Our eyes met and we both smiled as wide as the horizon, crashing into each other with a most long-overdue hug. The feeling now was obviously much different than those palpitations I'd once experienced by our lockers in the fluorescent-lit hallways of intermediate school, but there was a certain joy that you only feel when reunited with someone from your past, like some kind of reassurance that life really happened. We sat down and caught up for a bit, talking spouses and children and family, laughing at the trouble we used to get into, and doing a roll call of where all our old friends were now. The minutes flew by, but soon it was time for me to get ready to go play, so I asked Sandi to please stay after the show for a bit more catch-up over a beer or two. I ran out the door to write a set list and wait for the houselights to dim.

The roar of the audience as we hit the stage that night was the kind that can only be found at a hometown show. It was many thunderous decibels beyond any other gig on that tour, and it shook me to my core with emotion and pride. I had spent my childhood here, climbing trees, chewing tobacco, playing hooky, lighting fireworks, searching the creeks for crawfish, and spray-painting walls, so I knew these streets, these people, and they knew me. I played each chord that night with every ounce of my being to thank them for a lifetime of Kodachrome memories, returning the tidal wave of love that washed over me as we sang every song together. At one point, as I played a triumphant guitar solo from the lip of the stage to the sea of screaming faces, blazing the fretboard to a rapturous response, I looked down and saw Sandi standing there . . . in the exact same spot where she had been standing in the dream I had the night she broke my heart. I stopped and realized that I had vividly imagined this exact moment thirty years before as a thirteen-year-old boy, like a premonition, and now I was actually fucking living it! CRAZY AS IT MAY SEEM, MY TEENAGE ROCK AND ROLL DREAM HAD COME TRUE. With only one difference: Sandi wasn't sobbing uncontrollably, consumed with regret that she had dumped me.

No.

She was smiling that amazing smile of hers, ice-blue eyes shining, with her middle finger in the air as she mouthed these immortal words . . .

"Fuck you, asshole!"

THE SCARS
ARE ON
THE
INSIDE

"Don't you have a headache, David?"

Crouched in a ball on the cold, damp ground, I looked up at the horrified faces of my two neighbors staring down at me in terror as I heard the bloody golf club fall into the freshly cut grass of their backyard with a thud. Barely conscious, I replied, "Ummm . . . I guess so . . . ," as I rubbed the back of my head, not realizing that my shaggy feathered hair was already matted and wet with blood pouring from the massive wound that their father's old pitching wedge had just carved into my nine-year-old skull.

"Y-y-y-you should probably go home . . . ," they stammered in unison.

Slightly dazed, but feeling no pain, I gathered my strength, picked myself up off the ground, and began walking the hundred and fifty yards back to my mother's doorstep across the street. It was a sunny Saturday afternoon, and as it was on most weekends, our idyllic little suburban cul-de-sac was abuzz with youthful activity. Whether it was lawn mowers humming in the distance, bicycle bells chiming in time, or screaming kickball games in full swing, our neighborhood always rang with a chorus of happy children

playing outdoors. The exact type of true-Americana shit that inspired network television fodder like *The Brady Bunch* and *Happy Days*. After all, North Springfield, Virginia, was a community specifically designed after World War II for that exact aesthetic. House after little brick house, just big enough for baby boomers to raise a family of four on their meager federal salaries, stretching for miles in a grid of manicured lawns, cracked sidewalks, and tall white oak trees. Only minutes from the nation's capital, each morning the corner bus stop boasted a long line of balding men sporting beige overcoats and briefcases, reading the *Washington Post* as they waited to be carted off to the Pentagon or other faceless, monolithic federal buildings for another day at the desk. Life here was a reliable nine-to-five monotony. A Groundhog Day rat race with little more than a gold watch at the finish line. For those brainwashed by "white picket fence" syndrome, this was the comfortable reward of security and stability. For a hyperactive, mischievous child like me, it was the devil's playground.

Saturday mornings would usually begin with a few cartoons over a bowl of cereal before I peered out of our living room picture window onto the street to survey the day's activity. If there was action to be found, I would immediately throw on a pair of my Toughskins (bargain jeans from Sears that came in a rainbow of nauseating colors) with the haste of a fireman called to an emergency and head out with a high-pitched "Bye, Mom! I'll be back later!" A recluse, I was not. I much preferred the countless adventures waiting to be found outdoors, like crawling through dank drainpipes, jumping off rooftops, or throwing crab apples at unsuspecting cars from the bushes beside the road (an inadvisable prank that usually resulted in a frenzied high-speed chase, with me cutting through yards and hurdling chain-link fences with Olympic speed to escape certain low-life retribution). From early morning to the moment the streetlights came on, I would wander the pavement searching for thrills until I wore holes in my special sneakers, which had been altered with a lift on the left shoe to correct my crooked spine.

On this particular day though, I noticed that my two best friends, Johnny and Tae, were loading golf clubs into the trunk of their father's car. *Golf?* I thought to myself. *We never play fucking golf. That is some bourgeois rich-kid shit.* We had sticks! And rocks! And creeks full of crawfish! What did we need with funny hats and plaid trousers? I quickly suited up and skipped over to their driveway to investigate, only to find that they had planned a family outing to the local golf course, sadly leaving me to my own devices for the afternoon. As I waved goodbye in disappointment, I turned and sulked back to my house, impatiently waiting for them to return by biding my time with the much-dreaded chores of raking leaves and cleaning my room (which was truly an exercise in futility, as I had little regard for organization or basic cleanliness back then. I'm a little better now. A little).

Hours passed slowly until finally I saw their blue Cadillac coming up the street. I immediately stopped what I was doing and rushed over to their house to find them both in their backyard, swinging golf clubs wildly at a practice ball on a string that was staked into the ground like a miniature tetherball setup. Cool! As I drew closer, I was in awe as they chopped away at it like deranged lumberjacks, large clumps of dirt and earth flying across the yard with each swat. Having never tried my hand at this new sport, I waited patiently for my turn, summoning every ounce of discipline my adolescent body could muster until I was finally given the old, rusted club for my shot. *This thing is heavy . . . ,* I thought as I raised my skinny arms to swing as hard as I possibly could. Whiff. Miss. Whiff. Another miss. Giant chunks of sod shot off in every direc-

tion like shrapnel, until I finally connected, and with a perfect *ping* the ball spun in a circle around its post, bringing me an indescribable sense of satisfaction. My heart filled with pride. "My turn!" Tae said, and he took the club from my hands, teeing up the ball for another strike. *I knocked the shit out of that thing . . . ,* I thought. *Might want to make sure the post is still firmly planted into the ground after the hurtin' I just put on that thang . . .* I leaned down to push the post into the soft dirt, and . . .

WHACK.

If you've ever been hit in the head with great force, you surely remember the sound of impact as it echoes through your skull. Similar to the bounce of a basketball or the thump of a less-than-ripe melon (which mine was), it's a sensation that never leaves you once you've experienced it. And the silence that follows, usually accompanied by some pretty little stars and a few fairies, is deafening. I had just been clobbered, full force, by a teenager with an adult-weight pitching wedge designed to produce a "high-trajectory shot" on the course. With a nine-year-old boy's head, it produces a much different result: Helter fucking Skelter.

Little did I know, my head had been split open like an over-ripe pumpkin long after the trick-or-treaters have gone home. I felt nothing. Zip. Nada. So, as per Johnny and Tae's suggestion, I began my trek home, whistling nervously and thinking, *I'm in so much fucking trouble right now,* without realizing the severity of what had just happened. I was wearing my favorite T-shirt that day, a white ringer with the Superman "S" on the chest, and as I was crossing the street I looked down at the red and yellow logo, but to my shock, this was no longer my beautiful Superman shirt. I was now covered in a sticky, coagulated mass of my own blood, scalp, and hair. I quickened my pace in panic as I made it to my yard, still feeling no pain, but knowing that one drop of blood on the living room carpet could bring this situation to a head (couldn't resist that one). As I scaled the small steps to the house, I could hear my mother vacuuming inside, so rather than barge through the door in a screaming, gory mess, I stood on the stoop and gently knocked, doing anything I could to defuse the imminent hysteria. "Mom? Could you come here for a second?" I cooed in my calmest, sweetest "little boy who really fucked up this time" voice. "Hold on a minute . . . ," she replied, oblivious to the terror that awaited outside, finishing her vacuuming in the other room. "Ummm, it's kind of an emergency . . . ," I whimpered.

The image of my poor mother's face as she rounded the corner to find her youngest child standing on the doorstep covered in his own blood will forever be burned into my memory. Though I felt no pain, I felt hers.

But, truth be told, this was not the first time.

We always joked that the doctors at Fairfax County Public Hospital were on a first-name basis with me. As if I were Norm from the sitcom *Cheers,* they would all roar "David!" as I was wheeled into the emergency room with yet another injury that required a fresh new set of wiry black stitches. Over time, I became unfazed by the hot pinprick of a Novocain shot and the feeling of skin stretching as a doctor pulled a thin nylon thread tightly to close a wound. It became ritual. To this day, I have never completely shaved my head, but I imagine that underneath my mop of dark brown hair is something that resembles a map of the London Underground, countless lines intersecting in a tangled web of scars. Hands, knees, fingers, legs, lips, forehead . . . you name it, if it's still connected to my body, it's been repaired like an old rag doll. As traumatic as that may sound though, don't be fooled. I always looked on the bright side and saw an injury as a day home from school. And I would have done *anything* for one of those.

Here's an example: I once broke my ankle in a soccer game at a park near Lake Accotink, a picturesque retreat about a mile from my house. All of the sixth graders had convened on one stretch of grass to play that afternoon, and before long a furious game erupted, as most of us were lifelong soccer players for our neighborhood athletic club. (Fun fact: I was always assigned to be goalie in every sport I played, which I have to believe is some kind of premature psychological profiling, but that's for another story.) At one point, I made contact with the ball at the precise moment another player did, twisting my foot in a gruesome direction it wasn't designed to go in. Falling to the ground, I knew I had done real damage. So, what did I do? I walked a mile home, thinking up ways to pitch this injury to my mother in hopes that I could milk it for a day home from school, not realizing that I had actually broken my ankle. To my surprise, I woke the next day to a gigantic purple foot. "YES!!" I rejoiced! "NO SCHOOL!!"

"David!" the doctors shouted as I arrived.

The list is long. The frozen-solid chocolate Easter egg that I decided to cut into with the sharpest knife in the drawer, resulting in nearly severing my left forefinger. The hallway corner outside of my sister's bedroom that I ran headfirst into not once but *twice* over the course of my childhood years, tallying more than a few stitches in my intricately embroidered forehead. The bike crashes. The car accidents. Being *run over* by a car when I was four. (My response? "But I didn't get hurt, Mommy!") My childhood was a series of far too many ER trips, each usually resulting in a new scar, a day off from school, and a damn good story.

In hindsight, I realize that my relationship with consequences was always funny. I didn't seem to fear physical consequences. I only feared emotional consequences. Of all my brushes with grievous bodily harm, I never felt physical pain in any of those moments. None. I always walked home after getting hurt. I always put on my best game face, so as not to inconvenience my mother any more than life had inconvenienced her already, and I always tried to reassure her that whatever gaping wound I had suffered, it was just a scratch, no matter how many stitches were required. Call it a defense mechanism, call it a neurological shutoff, call it what you like, but I can only imagine it was learned from the sacrifices my mother made to raise two happy children, no matter what pain she may have endured. AFTER ALL, THE SHOW MUST GO ON.

There is a saying: "You are only as happy as your unhappiest child." I never truly understood what that saying meant until the day I had to take my own daughter Violet to the pediatrician for a shot. Up until then, her only cries had been simple signals of hunger or fatigue, or that it was time for a new diaper. She had spent most of her first six months in my lap, smiling and giggling as I bounced her up and down, cherishing her like the miracle that she is as she stared at me with her gigantic blue eyes, reducing me to a puddle of mush with every squeak. On this day though, the doctor asked me to sit her in my lap as they prepared to give her the shot, so I turned her to face me just as I would every day in my living room chair, the two of us smiling at each other and communicating with our eyes rather than words. Although, this time was different. I knew that what came next would hurt her. I tried my best to make her giggle and smile, but as the long, sharp needle sank into her tiny arm, her expression quickly turned from one of bliss and joy to one of immense pain. Her eyes, still locked on mine, widened and filled with tears, as if to say, "Daddy, why would you let them hurt me?" I was absolutely shattered. My heart broke into a million pieces, and in that moment I felt not only Violet's pain but my mother's pain as well.

Upon returning home (her tears were dry by the time we left the doctor's office, of course), I called my mother and told her that I couldn't shake this devastating feeling, explaining that this was the first time I had ever experienced my child's crying from real pain and how it had absolutely crushed my soul. Her response was as wise as I have now come to expect:

"God forbid she ever shows up at your doorstep covered in her own blood, then you'll really understand . . ."

Good thing my mother wasn't in attendance the night of June 12, 2015, at Gothenburg, Sweden's Ullevi stadium.

It was a beautiful Scandinavian summer evening. Clear skies, warm breeze, and fifty thousand Foo Fighters fans anxiously awaiting our tried-and-true, two-and-a-half-hour, twenty-five-song set list. At this point, our little band had graduated from arena to stadium level, becoming a tight, well-oiled machine that banged out song after song with little respite, and I had become more than comfortable with entertaining an audience of this magnitude, living out my innermost Freddie Mercury fantasies on a nightly basis. Hearing a time-delayed full-throated sing-along ricocheting from the farthest rafters of a football stadium is an out-of-body sensation, one that becomes oddly addictive over time, echoing in a chorus of sublime connectivity. The open air, hitting you in gusts that give your hair a perfect Beyoncé blowout while you inhale the aroma of sweat and beer that sometimes rises from the crowd in a foglike condensation. The roar of fireworks above your head as you take your final bow and sprint to the room-temperature pepperoni pizza waiting in your dressing room. Believe me, it is all that it's cracked up to be and more. I never fully embraced stadium rock until I experienced it from the lip of the stage, and to this day I have never taken a single moment of it for granted. It is an otherworldly experience, one that can be described in just two words: fucking awesome.

At one point before the show, a local promoter popped his head into the dressing room to wish me luck and to remind me that I had much to live up to, as the one and only Bruce Springsteen had played this stadium before and the audience were so enthralled that they "split the foundation" of the gigantic venue. No pressure! Never for a moment have I imagined rising to the level of "the Boss" himself, but I have to say, this pep talk did turn up the heat a little bit. *I'm gonna fuckin' give it to them good tonight,* I thought, and continued my pre-show ritual, which usually consisted of three Advils, three beers, and a room full of laughter. I confess, I have always been too embarrassed to do any sort of conventional vocal warmups and vocal exercises. Especially considering that the majority of my performance is screaming bloody fucking murder rather than any gorgeous, operatic croon. A few belly laughs and our version of "band prayer" (a nonreligious moment where we all do a shot of Crown Royal as we stare into each other's eyes) always does the trick.

The sun was still bright in the sky when we hit the stage that night, and as we opened with the first chords of "Everlong" (undoubtedly our most popular song), the crowd went wild. This song, which we usually reserve for the closing number, was the perfect selection to begin what would turn out to be our most unforgettable show, and we barreled through it with the excited force of a band on fire. Without hesitation, we quickly counted into the fast-paced rock of "Monkey Wrench" as I ran from one side of the stage to the other, banging my head and soloing like a kid with a tennis racket in his bedroom mirror. Stadium stages are not only wide but extremely high, in order for the audience to see the performers from hundreds of yards away, so each movement is a fifty-yard dash, leaving you with little breath to sing the next line when you race back to the microphone.

Midway through the song, I jolted forward for another trip to the wings (puns are indeed a specialty of mine) and my foot caught a cable that stretched across the floor, which sent me into a stumble only feet from the edge of the stage. My body lurched forward, and my balance was gone as I peered down at the twelve-foot fall before me. *No sweat,* I thought. *I'll just jump.* As I had done countless times from neighborhood rooftops as a child, I put my best foot forward (see?) and hoped everything would work out. But this was no rooftop overlooking a manicured suburban lawn. No. This was hard, unforgiving concrete with hard plastic walkways designed to protect the soccer field beneath them. My body slammed the ground with a gruesome BANG!, and a giant wave of panicked adrenaline instinctively kicked in. *How embarrassing!* I thought. I quickly stood up so as to play it off like another minor childhood tumble, no big deal, but as I took my first step I instantly knew something was wrong. As I put my weight on my right ankle, it felt warm and numb, with the sickening consistency of a sock full of mashed potatoes. It was just . . . mush. I fell to the ground again, holding my leg as the local security guards surrounded me. Blissfully oblivious to what had happened to me, the band played on above my head, out of view of the carnage unfolding below the steep stage. I somehow caught the attention of our band security guard, Ray, who was thirty yards away, and exaggeratedly mouthed the words "I JUST BROKE MY FUCKING LEG!" Ray immediately jumped to my rescue, his massive frame bounding toward me as the band stopped playing and the song ground to a halt.

I asked for a microphone, and from the narrow lane of the sweaty security pit I calmly declared, "Ladies and gentlemen, I think I just broke my leg. I think I really broke my leg . . ." There was a stunned silence in the stadium, as my faithful band was now looking down over the lip of the stage in bewildered shock, watching as I was quickly surrounded by paramedics calling for a gurney. My mind was racing as I tried to think of something to say that would defuse or remedy this ridiculous twist of fate. Here I was, barely two songs into a planned two-and-a-half-hour set, about to be carried away like an injured athlete off the field in front of fifty thousand fans. These people had all traveled from far and wide, spending their hard-earned money to be entertained for the evening. I was going to give them a Boss-level show, damn it. I thought, and then blurted out the first thing that came to mind: "You have my promise, right now, that the Foo Fighters . . . we're gonna come back and finish this show . . ." I LOOKED UP AT OUR DRUMMER TAYLOR, MY BEST FRIEND AND PARTNER IN CRIME, AND SAID, "KEEP PLAYING!!!"

As I was carried to the side of the stage, the opening notes of "Cold Day in the Sun," from our fifth album, rang through the stadium to a stunned audience. A young Swedish doctor by the name of Johan Sampson cut the laces of my high-top sneaker, and as he removed it my foot fell limp to one side. I had dislocated my ankle, tearing all of the ligaments that keep the joint in place, as well as snapping my fibula in a razor-clean break. He looked up to me and in his heavy Swedish accent said, "Your leg is probably broken, and your ankle is dislocated, so we must put it back in right now." Just then, my wife, Jordyn, and my tour manager, Gus Brandt, ran to my side in horrified concern, but all I could do was laugh at the absurdity of the situation. I instructed Gus to get me a tall Solo cup of Crown Royal and leaned over to my wife, taking the sleeve of her leather jacket and putting it between my teeth. "Go for it," I told the doctor as I bit down on the salty black material, feeling a strange pressure as they wrestled my ankle back into place like an old key in a rusty lock.

"Stay with me, stay with me, tonight you better stay with me . . . !!!" sang Taylor. The Faces classic that we had been playing for years echoed in the distance as another paramedic tried putting one of those Mount Everest Mylar blankets over me, assuming that I was in a state of shock. Can't blame her, really. Maybe I was. I was lying on my back laughing with a plastic cup filled to the brim with whiskey, showing no signs that I had just decimated my leg in a massive fall. The only thing I felt in that moment was the responsibility of finishing the show for the thousands of people who had come to see us tear this place down with our well-oiled stadium-rock machine. I imagined lines and lines of people, heading for the exits, hands hanging low in disappointment, cursing our name and vowing to never come see us again. I turned to Johan, who was carefully holding my foot in place, and asked, "Hey . . . can I go up and finish the show if I sit in a chair?" "You will need a brace . . . ," he told me. I asked if they had one on hand, and he informed me that we would need to go to the hospital and have a brace fitted there, and then we could return. "How far is the hospital from here?" I spat back. "Thirty minutes," he replied. *Fuck that!* I thought. There was no way in hell I was leaving this stadium without giving these people their money's worth. "How about this . . . ," I said. "*You* go to the hospital and get a brace, I'm gonna go sit down and play, and when you return, we'll put it on." He looked at me in frustration and very politely informed me, "If I let go of your foot, it will fall back out of the socket!" Without hesitation, and in a moment of pure, stubborn will, I loudly exclaimed, "Well then, you're coming up onstage with me, motherfucker!"

"Pressure . . . pushing down on me . . . ," Taylor continued in raspy perfect pitch, now singing the Queen/David Bowie classic as the doctor wrapped my ankle tightly in an Ace bandage, never losing hold of my annihilated limb, until I was lifted in a coordinated effort of multiple large men and carried back to the stage, where a chair waited for me in the place where I'd once stood.

Life has a way of gifting you serendipitous, poetic moments along the way, but as my ass hit that chair and my guitar was placed in my lap, I burst into the bridge of "Under Pressure" as I always had done, singing in my best falsetto, "Chippin' around kick my brains around the floor! These are the days it never rains but it pours . . . ," and the deafening roar of the crowd confirmed that this song and this lyric could not have been more apropos in this unforgettable moment. You just can't make this shit up. It was sheer joy. It was triumph. It was survival.

Next, I kicked into our song "Learn to Fly" and looked down at Johan kneeling in front of me, trying his best to steady my foot as I thrashed my guitar back and forth, adrenaline still pulsing through my veins. I noticed that he was no longer in a fixed state of worry but bobbing his head along to the music, so I winked with a smile and said, "This is pretty cool, huh?"

"Yeeeeeaaahhhh!!!" he said. Little did I know that he was also a rock musician, and that the thrill of being on a stadium stage was in no way lost on him.

It wasn't long before the ambulance returned with that brace, which turned out to be a full plaster cast that they slung on me with the speed of a NASCAR pit crew, and we continued on with the show. Hours and songs passed, and at one point I even crutched my way to the center of the stadium to sing "My Hero" and "Times Like These"; the amount of love and support that was returned by the audience in a rapturous sing-along brought me to tears. By the time we hit the final notes of "Best of You," I knew that we had just experienced a defining moment in our career. This band, born from the heartbreak and tragedy of our broken past, was a celebration of love, and life, and the dedication to finding happiness in every next day. And now, more than ever, it represented healing and survival.

I was quickly escorted to a car beside the stage, and we sped off to the hospital surrounded by a wailing police escort. Along the way, I noticed that my then six-year-old daughter, Harper, who had watched this entire series of unfortunate events play out, began to cry quietly. As the siren lights illuminated her face, I asked, "What's wrong, Boo?" She didn't speak. "Are you scared?" I said. She nodded her head slowly as the tears rolled down her beautiful face, and my heart sank in my chest. Though I felt no pain, I felt hers. "Everything's fine! We're just going to the hospital so that they can take pictures of my bones . . . it's really cool!" I said with forced, manufactured cheer. She did her best to smile and muster some courage, but I could feel the fear and empathy in her innocent little heart, and I was instantly focused on her well-being. After all, you are only as happy as your unhappiest child. Upon arrival at the hospital, I was placed in a wheelchair and sat her in my lap for the ride to the X-ray room, doing my best to make this bizarre moment fun.

Thankfully, she giggled.

Lying on the cold X-ray table, I was told to remain still as they moved the equipment around my leg to get a clean shot of my injury. Like an alien abduction, the white light filled the room, and there I was, alone, with only a window separating me from my tour manager and the technician. Silence. A low humming noise buzzed a few times, and I looked up to Gus's pained expression behind the glass. It was not what I'd hoped or wanted to see. He looked me in the eyes and mouthed the word "surgery." Fuck.

The pain had finally set in when I made it back to my hotel in Norway that night, and as I lay on the couch with my cast in the air, I couldn't help but think of those summer days I'd spent as a mischievous, hyperactive daredevil child, wandering the streets searching for thrills until I had holes in my sneakers, with no regard for physical consequences. Only emotional consequences. And as I looked at the texts pouring in on my phone, I wept at all the love and concern that my friends were sending me upon hearing the news. I knew what I had to do.

YOU PICK YOURSELF UP OFF THE GROUND. YOU WALK HOME. THE SHOW MUST GO ON.

TRACEY
IS A PUNK
ROCKER

"Tracey, they're here!"

In the extravagant foyer of my aunt Sherry's turn-of-the-century Evanston, Illinois, estate, I stood at the bottom of the long, winding staircase waiting to greet my ultra-cool cousin Tracey with a much-anticipated hug. Though we weren't technically related, I considered Tracey family as much as I did any blood relative. Our mothers had met as teenagers in high school and became lifelong friends, even forming an a cappella singing group called the Three Belles that performed at their local Boardman, Ohio, Kiwanis clubs, Women's City Clubs, and school functions in the early fifties (not to mention a morning TV cooking show where my mother drank milk for a commercial endorsement and almost threw up all over the set). Joined by their dear friend Jeralyn Meyer, the trio sang "Tea for Two," "Bewitched," and "Alexander's Ragtime Band" in perfect harmony, all smiles and matching outfits. With no real professional aspirations, theirs was more of a heartfelt passion, a way to pass the time and share their love of music with friends. After graduation, my mother and Sherry went their separate ways in life but vowed to reconnect every summer from then on, which we did, no matter the distance between our families.

Our seven-hundred-mile drive from Springfield, Virginia, to Evanston was no small feat. My mother, my sister, and I would cram our luggage, pillows, blankets, and cooler full of snacks into our baby-blue 1981 Ford Fiesta for the eleven-hour drive, usually stopping halfway in Youngstown, Ohio, for a few days to visit with my grandparents, not far from where I was born in the little town of Warren. It was the highlight of the year, driving up the Pennsylvania Turnpike into one of America's most beautiful corners, winding over rolling hills and through long mountain tunnels. I always enjoyed the trip, singing along to the radio with my mother from the front seat, pulling over at rest stops for souvenirs, and eating sandwiches that we had brought for the ride. It was my first real

taste of travel, and even then I could appreciate the gradual change in landscape as we barreled across the country toward the Midwest in our tiny little car, squeezed in like cosmonauts for hours on end. I can only think that the pleasure I found watching the long road ahead inspired me to follow those same highways later on in life.

After traveling from our sleepy suburban Virginia neighborhood, into the Pennsylvania hills, and past the long, flat cornfields of rural Ohio, the sight of Chicago's sprawling metropolis before our windshield was nothing less than triumphant. Like the Emerald City from *The Wizard of Oz,* the glorious vision of the Sears Tower standing in the distance always filled me with a sense of amazement and wild anticipation, wondering what this summer's trip would have in store. I absolutely loved Chicago. Its multicultural maze of subway cars and brick buildings seemed like a playground of opportunity, much more exciting than the quiet suburban environment of my home in Virginia. Along with my cousin Tracey, the most adventurous of my "cousins," there were her three older brothers, Trip, Todd, and Troy, who would always take me under their wing and show me a world outside of my own that I otherwise never would have experienced, from exploring the city to playing for hours on the warm beaches of Lake Michigan. This was my Fantasy Island, my Club Med, my Copacabana. This also became my life's first real taste of independence, as I eventually began taking the L downtown without my mother's supervision to explore the city's many corners, quickly finding my own sense of identity that stretched far beyond who I had been led to believe I could be. I was living a classic 1980s John Hughes coming-of-age film without realizing it, aesthetically and emotionally.

As I stood waiting for Tracey to bounce down in her usual shorts and polo shirt, I noticed an ominous sound from upstairs. The sound of chains clanging and leather creaking, boots hitting the floor with a thud in every step, like a Viking slowly approaching an intended victim. A home intruder? A Hells Angel? The Ghost of Christmas Past? My heart raced as the footsteps grew closer, now at the top of the staircase. *Boom. Clink. Boom. Clink. Boom. Clink.* And then she appeared . . .

TRACEY WAS NOW A PUNK ROCKER.

With shiny Doc Marten boots, black bondage pants, an Anti-Pasti T-shirt, and a shaved head, she was a terrifying yet glorious vision of rebellion. Long gone were the tennis shorts and sneakers from last summer; Tracey had transformed into something I had seen only on prime-time TV shows like *CHiPs* or *Quincy.* But this was no cartoonish, spiky-haired villain terrorizing a silly sitcom with reckless anarchy and a clamorous soundtrack in the background. No. This was fucking real. I stood in awe, as if I were face-to-face with an alien sent from another civilization, examining every spike, every safety pin, and every leather strap with joyous bewilderment. But my shock and surprise were calmed the instant she greeted us with her usual sunny smile. It was still Tracey, just turned up to 11 like a postapocalyptic superhero. To say that I was excited would be one of my life's greatest understatements. I was beside myself. Something had been awakened in me—I just wasn't yet sure what that was.

After the usual jolly catch-up, Tracey and I wandered upstairs to her bedroom, where she proceeded to show me the massive record collection next to her turntable stereo. Rows and rows of seven-inch singles and LPs, all neatly lined up and meticulously cared for, with band names that I had never heard of—the Misfits, Dead Kennedys, Bad Brains, Germs, Naked Raygun, Black Flag, Wire, Minor Threat, GBH, Discharge, the Effigies . . . too many to name here. This was a virtual treasure trove of underground, independent punk rock, something I had never known existed up

until that point. We sat on her floor as she proceeded to play record after record with the enthusiasm of a professor instructing a
hungry student ravenous for knowledge. "Listen to this one!" she
would say, and carefully drop a disc onto the record player. "Now
this!" she continued, playing one after another, blowing my mind
into outer space with each track. I had questions. So many questions. *How could I have not known that this existed? Does everybody
know about this? Is this even legal?* I examined the sleeve of each
record, eyes wide, gazing at the crude artwork, photos, and credits,
while Tracey blasted the loud, raw music filled with whiplash tem-
pos and bloodcurdling screams. Hours flew by, and everything I
knew about music up until that point went right out the window.

THIS WAS THE FIRST DAY OF THE REST OF MY LIFE.

Upon closer inspection, I noticed one glaring difference from
all the typical classic rock albums that I owned at home: none of
these albums were from any record companies I had ever heard of.
On the contrary, most of them practically looked homemade. They
featured xeroxed covers with dark, pixelated photos; handwritten
lyrics and credits; silkscreened logos and graphics, all clumsily
stuffed into plastic sleeves that sold for a mere three or four dollars.
This underground network somehow existed entirely outside of the
conventional, corporate structure and defied the ordinary manner
of manufacturing and distributing music. These people were doing
it THEMSELVES, Tracey explained. I was entranced, awakened,
and inspired. I no longer considered music an unattainable act of
wizardry, only possible for those who were blessed with the godlike
ability of Jimi Hendrix or Paul McCartney. I now realized that all
you needed was three chords, an open mind, and a microphone.
And the passion and drive to make it happen yourself.

That night, Tracey was planning on taking the L downtown to
see local Chicago punk band Naked Raygun play at a dive bar just

across the street from Wrigley Field called the Cubby Bear. Having just listened to their song "Surf Combat" that afternoon, I was dying to experience this radical lifestyle up close and in the flesh but couldn't imagine Tracey would invite me along, as I looked like a square thirteen-year-old kid who'd just fallen off the back of a public school bus. More Opie Taylor than Sid Vicious, I could only imagine Tracey's mortification if I were to walk with her through a room of Mohawks and spiked leather jackets. But, after a bit of cajoling from my aunt Sherry, Tracey graciously conceded and agreed to let me tag along. This was uncharted terrain, seriously foreign territory, and my stomach was in knots with nervous anticipation.

Not to mention . . . I had never been to a live concert before.

After all my years of watching MTV and staring at the KISS and Led Zeppelin posters on my bedroom walls, I foolishly thought that bands performed only on giant stages with smoke machines and massive displays of lasers and pyrotechnics. To me, that was rock and roll. Little did I know that all you needed was four walls and a song.

On the train ride into town, my mind was an electrical storm of dangerous premonitions, imagining the chaos and madness that awaited in that dingy hole-in-the-wall bar downtown. Just hours before, a truth had been unlocked in me that I couldn't wait to live out. I now identified with something, and it wasn't anything I had seen in my life back home. Those jagged record sleeves and distorted garage recordings that leapt out of Tracey's speakers had forced open a window to my soul, and I had finally experienced a connection that made me feel understood. Having always felt slightly removed from the norm, I never had anywhere or anyone to turn to for understanding and reassurance among my peers. I was a kid from a broken home, a mama's boy, an okay student at best. A ball of misplaced energy who was looking for his niche, his tribe. I was in desperate need of an existential makeover. I could feel it coming.

When we arrived at the Cubby Bear, I noticed a few punks hanging out on the street outside the club door and was surprised at how young they were. Teenagers like me, they weren't the menacing faces that I had seen on Tracey's album covers. Most were just skinny skater types in jeans, T-shirts, and Converse Chucks, bouncing off the walls with adolescent, hyperactive energy, just like me. Instantly relieved, we walked up and Tracey introduced me to her gang of outsiders. I soon picked up that everyone there that night knew everyone else, and it was a tight community of friends, all drawn together by their love of subversive music and the celebration of personal expression. Sure, there were some spikes, and leather, and colorful hair, and piercings, but I didn't see this as threatening. I felt like I was at home.

Like a bomb ready to detonate, the room was ripe with anxious tension as Naked Raygun prepared to hit the stage. As the houselights went out, I was immediately struck by the intimacy of the gig. Unlike what I saw in those posters on my bedroom wall, I was shoulder to shoulder with everyone else, standing only feet from the small stage as the singer gripped the microphone, ready to count into the first number. And when he did, the small room ignited like a powder keg in a frenzy of limbs and deafening volume. People on top of people. Slam dancing, stage diving, the crowd chanting the words to each song with fists in the air like an army of loyal sonic soldiers. I was stepped on. I was shoved and punched. I was thrown about like a rag doll in the melee of the crowd, and I fucking loved it. The music and violent dancing released an energy within me that had been pent up for years, like an exorcism of all of my childhood traumas.

THIS WAS A FEELING OF FREEDOM THAT I HAD WAITED FOR MY ENTIRE LIFE, AND NOW THAT I'D BEEN BAPTIZED BY SPIT AND SWEAT AND BROKEN GLASS, THERE WAS NO TURNING BACK. Song after thunderous song, I kept close to the small stage, bathed in the distorted glory of the music. Naked Raygun is considered by some to be the most important band in the history of Chicago punk, and their style almost resembled a hardcore Dick Dale type of surf rock. Of course, I didn't understand their relevance then. I just knew that this music was filling my head and my soul with something I needed more of. With no song longer than about three and a half minutes, each stuttered blast was met with a riotous response, and the pauses between songs seemed like an eternity as I waited for the chaos to resume. It was all over much too soon, and as the houselights came up, I walked over to the merchandise table and bought my first punk rock record: Naked Raygun's "Flammable Solid" seven-inch single. One of only a thousand made.

After the gig, we boarded the train and returned to Evanston with ears ringing and hearts made anew. In one summer day, I was forever changed, and now understood that I didn't need the pyrotechnics, lasers, or impossible proficiency of a virtuoso instrumentalist to become a musician. The most important element of rock and roll had been revealed to me in Naked Raygun's performance: the raw and imperfect sound of human beings purging their innermost voice for all to hear. This was now available to me, and I couldn't wait to return home to Virginia and spread the gospel to all of my friends, hoping that they would see the light, too.

Turns out, Tracey herself was the singer in a punk rock band named Verboten, and they had already recorded some original songs and played live gigs around Chicago. With an average age of about thirteen years old, the four-piece was just kids doing it all themselves, writing and practicing in Tracey's basement, booking their own shows, and making their own T-shirts to sell at their gigs. Guitarist Jason Narducy couldn't have been more than eleven years old at the time, and his Gibson SG dwarfed his tiny body as he banged out power chords to songs like "My Opinion" and "He's a Panther." This inspired me even more, seeing a kid even younger than myself stepping out and following his dreams. I knew that my guitar at home was in for a right banging once I got my hands on it again. Hell, if these kids could do it, I could too.

The days of our vacation flew by as I immersed myself in Tracey's library of music, studying each album, even discovering a few bands from my hometown in her collection: Minor Threat, Faith, Void, and my personal favorite, a group named Scream whose Bailey's Crossroads PO box address was just miles from my neighborhood! Mind. Fucking. Blown. Scream were a bit different from the other, less polished groups, though. With strong melodies and hints of classic rock and roll here and there, their fast, aggressive songs seemed a bit more crafted than everything else I had heard on that trip. And they didn't necessarily look like the punks I had seen on those other album sleeves and in those fanzine pages in Tracey's room. Dressed in jeans and flannels and with scruffy hair, they looked like they were . . . from Virginia. I joyously played their album on repeat with a sense of hometown pride, memorizing every word—and every drumbeat.

The rest of our vacation was spent going to shows, buying albums at Wax Trax! records, and hanging out with other punks, as I slowly learned this new language of records and tapes that circulated among them. I witnessed that this underground scene was a grassroots network of young music lovers like me, blissfully removed from the mainstream idea of a "career" in music. Like the Three Belles many years before, there were hardly any professional aspirations in this crew, but rather a heartfelt passion to share the love of music with friends. The reward? Usually nothing more than a sense of accomplishment from doing something you loved entirely on your own. And it was worth every drop of blood, sweat, and tears. There were no rock stars here. Only real people.

The long drive back to Virginia was like a metaphorical journey from my past to my future. I had left something behind in Chicago. Long gone was the little boy who could never imagine his songs, his words, or his passions someday residing deep within the grooves of a dirty black slab of vinyl. Long gone was the little boy afraid of being ostracized for seeming different from all of the cool kids. Armed with a Germs record, a Killing Joke T-shirt, and the "Flammable Solid" single I had purchased at the Naked Raygun gig, I was now determined to begin my new life as a punk rocker. I had finally shed that outer layer of fragile adolescent insecurity and begun to grow a new skin, one that would form into my true self, and I couldn't wait to show it to the world.

They'll rip your skin off
They'll flay you alive
You try to keep breathing
On this ride of your life

I got gear
I got gear
I got gear
I can use it

JOHN
BONHAM
SÉANCE

The altar was set. The candles were lit. The ritual was prepared. I quietly sat down on the floor facing the makeshift shrine that I had constructed by hand with scrap wood and leftover model paint, cleared my mind of all thoughts, and began to pray. I don't know exactly who I was praying to, but I did know exactly what I was praying for.

Success.

I sat quietly and meditated, trying to open myself to the universe and receive some sort of divine intervention, imagining that every cell in my body would be transformed and empowered, providing me with the supernatural abilities that my heroes must have had in order to transcend time and space with their music. There must have been some intangible, mystical element at play, I thought, and I was desperate to tap into that, so I performed my primitive rite with the intense, earnest conviction of a seventeen-year-old with nothing to lose.

The flickering candles at each corner of the board spilled their yellow light onto the cold concrete floor of my carport, illuminating the symbols I had drawn to summon the spirits that would guide me to my destiny: the John Bonham three-circles logo and the number 606, two emblems that held deep significance in my life. With my own form of telepathy, I listed my deepest desires in the hope that someone, something, somewhere, would heed my call and answer my prayers in time. Manifestation was not a practice I was well versed in, but I did have faith in the idea that if you can perceive it, you can achieve it. With the help of the universe, this was my intention. Or, to go toward the sacred:

What you think, you become,
What you feel, you attract,
What you imagine, you create.

Some refer to this as the "Law of Attraction," the idea that the universe creates for you what your mind focuses upon. As a

teenager, I knew nothing about this concept, but from an early age I did believe very deep down that anything was possible if I devoted myself to it entirely. At best, my options in life were slim at this point. With no high school diploma and no family money, I was destined to live paycheck to paycheck, with music being my driver, which was thankfully enough to keep my spirit from dying. All I could do was dream. So, dream I did. But I no longer just fantasized about someday "making it" as a musician. I was intent on subpoenaing the unknown to take me there.

What inspired me to take such drastic and extreme measures?

There is a theory out there that most musicians decide their creative path in life between the ages of eleven and thirteen. This is the golden window of opportunity where independence and identity intersect, a most treacherous phase in any child's life where you become your own person, no longer just your parents' accessory. A time to discover who YOU are, and if you happen to have any sort of musical inclination and drive, chances are you will decide this is who you will be for the rest of your life. A musician. I believe in this theory, because it is exactly what happened to me.

There was a time when music was just a sound to me. Simple nursery rhymes and radio jingles that I would mindlessly sing along to for fun, floating in one ear and out the other. Songs were just intermittent melodies and rhythms that would come and go like the wind, never completely taking hold of my heart, just moving the air that I breathed and filling time between life's more important moments. UNTIL ONE DAY THEY BECAME THE AIR THAT I BREATHED.

It's hard to explain this feeling to someone who doesn't share the same affliction. It's similar to being possessed, I would imagine, though I can't verify this by personal experience as of yet.

When your heart, mind, and soul cannot control or refuse the desire to create a sound, or lyric, or rhythm, and you are helpless against the burning impulse to purge these inner demons, you are forever committed to a lifetime of chasing the next song. If it weren't such a sublime affliction, it could very well be considered a curse.

By the time music got its hooks in me, I became hopelessly pre-occupied with every aspect of its construction, throwing all other childhood interests out the window. Nothing else fascinated and stimulated my mind as much as the composition and arrangement of a song, and every waking hour was spent unraveling this mystery. Having no true music training, I didn't refer to the sound as "notes" on paper; it became shapes that I could see in my head as I listened intently to the multiple layers of instruments. Like colorful building blocks stacked upon each other, music became something that I could "see," a neurological condition known as synesthesia, where when one sense is activated (hearing) and another un-related sense (vision) is activated at the same time. My inability to read music sharpened my musical memory, because the only way I could retain information was to take a mental snapshot of it in my head, which honed my ability to focus. It was the handicap of not having lessons or even an actual drum set to learn on that challenged me and made me work even harder to get better, to find a way to succeed. I know that now.

At an early age, I started to play the drums with my teeth, sliding my jaw back and forth and chomping up and down to simulate the sound of a drum set in my mouth, doing drum rolls and grace notes as if I were using my hands, without anyone ever noticing. As I walked to school every morning, I would hum melodies and perform drum parts with my teeth, playing my favorite songs and writing original compositions until I walked through the front door and unloaded my backpack into my locker. It was my best-kept secret, almost as if I was silently practicing drumming all day long in my head, which taught me new tricks to try once I sat down at an actual kit. During one childhood visit to the dentist, the doctor inspected my pearly whites, backed up, and asked, "Do you chew a lot of ice?" Puzzled, I replied, "Ummmm . . . I don't think so?" He informed me that I had an unusual amount of deterioration from something wearing down my teeth, and I immediately knew the culprit. "I can play the drums with my teeth!" I proudly exclaimed. Baffled, he stared at me as if I were a crazy person, so I told him to come closer, and he bent down, putting his ear just centimeters from my mouth. I proceeded to perform Rush's "Tom Sawyer" for him, my jaw moving back and forth at lightning speed, the sound of calcium and enamel being chipped away like a tap dancer on a brittle stage, and his eyed widened as he stepped back in shock, telling me that I might want to reconsider this strange and orally detrimental habit. But there was no turning back. I was cursed to a lifetime of orthodontic percussion.

I have only met one other person in my life who followed this same abnormal practice: Kurt Cobain. It is most noticeable during our *MTV Unplugged* performance that we filmed in New York City in November 1993. You can see Kurt's jaw clenching and moving side to side at certain points in the show, because it served as a sort of metronome while he strummed his guitar. To me, this made perfect sense, as every musician creates his own individual "feel." There is an internal rhythm that each musician follows, and no two are the same. As I wrote in the foreword of Chad Kushins's John Bonham biography, *Beast,* this concept is hard to define:

*Every musician plays differently, we know this, but there
must be something intangible that differentiates the music
written on a chart from what is created by one drummer to
the next. Is it the way that each mind interprets a pattern?
The internal clock that is defined by one's physical and
emotional construct? The way they see the space between
the notes? I have watched many producers try to explain
and manufacture "feel," but I am convinced that over-
intellectualizing it is futile. It is something divine that only
the universe can create, like a heartbeat or a star. A solitary
design within every musician that is only their own. I liken
"feel" to the cadence of poetry, sometimes comforting, other
times unsettling, but always a gift from one soul to another.
A romance between the giver and receiver which serves as the
punctation of one's truth.*

And it was John Bonham's "feel" that brought me to that fateful night in front of my makeshift altar in the carport.

I had been listening to Led Zeppelin since I was a little kid, as
their songs were on permanent rotation on the rock and roll stations
of my youth, but it wasn't until I became a drummer that I noticed
the confounding mystery of John Bonham's sound and fell head
over heels in love with their entire catalog. When I listened to his
drumming, I literally heard voices speaking to me, sometimes in a
whisper, sometimes in a scream. This was something that I never
experienced while listening to any other drummer, and at times it
almost scared me. There was something about the space between
his notes that made the electrical impulses in my brain stutter, and
time would slow in the milliseconds before each snare drum hit, as
if I were falling into a crushing black hole over and over again. The

weight behind his groove was more than physical, it was spiritual, and as hard as I tried to emulate his playing, I finally realized that it was no use because this was more than drumming, it was a language of his own, his irreplicable DNA laid bare on vinyl.

Though he was technically mind-boggling, I wasn't so concerned with *how* he played what he played; I was more interested in *why* he played what he played. What was his intention? Why did his signature groove seem so much more natural than that of any other drummer, like the ocean tide, sometimes crashing against towering cliffs, other times gently lapping the shore? What was it about his feel that spoke to me? And did I have a feel of my own? I eventually deduced that this was the work of the universe, and I was going to need to get to the bottom of that question by offering myself up.

At this point in my life I was exploring mysticism and the notion that a person could become one with god or the Absolute, so I was open to investigating how that might happen (I was also exploring hallucinogens at the time), but I followed no particular creed in my selfish quest. And, though I understood the basic concept of organized religion, I wasn't raised in a religious environment and would only go to church with my Episcopalian father once a year on Christmas Eve, when we would attend mass at DC's historic St. John's Church. I certainly connected with the spiritual aspect of it and found the ceremony to be beautiful and quite uplifting, but that particular set of beliefs had not been ingrained in me from an early age, so it all remained a mystery to me. It wasn't until I was sent to a Catholic high school (for reform, not religion) that I studied the concept of faith and began to understand what it actually meant.

Among my numerous classes in Catholic religion, such as "Old Testament," "New Testament," and "Christian Scriptures," there was one that I enjoyed the most, called "Understanding Your Faith." More than just lists of psalms and verses to memorize, this was an exploration of the concept of faith, the unconditional belief in something that defies logic and guides your life. Now, *that* was something that I could relate to, though in a much different context. THERE WERE CERTAIN THINGS IN MY LIFE THAT I RELIED ON UNCONDITIONALLY AND IN WHICH I HAD UNWAVERING FAITH—THE LOVE OF MY MOTHER, MY LOVE FOR HER, AND THE LOVE THAT FILLED MY HEART WHEN I PLAYED MUSIC. And so, without the conventional structures and rules that usually went along with such things, I considered music my religion, the record store my church, the rock stars my saints, and their songs my hymns.

It was that unconditional faith that I meditated upon as I sat before the flickering candles of my punk rock tabernacle.

Was it witchcraft? I have attended a Wiccan ceremony and found it to be quite similar to my innocent teenage experiment all those years ago, but I can only call my little ceremony what it was to me at the time, an appeal to harness the power of the universe to achieve my greatest desire. It's easy to chalk it all up to coincidence, but as I write this today, having tattooed both the three-circles logo and a gothic "606" into my skin, I have to think that I manifested my destiny that night, utilizing the Law of Attraction, calling upon the universe, tapping into a higher power, or whatever. I just know that today, the success I prayed for in my carport that night has found me.

Or maybe I sold my soul for rock and roll?

PART TWO

THE BUILDUP

YOU'D
BETTER BE
GOOD

"Okay . . . so, you wanna play some Zeppelin or AC/DC or something?"

Hunched over in a chair positioned directly in front of my drum set was none other than the one and only Franz Stahl, legendary guitarist of DC's coolest hardcore punk rock band, Scream. As a seventeen-year-old mega-fan I could barely contain my excitement, practically shaking on my drum stool while my callused hands gripped my splintered drumsticks in white-knuckled anticipation, dead-ready to jam with my personal hero. It was painfully clear that this otherworldly feeling was not mutual. Franz seemed about as enthusiastic for this audition as if it were a trip to the dentist for a double root canal.

"No, man . . . let's do Scream songs!" I practically yelled. Somewhat shocked, he looked up from the guitar in his lap with his big blue eyes and asked, "Oh yeah? Which ones do you know?"

This was the moment I had been waiting for. I stared Franz straight in the eyes and, in my best Clint Eastwood–catchphrase tone, brazenly said, "I know them all . . ."

Soon the dingy, underlit basement of this Arlington, Virginia, head shop exploded in a deafening fury of wailing guitar and astronomical BPM. Franz and I blasted through their entire catalog, album after album, even playing tunes that hadn't been released to the public yet (yes, I may have had a few bootlegs). With each song, I could see Franz's mood lift, as I needed little to no instruction for any verse, chorus, or finale to guide me. He didn't know that his songs had been burned into my memory. After all, barring my one lesson from a local jazz drummer ("You're holding your sticks backward, David"), I'd basically learned to play the drums by listening to Scream.

My punk rock baptism had occurred just a few years before, and I had begun collecting records with the ravenous fervor of a crackhead in heat, spending all of my hard-earned money on any album that I could find in the hardcore section at Olsson's Books and Records in Georgetown, one of the few local record stores that actually carried underground music. Every last penny of my Shakey's pizza and landscaping salaries was spent amassing a collection of loud, fast, and beautifully primitive albums that I would excitedly purchase with crumpled bills and carefully counted coins, racing home to throw them on my turntable, inspecting every detail from the artwork to the credits as I played them on repeat at concert-level volume. My mother was a very tolerant woman, allowing me to listen to whatever music I pleased (even the occasional Satanic death metal band).

Scream were different, though. Their sense of musicality and dynamics was a bit deeper and wider than that of most other hardcore bands, dipping into classic rock, metal, ska, and even reggae with ease. More important, their songs were full of incredibly catchy melodies that seemed to awaken the Beatles fan in me, something that most other punk rock bands had to substitute with atonal noise out of sheer songwriting inability. Plus, their drummer, Kent Stax, was a rudimental force of nature. It was clear that he had a deeper knowledge of the drums than most self-taught punk rock drummers, as his speed and precision were virtually unmatched. Like he was Buddy Rich in Doc Martens and a leather jacket, you could tell the dude had practiced his paradiddles.

With my pillows and a pair of oversized marching band drumsticks, I would sit and play along to my Scream records until there was sweat literally dripping down my bedroom windows, doing my best to try to emulate Kent's lightning-speed drumming, which was no easy task. I had no band of my own at the time, much less a drum set, but it didn't matter. I could close my eyes and imagine in that moment that I was the drummer of Scream, thrashing away to my favorite songs as if they were my own.

Having formed in 1979 after seeing the legendary Bad Brains play in a tiny venue downtown called Madam's Organ, Scream were a group of lifelong friends who met in high school and went on to form one of America's most seminal punk bands, and were much older than me. Over the years, they had become local heroes, respected by all musicians in the scene, and I would go to see them any chance I had. Lead singer Pete Stahl stalked the stage like a vagabond Jim Morrison possessed, bassist Skeeter Thompson held down the grooves with concrete time, and guitarists Franz Stahl and Harley Davidson (yes, you read that correctly) were a blinding duo of crunchy rhythms and solos. As morbid as it may sound, I would often fantasize that I would be in the crowd at a Scream gig and an announcement would come booming over the PA system— "We apologize for any inconvenience, but due to an emergency with their drummer, Scream will not be able to perform tonight. That is . . . unless there's someone in the audience who can fill in for him . . ."—and I would jump up on the drum set and save the day. Juvenile, I know, but hey . . . a kid can dream . . .

Eventually, my prowess as an amateur pillow percussionist out-grew the confines of my ten-by-ten bedroom, and I started playing an actual drum set in actual bands, with names like Freak Baby, Mission Impossible, and Dain Bramage. My skills were grow-ing exponentially, and I was implementing all of the tricks I had learned from playing along to my favorite records, eventually show-casing my own bastardized versions of all my favorite drummers. I was terribly heavy-handed when I sat down behind a real drum set, given my pillow-beating training, the equivalent of an athlete's running in the sand. I broke skins and cymbals at an alarming and painfully expensive rate, so much that I became a regular at the neighborhood music store, constantly replacing my demolished gear as the jaded employees gleefully took my money, week after week.

One day, as I passed the bulletin board full of flyers and advertisements on the wall by the front door of the music shop, I noticed a xeroxed sheet of paper out of the corner of my eye that read:

SCREAM LOOKING FOR DRUMMER. CALL FRANZ

This couldn't be, I thought. First of all, why on earth would Scream, an internationally known band, be advertising for drummer auditions in a dumpy Falls Church, Virginia, music store? And second, how could they possibly find a drummer who could even get close to how Kent Stax played on their incredible records? I incredulously took down the number and decided that I would call, even if just to tell my friends that I had spoken with THE Franz Stahl on the phone. At the time I was seventeen years old, still in high school, and in a band with two of my closest friends called Dain Bramage, so I was surely not qualified nor ready to commit to actually joining a band as established as Scream, but I couldn't pass up the opportunity to at least jam with them once for bragging rights. My ridiculous, juvenile fantasy of swooping in and saving the show had perhaps manifested this unexpected twist of fate. Deep down I felt that I had to let the universe take its course.

I raced home and nervously dialed the number from the phone on my mother's desk, pushing aside the ungraded school papers. To my amazement, Franz answered, and after a stammering presentation of my imaginary résumé (lies), he told me that the band had nowhere to practice at the moment, but he'd keep my number and call me back when they could jam. I took that as a good sign and

waited for him to get back to me. Of course, I failed to mention a few rather important things on that first call. The most glaring omission? My age. I couldn't imagine that he would let a seventeen-year-old high school junior without a car who still lived with his mother try out for his band, so I did what any ambitious young rocker would do: I fucking lied and told him that I was twenty-one.

Weeks passed without word from Franz, so I thought I'd give it one more shot, calling his number again in hopes that he had misplaced mine. His girlfriend answered and, after a long chat, promised that she would have him call me. (As I have now learned in my wise old age, if you want something from a musician, ask their girlfriend.) It worked, and within hours he returned my call. We set a time and date, opting for that dingy basement in Arlington.

I begged to borrow my sister's 1971 white VW Bug for the evening and miraculously managed to stuff my entire drum set into it like thirty clowns playing an expert-level game of Tetris. There was barely enough room to breathe, much less move the gear shift as I drove, but nothing was going to keep me from that audition. My mind was racing with excitement as I barreled down the highway, imagining just being IN THE SAME ROOM as Pete, Skeeter, Harley, and Franz, blowing their minds with my next-level shit, living out my rock and roll fantasy.

When I arrived, I was greeted by Franz and only Franz. Having few to no expectations based on my nerdy, clearly not twenty-one-year-old voice over the phone, I'm sure that he'd informed the others that my audition was probably a waste of their time and spared them the torture. My dreams of a one-night stand with the almighty Scream were instantly dashed, but that didn't stop me from playing like my life depended on it.

Because it did.

Afterward, Franz seemed surprisingly impressed and asked if I'd like to come back and jam again sometime. I couldn't believe my ears. I had passed round one at least. Feeling like I had just won the lottery, I happily agreed, methodically crammed my drum set back into the VW Bug, and drove home with a heart full of pride.

The next audition was with the full lineup. Apparently, Franz had told the band that I was worth listening to, and the others joined in, curious to see this skinny, no-name kid from Springfield who knew every one of their songs beat the living shit out of his cheap Tama drum set like he was in a stadium full of people. Now I was truly barking with the big dogs, surrounded by faces that I had seen only on record sleeves or from the crowd while dancing my heart out and singing along at the top of my lungs. That dingy basement was shaking with the awesome sound of Scream, though Kent's rudimental drumming was now replaced by my relentless Neanderthal wallop, strengthened from years of running in the sand.

After another triumphant rehearsal, I started to see that my intention of jamming with Scream for bragging rights was turning into something more serious. They unanimously agreed that I was the drummer they had been looking for, so I was now faced with the real-life opportunity to join an established band that had made a name for themselves with a killer catalog, had amassed a loyal following, and toured not only around the country but internationally as well. My dream was coming true.

I WAS AT A CROSSROADS. High school was going nowhere for me, and my future was looking more and more like a life of manual labor and suburban monotony with each dismal report card. My heart was entirely devoted to music, my one and only passion, so my grades (and my attendance) had by now slipped to the point of no return. A bitter pill to swallow considering that my mother was a much beloved teacher at our neighborhood high school, and I, her only son, was racing down a dead-end street on a collision course with the school guidance counselor at best, expulsion at worst. Then there was my father and his dreams of my becoming an upstanding Republican businessman, the most implausible of all scenarios. At this point, I'm sure that he had given up any hope for my future on Capitol Hill, but he was my father after all, and he had instilled a fear of disappointing him in me from day one. Then there were my good friends in Dain Bramage. I had known Dave Smith and Reuben Radding for years, and our little three-piece made one hell of a noise. We had yet to really tour and hadn't even gathered much of a local fan base, but we were indeed a young band giving it our best try. In hindsight, I like to think that we were "before our time," as our sound would have fit right into the underground explosion of the early nineties, mixing the energy of punk rock with the melodies of REM, Mission of Burma, and Hüsker Dü. But at that time, we were still just kind of floating.

For me to upend my life and join Scream would mean leaving school, to the dismay of my public school teacher mother; sacrificing the already strained relationship I had with my disapproving father; and quitting the band I had started with my two close friends. It was a gigantic leap of faith, to say the least, with no guarantee of any kind of safety net. It was some scorched-earth shit. After much consideration and soul searching, I just didn't have the courage. Perhaps because I had no faith in myself. So, I politely declined, thanking them, and my life went on as I barreled ever faster down my dead-end road.

A few months later, I saw that Scream was playing a gig downtown at the 9:30 Club, a Washington, DC, landmark for underground music. With a legal capacity of only 199 people, it was a dark, dingy dive bar, but it was our church, and I had seen dozens of shows there over the years, even playing a few myself. I decided to go to the show, as I now considered the guys my friends, but deep down I knew it would be heartbreaking to watch a band I could have joined but hadn't, simply out of fear. Fear of change. Fear of the unknown. Fear of growing up.

The houselights went down, the band took their places, and Kent Stax started the walloping snare drum intro of "Walking by Myself," a more recent song that summoned the fire of the Stooges and the MC5 in a wall of guitars and heavy groove. The energy in the packed club was like a tightly wound coil ready to pop, and when the full band kicked in, the room absolutely fucking exploded . . .

Hey you!
Well take a look at me
Have you forgotten what's real or what started our scene
I'll tell you what I mean
Am I screaming
For something to be?
Have all my friends
Turned their backs on me?
I'm out here walking by myself
I'm out here talking to myself . . .

I sang along to these words at the top of my lungs and suddenly everything made sense. I instantly regretted my decision to not be a part of something so cathartic. My heart leapt into my throat like it had been shot out of a cannon, and I decided right then and there that this was my destiny, this was my band, this was my future, and this was my life. The crossroads I was faced with in my dead-end suburban life suddenly vanished and I decided to take that leap of faith, leaving everything behind for the feeling that shot through my veins when the two hundred people in that room erupted in a wave of chaos and joy.

After the show, I told the band I had made a stupid mistake and wanted back in. After a bit of cajoling and convincing them that I was 100 percent committed this time, they welcomed me with open arms. Kent had recently become a father and chose to devote his life to his family. His decision to follow a new path opened up one for me.

Now all I had to do was turn my life upside down.

My biggest concern was my mother, of course. The woman who'd sacrificed so much for me, devoted every second of her life to my personal well-being, and shown me nothing but love from the day I was born. I never wanted to disappoint her, because aside from being my mother, she was my best friend. I couldn't let her down. I like to say now that she disciplined me with freedom by allowing me to wander, to find my path, and ultimately find myself. I never wanted to sacrifice her trust, so I respected her and always kept it cool. I knew that my leaving school at such a young age would break her heart, but I also knew that staying would break mine.

We sat at her desk, and with my head hung in shame, I explained that I wanted to drop out of high school and tour the world. Her response?

"YOU'D BETTER BE GOOD."

I can only think that, after twenty-five years of teaching underachievers like myself, my mother knew deep down I was not college material. But she did have faith in me. She saw the light in me and understood that my heart, soul, and drive were not things you learn from any blackboard or textbook under the hypnotic buzz of the classroom lights. She would often say, "It's not always the kid that fails the school. Sometimes it's the school that fails the kid." So, as she always had, she gave me the freedom to wander, find my path, and find myself.

My father was a different story.

Sitting in the principal's office flanked by my parents, I was read the riot act and given a most hopeless life forecast of poverty and despair by my father and the guidance counselor. I was a worthless punk in their eyes, a hoodlum rat with nothing to offer other than to fill their tanks with gas on the weekends or shine their loafers at the airport as they waited for their next flight, but I sat there and took it all like Rocky Balboa, thinking, *Fuck you. I'll prove you both wrong.* My favorite line? "You probably do all the things that a kid your age shouldn't do, like smoke cigarettes and drink coffee." Coffee? Since when was coffee considered a class A drug? I proudly confessed to both.

As we walked to our separate cars in the parking lot, my father got one more jab in before officially disowning me for good, screaming, "AND STAY OFF THE DRUGS!!!" It was the most trembling, Bob Dole–esque display of tight-ass Republican fury I have ever seen, still to this day. I could only laugh. His degradation couldn't hurt me anymore. I was finally off the hook, and so was he (I seem to remember his driving a new, forest-green Plymouth Volare soon after I left school and can only conclude that the meager college fund he had set aside for me was immediately withdrawn and blown on this most pimp-ass ride). The cord was officially cut, and I was free to bolt.

I'D BETTER BE GOOD, I THOUGHT.

As for my friends in Dain Bramage, well . . . they were pissed. I left them in a shitty spot, and primitive voodoo dolls adorned with my face may have been impaled over stacks of burning Scream records for years to come, but I am happy to say that to this day we are all still friends, and we try to see each other whenever possible. Our lone LP, *I Scream Not Coming Down,* was recorded during a biblical electrical storm over Crofton, Maryland, in July 1986 and is a temper tantrum of spasmodic rhythm and beautiful melody. I will be proud of this album forever, not only because it was my first, but because of its wonderfully unique qualities. There was no one like us.

With my life completely upended, I took a job at a local furniture warehouse prepping trucks full of gaudy entertainment centers and recliners for delivery and began rehearsing with Scream on a regular basis. We spent months honing our sound and writing new material before finally debuting the new lineup July 25, 1987, at a benefit show for Amnesty International at Johns Hopkins, which was to be followed by a silent candlelight march past several international embassies to draw attention to human rights abuses worldwide. This was the most nervous I had ever been to perform, not only because of the size of the audience (anything over twelve people was considered stadium rock to me) but because the room was filled with all of my local heroes. Members of Minor Threat, Fugazi, and Rites of Spring all looked on to see if I had what it took to fill the giant shoes of the great Kent Stax, and I felt that it was my personal responsibility to do the band proud. After all, Scream were their heroes, too.

Sights were set on a fall tour of America, which was to begin in October. Scream had made this six-thousand-mile lap around the country multiple times before, but this was to be my first, something I had dreamed about ever since I picked up my first instrument. The idea of traveling town to town with no other responsibility than to rock you night after night almost seemed too good to be true.

The proposed itinerary read like the back of an old Grand Funk Railroad concert T-shirt, with a quick twenty-three shows in a little over a month taking us up the Eastern Seaboard, across the Midwest, over the Rockies to the West Coast, and back home through the South. The farthest I had been from home at that point was Chicago, on one of our epic family road trips, so to see cities like Kansas City, Des Moines, San Francisco, Austin, Tacoma, and Los Angeles on the schedule absolutely blew my fucking mind. I was not only over the moon, I felt like I was traveling to it in a Dodge van.

The van.

Historically, vans have always been the preferred and most economical mode of travel for young, independent bands that need to get from point A to point B with little to no money. From the Beatles to Bad Brains, all bands start here, or at least they should. Not only does the van serve as your equipment truck, carefully packed to fit an entire backline of gear inside (multiple amplifiers, guitars, and drums), but it also becomes your home away from home. A place to sleep when there is no hotel room (there never is), a place to warm up when there is no backstage, and a place to establish lifelong bonds with your bandmates on those epic, cramped trips across the country. It's not for everyone, I can tell you that. It takes a certain type of person with a certain type of disposition to survive months in what seems like a miniature submarine with wheels, but if you can take it, it becomes a formative experience that you will forever rely on for life perspective.

With five people in our band (plus one roadie, none other than my lifelong friend Jimmy Swanson), we had to methodically manage the space in our van down to the last square inch. Scream were veterans of this DIY science, so designing an interior layout that would successfully fit each person *and* all of our equipment wasn't impossible, it just required some serious engineering (courtesy of lead singer Pete Stahl) and multiple trips to the hardware store. The design involved building a platform from two-by-fours and plywood sheets that would act as an area to sleep on, while all the gear would fit comfortably underneath. This was not a glamorous setup by any means, but it was efficient and functional. Once we found the perfect configuration to pack the gear underneath the platform, it could never deviate from that carefully calculated puzzle, otherwise the shit wouldn't fit. Even though that tour was over thirty years ago, I can still vividly remember how to load that old bucket of rust with the speed and efficiency of a fire station on call.

When the day finally came to embark on our cross-country journey, the van sat parked in the driveway of the old Bailey's Crossroads house where we'd rehearsed for months, and one by one each member showed up with his duffel bag and sleeping bag in tow, ready to shove off. I was the youngest member of the band by almost ten years, and this was to be my first tour, so to say that I was green would be generous at best. "Hey!" Harley barked at me from the front seat as we were climbing into the van. "Don't be asking me to pass you stuff from the back every ten seconds, you hear me?" Ken Kesey's *Further* was quickly turning into the river patrol boat from *Apocalypse Now,* and we hadn't even backed out of the goddamned driveway yet. Fuck.

I had finally let it slip in an interview a few months before that I wasn't actually twenty-one, I was only eighteen, forgetting that I'd lied about my age on that first call with Franz. The others had looked at me in shock, but at that point we were such a well-oiled rock and roll machine from all of those sweaty rehearsals in that tiny basement, it made no difference. There was no turning back. The only problem my lie posed was that I wasn't legally allowed inside some of the bars that we were booked to play in, so we kept our mouths shut, and if anyone ever found out, I would sit in the van patiently waiting to play, jump onstage when it was time and tear the roof off the joint, then scurry back to the van immediately after the show, soaked in sweat.

Like a row of smelly sardines in a can, we would lie across that squeaking, quaking platform in our musty sleeping bags, reading, listening to music, laughing, farting, and passing the time any way we could on those long drives. Being confined to such a small space with so many people for such long periods of time actually benefits the little time you have onstage, because when you finally set up and plug in, you just want to fucking explode. Any angst, frustration, homesickness, or depression that you may feel is taken out on your instrument in a primal fit of rage for that fleeting hour of performance, and if you're playing loud rock and roll, it doesn't get any better.

One of the first stops on that tour was CBGB's in New York City. Having been to New York City only once before on a family trip that my mother paid for by taking on an extra job as the JV girls' soccer coach for four hundred dollars (it was a miracle of couponing and all-you-can-eat buffets), I was boiling with excitement to return, and to the legendary CBGB's no less! This was punk rock ground zero, the epicenter of the soundtrack of my youth, and I would soon be standing on that stage myself, playing my heart out for the ghosts of those who had paved the way for young punks like me. The Ramones, the Cramps, Talking Heads, Television, Patti Smith, Bad Brains—this was hallowed ground, and it was my life's greatest achievement that I had even made it this far.

Upon arrival, the sight of the iconic awning above the front door sent shivers down my spine. I was overcome by its beauty, weathered and decayed from years of the Bowery's filth, just as I had seen in decades of black-and-white photographs. A crowd of punks had already gathered on the street, and we conveniently (incredulously) found a parking space directly in front of the club, spilling out of our van like Jeff Spicoli after hours of smoke and confinement. We were greeted by the infamous Harley Flanagan, bassist of New York's most notorious band, the Cro-Mags. I was starstruck. Their album *The Age of Quarrel* was in my top ten punk records of all time, and here I was face-to-face with the most terrifying-looking punk rocker I had ever seen. You needed only take one look at the guy to realize he should not be fucked with. Ever. Plus, he had a pit bull on a leash that was almost as vicious as he was, so the combination of these two together made me keep my distance, until he spotted Skeeter and Pete and it instantly turned into a reunion of old friends, all smiles and handshakes and mutual respect. I was introduced and must have seemed like a schoolgirl at a Beatles concert, meeting what I would consider a "rock star." We invited Harley into the gig, but he declined, having nowhere to put his dog, so we kindly offered to let the dog stay in our van out front as we played. Problem solved. We began to set up our gear for our afternoon slot on the bill.

As I was nervously setting up my drums in front of a full house ready for us to begin, I couldn't for the life of me find my drum key (a most important tool to tune, tighten, or adjust any piece of drum hardware) and eventually realized that I had left it in the van. I screamed at Pete, "Dude! I need the keys to the van really quick!!" He tossed them to me from across the stage and told me that we were on in five minutes, so I elbowed through the crowd all the way to the front door in a flash and ran to the van parked out front. Fumbling with the keys as if I were disabling a time bomb, I finally slipped it into the keyhole, flipped the lock, grabbed the handle to open the door, and "RAHAHARAHHAHARAHA-HAH!!!!!!!" The face of the most demonic, bloodthirsty pit bull filled the window in a murderous fit of fury that almost made me soil myself. *Fuck!* I thought. There was a club full of people ready for us to start any minute, and the only thing between me and that fucking drum key was a horrifying fifty-pound mass of muscle and teeth. I needed to find Harley, and I needed to find him fast. I ran back into the club, scanning the dark room for his unforgettable sneer until I spotted him and begged for his assistance. When I opened the van door with Harley by my side, I was greeted by not Satan's hound from hell, but an adorable puppy wagging its tail in excitement to see its best friend, squealing and licking his face until I found the drum key, locked up once more, and made it to the stage in time to tear CBGB's a new asshole. If it weren't for Harley Flanagan, not only would there have been no show, but I probably wouldn't have a nose or lips right now.

Next, we headed toward the Midwest for shows in Chicago and Detroit. I was no stranger to Chicago of course, but I considered Detroit somewhat exotic, uncharted territory. Of course, everybody knows its rich history of music, but many don't realize it was America's murder capital for the two years prior to my first visit (rivaled only by Washington, DC), so there wasn't much sightseeing to be done unless it was from the safety of the van. Not only was this one of America's roughest towns, but Detroit was home to some of America's roughest bands—it's not a coincidence that the MC5 and the Stooges were both from there. Our gig that night was with local heroes Laughing Hyenas at a bar called Paycheck's in Hamtramck, a predominantly Polish neighborhood about five miles from the center of Detroit. A hard act to follow, the Hyenas were as abrasive and mean as their hometown would suggest but kind enough to invite us to stay at their place after the show. They lived in a group house in Ann Arbor, which was about an hour west of Detroit, so seeing as how we were heading in that direction anyway, we took them up on their most generous offer.

Heading out of town, I was on cloud nine as we stopped at a desolate, bullet-ridden gas station to fill up the tank before the drive, because that night I had met another hardcore hero of mine, Laughing Hyenas lead singer John Brannon, who was once the singer of my favorite Detroit band, Negative Approach. I was living out my punk rock dream, not only meeting the faces of my record collection but now sleeping on their fucking floors.

The party started the minute we arrived, and soon everyone was drinking (among other things) furiously while watching Super 8 films on a small screen in the living room. Exhausted from the show, I decided to pack it in early, opting to chill in the van parked out front to get a good night's sleep somewhere quiet rather than toss and turn in this house of horrors all night long. Sleeping in the van was common practice, mind you, even if you were lucky enough to have found a house to crash in, because there was always the chance that someone would break in and steal all of your equipment, rendering you dead in the water far from home. So I volunteered to guard our livelihood with my life, headed out to the van, and passed out in the comfort of my Kmart sleeping bag.

I awoke hours later to the feeling of the van rumbling down the highway. Confused, I sat up from my sleeping bag and looked around, but everyone was gone, except for Pete, who was quietly driving, his face silhouetted with each passing streetlight. "Dude, where is everybody? Where are we going?" I croaked as I wiped the sleep from my groggy eyes. In his classic Southern drawl, Pete looked at me and said, "Do you believe in miracles?" Hours before, as we were filling up our tank to begin our journey westward, Pete had left our "float bag" (a small bag with all the cash we had to our names, around $900) on top of the gas pump back at that desolate, bullet-ridden gas station in one of the worst parts of town. Realizing that it was gone, he'd jumped in the van and doubled back to Detroit at top speed in the unlikely event that it was still there.

Miraculously, it was, and we continued on. I began to realize that at any moment, this whole thing could fall apart. That sense of suburban security I had been conditioned to aspire to was now in my rearview mirror, and the thrill and mystery of this new freedom fit me like a glove.

After a few shows, we had managed to cross the Mississippi River, the farthest I had ever been from home, and I was beginning to settle into this new life of truck stops and tollbooths quite comfortably. To really see America, you need to drive it mile by mile, because you not only begin to grasp the immensity of this beautiful country, you see the climate and geography change with every state line. THESE ARE INDEED THINGS THAT CANNOT BE LEARNED FROM AN OLD SCHOOLBOOK UNDER THE COLD CLASSROOM LIGHTS; THEY MUST BE SEEN, HEARD, AND FELT IN PERSON TO BE TRULY APPRECIATED. The education I was getting out here on the road proved to be far more valuable to me than any algebra or biology test I had ever failed, because I was discovering life firsthand, learning social and survival skills I still rely on to this day (e.g., knowing when to speak and when to shut the fuck up).

Though I was finally free to follow my lifelong dream, I would still occasionally call my mother to reassure her that she had made the right decision in letting me go. Even thousands of miles apart, I was closer to her than anyone and wanted her to know that the gamble she had let me take with my life was paying off.

Kansas City, Boulder, Salt Lake City—the cities flew by as we wound our way out to the West Coast, leaving a trail of beer cans and blazed stages in our wake. Within weeks, we were driving through the cold drizzle and towering evergreens of the Pacific Northwest, headed to our gig at Tacoma's Community World Theater, where we would play with a young band by the name of Diddly Squat. Great name, but even greater bass player, who I would meet years later to form a band of our own. Yes, Foo Fighters bassist Nate Mendel was a teenage punk just like me, and our paths actually crossed a few times without formal introduction, but that's how these things tend to happen; you just have to let the universe take the wheel. Thank goodness it did.

I have to say, I didn't find the Pacific Northwest very appealing at first, and that's being kind. The oppressive blanket of low-lying, gray clouds that permanently blocked out the sun in the fall seemed to drain not only my energy but also my mood. Not to mention the "aroma of Tacoma," a smell that emanated from the industrial paper mills in town, redolent with subtle notes of boiled broccoli farts and dog shit, which moved through the city depending on the direction of the shifting wind. Lovely. How anyone could permanently live somewhere so depressing was beyond me, but then again, this was a corner of the country that I knew absolutely nothing about . . . yet. One thing was for certain, though . . . the weed was getting better and better with every mile farther west.

My career as a dusk-to-dawn stoner was in full swing now; I was smoking it if I had it, searching for it if I didn't. This posed perhaps life's greatest challenge on the road. Not only did you have to budget it into your $7.50-a-day per diem (cigarettes, Taco Bell, weed) but you had to have a keen sense of party radar to scope out who was holding and who wasn't at all times. Jimmy and I were constantly on the lookout for any lanky metalhead with a Slayer patch on the back of their leather jacket or crusty hippie-punk with dreadlocks tucked into a knit cap milling around the gig. When we rarely scored, we would run back to the van and inspect the bud, marveling at its superiority to the brown dirt weed we were used to smoking back home, and then proceed to get high as two Georgia pines right before the show.

It was finally time to head to California, somewhere I never in my wildest dreams thought I would see. To be standing in front of the Hollywood sign 2,670 miles away from my little idyllic neighborhood made as much sense to me as planting a fucking flag on Pluto. Unfathomable. All I knew about America's most glamorized state was what I had seen on television and in movies, so I imagined all the police would look like they were in the Village People, all the kids would look like they were in *The Bad News Bears,* and all the women would look like Charlie's Angels. (Turns out I was right.)

With five days until the next show, we took our sweet time heading down to our next destination, Santa Cruz, another town I knew virtually nothing about other than it was where Corey Haim's vampire masterpiece *The Lost Boys* was filmed. Scream had become close friends with a band from Santa Cruz called Bl'ast years before, and as most everyone was in this underground network community, they were generous enough to offer a place to crash until our next show, in San Francisco. The eight-hundred-mile drive was a killer, but the scenery made up for our claustrophobia. We wound through the mountain passes of the prehistoric Pacific Coast Ranges until we finally made it to the Pacific Coast Highway, where we threaded through the mighty redwoods as giant waves crashed along the cliffs. I was in awe. Having watched the landscape evolve into this natural beauty over long, arduous weeks and thousands of miles, I considered this the payoff. I felt so lucky, so alive, so free.

Stopping at a pay phone as we got closer to town, Pete called ahead to our host, Bl'ast buddy Steve Isles, and gave an ETA for our arrival. He returned to the van with wonderful news: Steve's mother, Sherri, was making a huge pasta dinner for us all and we would be crashing at their beautiful A-frame house just down the street from the beach for the next four days. This wasn't tour anymore, this was Club Med. We bought Sherri a bouquet of flowers and a bottle of wine at the grocery store and raced to our new accommodations, ready to break free from the confines of our van and feast like kings.

We were greeted like family, and before long the mountains of pasta were being devoured and fat joints of the most incredible marijuana I had ever seen were being passed around the table, the thick, sweet smoke wafting in the air as we drank and told stories from the road. To my amazement, even Sherri was smoking! Now, THIS was California. I thought MY mom was cool. For Sherri to take in this vagabond group of disheveled punk rockers, feed us, smoke us out, and give us somewhere warm to sleep was nothing short of sainthood-level charity. It was the most selfless act of hospitality I had ever experienced. I passed out in my sleeping bag with a foggy smile and a full stomach.

The next day, Sherri was leaving town but instructed us that the leftovers were in the fridge and the weed was in the cupboard. Jimmy and I looked at each other and immediately made a beeline to the cupboard, where we found a large mason jar packed with the kind of weed you only see in a *High Times* centerfold. We grabbed a hairy, fluorescent-green bud and headed down to the beach on two Vespa-like scooters that we found in the garage, and there it was . . . the Pacific Ocean. I walked across the sand to the shore break and let the freezing water rush over my feet as I watched the sun set on the horizon. I had made it. FROM ONE OCEAN TO THE OTHER, I HAD CROSSED THE COUNTRY ON NOTHING MORE THAN THE LOVE OF MUSIC AND THE WILL TO SURVIVE.

Surely, it could never get any better than this.

SURE,
I WANNA
BE YOUR
DOG!

SCREAM

SCREAM

Spring Tour, 1989

March 31...Richmond, VA
April 4....Columbia, S.C.
        5....Orlando, Fla.
        6....Tallahassee
        7....Miami
        8....Gainesville
        9....Atlanta, GA

        10
        11
        12...Hattiesburg, Miss
        13...Memphis, Tenn.
        14...Fayetteville, Ark.
        15...Little Rock
        16...New Orleans, LA
        17.
        18.
        19...Austin, TX
        20...Houston
        21...Dallas
        22...Tulsa, OK
        23...Oklahoma City
        24...
        25...Albuquerque, N.M.
        26...Las Crusas
        27...Tuscon, Ariz.
        28...Phoenix
        29...Los Angeles, Calif.
        30...SanFrancisco
May 2....L.A.
        3....L.A.
        4...LasVegas, NE
        5...Salt Lake City
        6...Berkley, CA
        7...
        8
        9...Chico
        10...Arcadia
        11...University of Oregon
        12...Portland
        13. .Seattle, WA
        14...Vancouver

Toronto, Canada. June 22, 1990. A sunny afternoon in "the 6."
Scream had just set sail on yet another North American tour in
our trusted (but funky) Dodge van, beginning with a jump over
the border for a short run of Canadian shows in two of my favorite cities on earth, Montreal and Toronto. Over the years, Scream
had established a small but loyal fan base up in the Great White
North, while making friends with a network of amazing people
who kindly hosted us in their various warehouse lofts and shared
apartments every time we came to visit (far more comfortable accommodations than we were used to at the time). From my first
tour at the age of eighteen, I always loved traveling to Canada. The
hash was good, the girls were cute, and the shows were consistently
wild, usually pulling in enough paid entrants to get us to the next
stop without much trouble. But it was the post-show parties with
our Canuck buddies, unrivaled in hilarity, that really made the
trek worthwhile. Because, let's face it, Canadians are fucking awesome. Laid-back, genuine, and funny as all hell. I defy anyone to
walk one city block without making a fast friend in Canada. We
were always welcomed there with open arms by our extended fam-

ily of freaks and geeks, and they never failed to show us a good time, whether drunkenly wandering the streets of Montreal well past midnight in search of smoked-meat sandwiches and poutine, or getting high until the sun came up while watching *Night Ride*. (Still to this day one of my favorite shows, *Night Ride* was literally just a camera mounted on the dashboard of a car, driving around town for an hour with a jazz flugelhorn soundtrack. Part of a genre hilariously referred to as "slow television," if paired with a little smoke and drink, it became a surreal, absurdist meditation. Very popular with prison inmates . . . or so I hear.)

Of all the venues in Toronto, the Rivoli on Queen Street West was perhaps the coolest club in town. Known for hosting the hippest bands on the underground touring circuit, with a capacity of around 250 people, it may not have been Royal Albert Hall, but it well suited a band like ours, and we would undoubtedly tear the roof off the fuckin' joint with a triple-digit decimal attack come showtime. As we loaded in and unpacked our gear onto the tiny little stage for an early soundcheck, I noticed that the bartender was putting up promotional posters for Iggy Pop's new album, *Brick by Brick,* all over the sticky, nicotine-stained walls. *Strange,* I thought, but since it had nothing to do with our gig, we all proceeded to plug in and crank up our high-octane punk rock and roll, getting our PA and monitor levels correct for that night's performance as best we could. Our road crew at the time consisted of one roadie, Barry Thomas (very Canadian), so the process of assembling our backline of equipment was mostly left to the band. No sound engineer, no lighting engineer, just the four of us and Barry. Typically, a club soundcheck was a late afternoon affair just before doors opened, as set times were usually in the later hours of the evening. But, for whatever reason, on this particular day we were asked to come in much earlier, at noon for our nine P.M. show. Kind of un-

National Bowling Hall of Fame and Museum

St. Louis

This 1936 Studebaker bowling pin car was created by a Cleveland, OH, proprietor. National Bowling Hall of Fame & Museum, St. Louis, MO

HOWDY MOM — JUST HANGIN OUT
AT THE BOWLING HALL OF FAME,
EATING HOT DOGS AND BUYING
T-SHIRTS. WE PULLED INTO ST.
LOUIS AROUND 11:00 LAST NIGHT
AFTER DRIVING FOR ALMOST 12
HOURS. THIS IS WHERE JENNIFER
AND I SORT OF BECAME AN ITEM,
SO ITS OUR LITTLE WALK DOWN
MEMORY LANE. TODAY WE DRIVE TO
OKLAHOMA CITY, PROBABLY ANOTHER
10-12 HOUR DRIVE. I'LL CALL YOU
THIS WEEKEND.
          XXXXOOOOO
          XXXXOOOOO
              LOVE
                DAVID

#3041 Art Grossmann Photo © 1989

MADE IN U.S.
ART GROSSMANN PHOTO MARKETING

POST CARD

HOUSE OF MOM

USA 29

I pledge allegiance...

0 277315 5

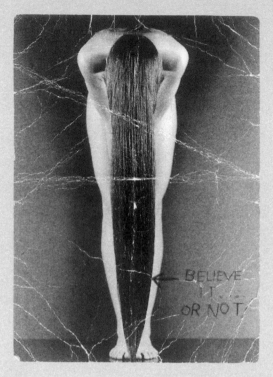

← BELIEVE
IT...
OR NOT

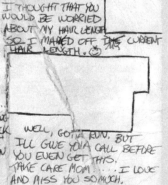

MOM—
    WASSUP? I'M SITTING HERE
IN A LITTLE HOUSE IN ANN ARBOR,
THINKING ABOUT HOW DIFFERENT
EVERYTHING IS AROUND HERE.
THE PEOPLE, THE PLACES........
EVEN THE DUNKIN DONUTS SHOPS
ARE DIFFERENT COLORS. ITS
GOOD TO SEE THE COUNTRY
LIKE THIS THOUGH, THERES SO
MUCH MORE TO LIFE THAN
BACKLICK SHOPPING CENTER
AND SPRINGFIELD MALL. I LOVE IT....

    I REALLY DO MISS EVERYTHING
THOUGH, I CANT WAIT TO GET BACK
AND DRIVE THE HONDA! ALL IVE
BEEN DRIVING LATELY IS THE VAN
(OCCASIONALLY) AND ITS SERIOUSLY LIKE
A HUGE TANK. BUT I SUPPOSE
THATS JUST WHAT WE NEED.

OH YEAH— ABOUT THIS
POSTCARD............
I THOUGHT THAT YOU
WOULD BE WORRIED
ABOUT MY HAIR LENGTH
SO I MARKED OFF THE CURRENT
HAIR LENGTH. ☺

    WELL, GOTTA RUN, BUT
ILL GIVE YOU A CALL BEFORE
YOU EVEN GET THIS.
TAKE CARE MOM.....I LOVE
AND MISS YOU SO MUCH.

                DAVID

usual. Nevertheless, we dutifully complied. As I tuned my drums and watched more and more Iggy posters go on the wall, I had a sneaking suspicion that something was up, so I stopped what I was doing and asked the bartender, "Hey, man, what's the deal with all the posters?"

"Iggy's having a record release party here before your show," he nonchalantly replied. "And he's performing."

My head practically exploded. This was a blessed miracle of musical destiny! Talk about being in the right place at the right time! I was soon to be in the same dingy little room as the godfather of punk, IGGY FUCKING POP! The artist formerly known as James Newell Osterberg Jr., this man was the Adam AND the Eve to what we now refer to as punk rock, and he would soon transform this little hole-in-the-wall club into a sonic Garden of Eden! The term "living legend" doesn't even begin to describe his importance and relevance. I mean, the guy is credited with inventing the fucking stage dive. Top that!

"But you guys have to clear out after soundcheck. It's record company only."

In an instant, my dreams of meeting this musical enigma were dashed. I begged. I pleaded. I held back the tears of a thousand Cure fans and furiously racked my brain to come up with any and every excuse I could think of to convince him that we should stay. "But, but . . . what about our equipment? We need to be here to make sure nobody steals anything!" I blurted out, hoping he would take the bait and give us a pass. "The gear will be fine," he said. "It's just a bunch of record company types."

Drowned in disappointment, we finished our soundcheck and retreated back to our old rust bucket in the alley, licking our wounds and cursing corporate, major-label record release parties to the fiery pits of hell. Banished from this once-in-a-lifetime experience, we were feeling pure heartbreak and rejection, rivaled only by the time I was dumped at a senior homecoming dance (which was on a boat, meaning I was therefore trapped in teenage purgatory until we docked hours later). Had the term "FOMO" existed in 1990, it most definitely would have applied here. Now our only options were to wander the city looking for a drink or sit in the van for nine fucking hours eating pizza and listening to the radio. Slightly hungover from the night before, I went with option B.

A short time later as we relaxed in the van, a black stretch limo appeared. Like a rock and roll secret service operation, it stealthily pulled into the back alley, stopped, and popped the trunk as the club door simultaneously swung open, a security guard awaiting the chauffeur's precious cargo with the choreographed attention to detail that would be offered for a sitting president. Peering out from the comfort of our homeless shelter on wheels, we craned our necks in excitement to see our hero in the flesh. And then, like Daniel's vision of the angel . . . he appeared. Just a short distance from our parking space, he emerged from the car, all five feet and seven inches of rock royalty poured into old jeans and a T-shirt. He walked to the trunk, grabbed his guitar case, and scurried inside. THIS WAS THE CLOSEST I HAD EVER BEEN TO A BONA FIDE ROCK STAR UP TO THIS POINT IN MY LIFE. His beautiful, crooked image had been burned into my brain from years of studying his work, but this was no one-dimensional album sleeve or bedroom poster. This was the living, breathing embodiment of cool, in the flesh. And, just like that, the backstage door closed behind him.

I have waxed poetic about the thrill of human interaction many times before, particularly as it applies to live music, because it takes us from the one-dimensional virtual experience to the three-dimensional tangible experience, ultimately reassuring us that this

WEST PALM BEACH

FLORIDA IMPRESSIONS
LASER PRINTS

HOWDY GUYS, I'M IN PALM BEACH NOW, ON MY WAY TO GAINESVILLE FLA. SO FAR WE'VE PLAYED ORLANDO, TALAHASSE, AND MIAMI. WE SPENT SOME TIME ON THE BEACH IN MIAMI, GOT ALOT OF SUN AND DID SOME GOOD SWIMMING. IT SEEMS LIKE MORE OF A VACATION THAN A TOUR SO FAR. AFTER TONIGHTS SHOW WE HAVE 3 DAYS OFF AND THEN OFF TO TENNESSEE(?). EVERYONE HERE IS FILTHY RICH AND VERY TAN. WE ATE IN A LITTLE LUNCHONETTE TODAY THAT THE KENNEDYS USED TO COME TO. KIND OF EXPENSIVE BUT COOL PEOPLE. I'M HAVING A GOOD TIME WITH EVERYONE, AND THE SHOWS HAVE BEEN O.K.. I'LL WRITE AGAIN SOON. I MISS HAVING AROUND YOU GUYS ALOT. SEE YOU SOON.

THEM GROHLS

Jack London
KINA, ITALY

WEST PALM BEACH, FLORIDA... Beautiful Waterways and
Beaches Make this a Favorite Vacation Spot.
Photo by Werner J. Bertsch

© SCENIC FLORIDA DIST
305-963-7694

DAVID

HEY— ITS THE 24th OF APRIL IM FINALLY SENDING THIS

life is real and that we are not alone. Even just a chance encounter with a person you've grown up listening to, gazing at their album covers for hours on end, learning to play the drums from studying their jagged, tribal grooves, can send the matrix on its side. That's all it took for me that night. My faith in music was rewarded, just by watching Iggy walk the short distance from his car into the same dark door I had just exited. My world was now a little bit brighter. And that was that.

A bit later, there was a knock at the window of the van. "Which one of you is the drummer?"

If I've learned one thing in my thirty-three years of being a professional touring musician, it's that nothing good ever comes from this question. More often than not, it's followed by either handcuffs, a subpoena, or a swift punch in the teeth. Not the type of thing you want to hear when you're parked in a litter-filled alley-way, eight hundred miles from home, in another country. My head shot up from my musty sleeping bag in the back of the van, eyes widened in fear, awaiting fierce retribution for god only knew what crime I had committed to warrant this damning inquisition. Frozen in shock and mind racing, I immediately began to review all of the regretful possibilities that had brought me to this fate. Had I left a lit cigarette on the drum riser at soundcheck, sparking a raging inferno that had proceeded to burn the venue to the ground with Iggy Pop inside? Maybe made a smart-ass remark about another local band in a blurry fanzine interview, to the dismay of an angry, struggling fellow musician? Perhaps a vengeful ex-boyfriend had waited for this moment ever since the day his girlfriend left him to be with me? (Least likely scenario. I fucking lived in a van, for Christ's sake.) I sheepishly raised my hand and with a trembling whimper replied, "Ummmm . . . that's me?"

"WANNA PLAY DRUMS WITH IGGY POP?"

This took being in the right place at the right time to a whole other level.

Confused at such an unimaginable proposition, I paused a moment. Like most musicians, I had fantasized that someday I would be called to the stage by my favorite band to fill in for their drummer, who, for whatever reason, could not perform. I had fantasized about that happening with Scream, back before I joined. Now it was actually happening. Since I learned to play the drums by listening to my favorite bands' records, I could replicate any of their albums note for note, Iggy and the Stooges included. This opportunity was, simply put, a dream come true. My heart retreated from my stomach in a rush of relief, and I screamed, "FUCK YEAH!" as I jumped out of my makeshift bed. I scrambled to collect myself as my bandmates looked on in wild amazement, tumbling out the side door onto the street in a rolling wave of excitement, racing to that backstage door as if I were on fire.

Once inside, I could hear a loud, distorted electric guitar being primitively strummed, feedback filling the room with deafening frequencies. As I turned the corner, there stood Iggy, guitar in hand, face-to-face with a full Marshall stack that towered over him like a monolith from *2001: A Space Odyssey* as he played jangly, dissonant chords and fiddled with the knobs to find his tone. First impression? He was wearing glasses. Not cool fucking rock star glasses, mind you. No, I'm pretty sure they were readers. *Thank god for that,* I thought, as it instantly defused some of the mortifying tension that had overcome me as I inched toward the stage. Before I could properly introduce myself, the man who had summoned me from the comfort of my sleeping bag blurted out, "Here's the drummer kid from tonight's band." Iggy turned with outstretched

POST CARD

HI GUYS. THIS POSTCARD IS'M
ACTUALLY FROM OCEAN CITY. A FRIEND
OF MINE MADE IT. AND SINCE I
HAVE NO OTHER I SHALL SEND
THIS. AINT IT PRETTY? SITTING IN
THE VAN OUTSIDE OF THE LIBRARY
IN MOUNT VERNON, WA. PETE HAD
TO PICK UP TAX FORMS (WE HASNT
EVEN DONE IHS YET) CAUSE HE'S
IN BIG TROUBLE. OH WELL, WE'RE
ON THE RUN ANYWAY. MY JOURNAL
IS GETTING FAT WITH NEW ENTRY'S
EVEN THOUGH WE HAVENT DONE
MUCH BUT EAT, SLEEP, + DRIVE.
CANT WAIT TO PLAY TONIGHT.
OUR FIRST 2 SHOWS WERE
GREAT, LETS HOPE THE
REST ARE AS WELL.

CATS, DOG, + GROHLS

I'M GROWING A MUSTACHE
AND GOATEE, BUT IT'LL
PROBABLY BE GONE BY THE
TIME I GET HOME. I'LL
SEND PICTURES.
TAKE CARE + SEE YOU
SOON. XXXXX LOTSA LOVE
DAVID

hand and said, "Hi, I'm Jim." I nervously clasped his hand, the same one that had penned the lyrics to such classics as "Lust for Life," "No Fun," "Search and Destroy," "I Wanna Be Your Dog," and so many more.

"Hi, I'm Dave," I said, like a kid meeting his teacher on the first day of school.

"Do you know my music?" he asked in his familiar Midwestern drawl. Now, ever since I was a child, I had always been told that there is no such thing as a stupid question, but no level of humility could spare Iggy the ridiculous "duh" face that I gave in response to this doozy. "Yes. I know your music," I said with a smile. "Wanna jam?" came next. Strike two. "YES," I obviously replied. I crawled back to my drum stool, and with Iggy fucking Pop standing a mere six inches from the yellow Tama drum set that I'd bought with money made from painting houses and mowing lawns, we started to jam. The rolling riff of "1969" was soon filling the empty room, and I joined in with its well-known tom-tom pattern, note for note, just like the record. Only guitar and drums, our stripped-down version of the song was even more raw than the classic album version (eat your heart out, White Stripes). Next up, the devilish "I Wanna Be Your Dog," perhaps my favorite from the Stooges' 1969 debut. Then, a curveball: he started showing me a song from his new record I had yet to hear, called "I Won't Crap Out." With the passion of a man performing to a sold-out stadium, he sang:

I'm standin' in a shadow, hating the world
I keep a wall around me, block out the herd
It's a nerve-wreck place to be, it kills real quick
You gotta scrape the concrete off your dick . . .

Having never heard the song, I followed along as best I could but had to wonder why the hell he was going to all the trouble of teaching me something that no one would ever hear. Maybe he was just lonely and wanted to jam? Maybe he was graciously making some no-name kid's dream come true by inviting me to play along with him, knowing that it was a story I would get to tell for the rest of my life? As strange as it seemed, I kept focused on his strumming hand and locked into the arrangement, banging it out like we WERE in a sold-out stadium. We ended in unison on a triumphant final crash.

"Great," he said when we finished. "We go on at six o'clock."

Wait, what? Us? This? Tonight? This was not at all what I was expecting. Never for one second did I imagine he would want to perform these songs with me IN FRONT OF PEOPLE. I thought this was just an impromptu jam session, something to pass the time fucking around as I had done a thousand times before with friends in basements and dusty garages filled with gasoline cans and gardening tools. I didn't realize this was a fucking audition! My jaw dropped, and with an incredulous stare I said, "You wanna do this tonight?" Iggy stood there smiling and said, "Yeah, man!" "Ummmm . . . should we have a bass player?" I asked. Seeming rather surprised, he said, "You got one?" I ran top-speed out to the van to grab our bassist, Skeeter. I couldn't wait to share this life-changing experience with another bandmate, knowing that he would appreciate it as much as me. Skeeter was a huge fan of Iggy and the Stooges as well (not to mention a phenomenal bass player with perfect time and feel), and the three of us were rehearsed and ready in no time. It was official: we were now Iggy Pop's rhythm section, at least for one night in Toronto.

As the record company filed in, we hung with Iggy in the tiny dressing room offstage, smoking cigarettes and listening to stories from his fabled career. THIS MADMAN, REVERED FOR LIVE PERFORMANCES WHERE HE SMEARED PEANUT BUTTER ALL OVER HIS BODY, CUT HIMSELF WITH SHARDS OF GLASS, AND EXPOSED HIMSELF TO THE AUDIENCE, WAS NOTHING BUT A FRIENDLY, WARM, DOWN-TO-EARTH GENTLEMAN. As if things couldn't get any weirder! He made us feel entirely welcome, and soon our nerves turned to excited anticipation. Every now and then there would be a knock at the door, and a label representative would ask, "Need anything?" Skeeter and I quickly realized that these people thought we were ACTUALLY Iggy's band! So, without hesitation, we began to see how much we could milk this already unimaginable experience. "A pack of smokes?" Done. "A case of beer?" No problem. "A carton of smokes?" Absolutely. It then hit me: This is what it feels like to make it. No sleeping in a freezing van with four other guys, lined up like sardines in sleeping bags on a plywood platform, rationing a $7.50 per diem on Taco Bell and shitty weed. No going home and begging for my job back every time a tour was over, patiently waiting for another to take me away from my high-school-dropout reality. No waiting in littered alleyways for your shot at some imaginary stardom. I knew that this feeling of success was fleeting, so instead of just a taste, I took a mouthful.

We hit the stage and were greeted with applause like I had never experienced before: Iggy Pop–sized applause. "FUUUUCK YOOOOU!!!" he screamed into the mike as we counted into the first song, "1969," and the crowd went wild. No longer that warm, down-to-earth gentleman I had just befriended backstage, he was instantly transformed into the Iggy punk fans all over the globe know and love. Tearing through song after song, I barely had time to reflect on the full-circle nature of this incredible twist of fate, so with head down, I surrendered to the moment and beat the living shit out of that big yellow drum set like it was my last night on earth. Every now and then I would look up through my greasy hair to see his chiseled, crooked frame stalking the stage like in all of those iconic one-dimensional photos and videos I had seen a thousand times before. Except now, he was three-dimensional, reassuring me that life is indeed real and that I am not alone. It was over within a matter of minutes, far too soon, and with free cigarettes and beer in in hand, we thanked Iggy and went our separate ways. I HAD FINALLY "MADE IT," EVEN IF ONLY FOR ONE NIGHT, AND IT WAS JUST LIKE I'D ALWAYS DREAMED IT WOULD BE. Too good to be true. So, without the least bit of disappointment, I appreciated it for the beautiful experience that it was. It was practically delusional to expect I would ever be in the right place at the right time again. What were the odds?

Our Scream tour continued, though not without complication. The shows that we were to play throughout the Midwest in order to get us to the West Coast were canceled, meaning we had to make the four-thousand-mile drive to Olympia, Washington, with nothing but those free cigarettes and the cash in our pockets. Having nothing left to lose, we decided to go for it. After all, we had made it this far; what was another long trip across America?

Little did we know it would be our last.

EVERY
DAY IS
A BLANK
PAGE

RAS RECORDS
P.O. Box 42517
Washington, D.C. 20015
(301) 564-1295

SCREAM
P.O. Box 4965
Falls Church, Virginia 22044-0965
U.S.A.

PETER MARC STAHL — *VOCALS*

SKEETER — *BASS*

DAVE GROHL — *DRUMS*

FRANZ STAHL — *GUITARS*

PHOTOS BY: TOMAS

For Bookings in the United States:
Doug Carin, Tripple XXX Entertainment
6715 Hollywood Blvd., Suite 287
Hollowood, California 90028
(213) 466-8730

For Bookings in Europe:
Tos Niewenhausen
P.O. Box 14570, 1001 LB
Amsterdam, Holland
Tel. 31-20-882-152

"Anyone seen Skeeter?"

A bit hungover from another wild night in Laurel Canyon, we all began to rise from our sleeping bags on the crowded living room floor of the dilapidated Hollywood bungalow that we had been sharing with a few Hollywood Tropicana mud wrestlers and took a head count. Pete, check. Franz, check. Barry, check. But Skeeter was nowhere to be found. *There's still time,* I thought, as we didn't need to be at soundcheck for that night's gig until later in the day, so crawling back into the comfort of my little cocoon for another few hours of sleep, I closed my eyes and crossed my fingers that, first and foremost, Skeeter was okay, but also that he hadn't left us stranded on tour thousands of miles from home with no money and no way back. A legitimate concern, considering that he'd pulled a disappearing act before.

By 1990, my travels with Scream had taken me from Louisiana to Ljubljana, Memphis to Milan, San Francisco to Stockholm, and at this point I had become a hardened road veteran, no stranger to the occasional crisis or conflict, so having one member missing in action was just another day in the life on tour. What had once been a crash course in how to survive on less than $10 a day in a van was now a familiar, comfortable routine, and I had assimilated into the life of a wandering vagabond quite easily.

The European tours were especially exciting; we visited countries that I had seen only on the nightly news or read about in my painfully neglected textbooks. But rather than the usual historic tourist sites that most people experience when traveling overseas, I was discovering the world from the seedy underbelly of the underground punk rock scene. Since Scream had toured Europe once before I joined the band, they had already established a network that took us in like family, giving us places to stay, food to eat, and equipment to use on tour since we had no money to ship our own instruments from home. Most of those friends were musicians as well, and most lived in squats, abandoned buildings that were filled with punks and anarchists, often pirating utilities from the city grid to survive. These communities of radicals were not only intriguing to my young, impressionable mind but also inspiring, as life in these makeshift communes was broken down to the most basic human elements, forgoing the trappings of conventional existence (materialism, greed, and social status) for a life of protest, freedom, and the understanding that we all need each other to get by. I found it all to be quite beautiful, worlds away from the suburban white-picket-fence syndrome I had left behind at home. The simple trade of a warm bed for a song created the foundation for my appreciation of being a musician, one that I still rely on to this day and use to get perspective when I feel lost in the tsunami of my now much more complicated life.

Amsterdam had become our home base for plenty of reasons, some obvious (weed), some simply logistical (proximity to northern Europe). We would usually save up our hard-earned money working our menial day jobs at home and fly standby on a Dutch airline called Martinair for ninety-nine bucks a pop, arrive at Schiphol international airport, steal a bike the first night, and spend the next few weeks preparing for our tour by making phone calls with a pirated phone card, rounding up gear, and renting a van that would become our home for the next few months. For extra cash, we would return bottles at the night shop, try our hand at the gambling machines in the bars, and even take odd jobs here and there to make ends meet. (I once worked at a small mail-order record company named Konkurrent, stuffing boxes full of albums to be shipped all over the world, just to support my weed habit until the tour started.) It was bare bones, but the hospitality and camaraderie shown to us by our gracious friends made us feel like we were living in the lap of luxury, and I eventually fell in love with the city so much that I even attempted to learn Dutch, a language that I'm convinced is impossible to speak if you weren't born in Holland.

BUT, MORE THAN ANYTHING, I WAS FREE, AND THERE WAS ADVENTURE AROUND EVERY CORNER.

One night in Amsterdam as we were all hanging out drinking on the sidewalk in front of our favorite punk rock bar, De Muur, there was a sudden burst of energy across the street at the Vrankrijk, one of Holland's most infamous squats. An army of skinheads and right-wing fascists had organized an attack on the building, and as they came marching up the small street, the residents of the Vrankrijk prepared for battle. Blinding floodlights turned on from the balconies, and chicken wire came down over the windows as punks began pouring out of the squat with makeshift weapons and shields. A full-on riot broke out, and before long we all joined in, throwing our glasses of beer high into the air, raining them down on the crowd of angry fascists in explosions of shattered glass like catapults launching warm malted grenades. Within minutes, the intruders surrendered and ran off, and we continued on with our night, now celebrating the rebellion like Vikings home from war. This wasn't rock and roll. This was medieval shit.

And that was just a Tuesday night.

Traveling Europe's gorgeous countryside became my favorite pastime, more so than rolling down the long, monotonous super-highways of our American trips, but it came with its own unique set of challenges. As we jumped from country to country, we were faced with a new language every week, and communication was reduced to a primitive version of sign language that bordered on ridiculous miming. That being said, I was learning about languages and cultures I never would have experienced in school, and the physicality of actually being in these places deepened my understanding of the world as a community, which is much smaller than most imagine. But the border crossings were always interesting . . . imagine the delight of a customs official when a gang of young punks would pull up in a van bearing Netherlands license plates (big red flag) and filled with guitars and amplifiers (bigger red flag). Like shooting fish in a barrel, they would line us up like convicts on the sidewalk and tear our van to shreds looking for any and all contraband. (I must admit, I've been subjected to more than a few body cavity searches over the years.) Though, having watched the 1978 film *Midnight Express* one too many times, we were all responsible enough to know to smoke up all our weed or hash before crossing any border, for fear of rotting away in a dark, dank prison. That being said, there was always a way to get around "the man." Whether stuffing our speaker cabinets full of Scream T-shirts to sell at shows (our bread and butter on the road) to avoid taxation from country to country or hiding small chunks of hash in Skeeter's dreadlocks so that we'd all have something to smoke on the long drives between shows (nothing like watching our bass-ist play with the drug dog at the border, knowing full well that his tangled mop was filled with ounces of spicy black hash), we did what we had to do to get by. But not without a few close calls along the way.

Once, when walking down an alleyway in Amsterdam with my old friend Marco Pisa, an Italian tattoo artist who I had met in Bologna when I painted his tattoo studio in exchange for a beautiful branding on my left shoulder, we were approached by two junkies trying to sell us heroin. Neither of us were fans of heroin (or junkies), so Marco politely declined with a stern "Fuck off!" and we kept walking. They persisted, following us closely, tapping our shoulders, and in a flash, Marco whipped out a switchblade with ninja speed and repeated, "FUCK OFF!" Stunned, I turned to walk away, but in the corner of my eye noticed one of the junkies about to hit me full force in the head with a metal pipe he had picked up from a construction site we were walking past. Marco and I took off like a shot, chased by a pack of screaming zombies, barely outrunning them before having a nice Thai lunch by the scenic canals.

It was enough to make anyone want to pack up and fly back to the comfort of their warm bed at home, but it was this element of danger that kept me from doing exactly that. FROM DODGY RENTAL VEHICLES DRIVING THROUGH APOCALYPTIC SCANDINAVIAN SNOWSTORMS AT NIGHT, TO PASSPORTS BEING STOLEN FROM YOUR ROOM AS YOU SLEPT, TO FISTFIGHTS WITH DRUNKEN ASSHOLES TRYING TO STEAL GEAR OR SWAG FROM THE VAN, EVERY DAY WAS A BLANK PAGE, WAITING TO WRITE ITSELF.

Even in the depths of my frustration and starvation, I never once entertained the idea of surrender. What did I have to go back to? Begging my boss at the furniture warehouse to let me come back to ten-hour days of coating garish sleeper sofas with toxic

3M chemicals? A lifetime of crippling rush-hour traffic, counting the strip malls and fast-food restaurants on every corner? I would rather have lain delirious in a tiny Spanish apartment, shivering in a pool of my own sweat from a debilitating flu as the sound of Barcelona's bustling Las Ramblas district echoed below. I'd rather have slept on a cold nightclub stage in Linköping, Sweden, after the show as paramedics rushed in to save someone dying from a drug overdose. I'd rather have pulled in to play a squat in Italy where they were burning their linens outside after a scabies outbreak, or been warned not to eat the pasta prepared by a local promoter who was attempting to poison us in retribution for a broken toilet.

Ride or die, as they say.

But perhaps it was this life of instability that made Skeeter abandon us the first time. On what would ultimately be my last European tour with Scream, in the spring of 1990, he decided that, for whatever reason, he just couldn't hang and flew home, leaving us stranded on another continent thousands of miles away. Fortunately we had our good friend Guy Pinhas fill in for a few shows so that we could finish the tour with just enough money to catch the standby flights back on El Al airlines, but I was beginning to think that maybe Skeeter's dedication to the band wasn't the same as Pete's, Franz's, and mine. We would have done anything and everything to keep the wheels from falling off.

Though none of us were irreplaceable, the chemistry between the four of us was undeniable, and Skeeter and I had a certain groove together, something that he had instilled in me years before at one of our early rehearsals, and something that was sorely missed when we played with a substitute bassist. I was like a wild pony when I first joined Scream, playing as fast and as hard as I could, placing meaningless drum fills at the end of every phrase to impress anyone within earshot. One day, Skeeter sat me down, rolled an enormous joint from the paper wrapper of a tampon found in the bathroom, and got me so fucking high I could barely see straight. "Okay, we're gonna play one riff, the same riff, for thirty minutes and you're not going to do one drumroll," he said. *Easy,* I thought. I sat down behind my kit and he began to play his silky bass line, part reggae, part Motown, and I confidently joined in. It wasn't forty-five seconds before I felt the urge to do a drumroll, but he shook his head and warned me not to do it, so I continued on with the groove. A minute later, I again felt the insatiable need to do a crazy drumroll, almost like a form of musical Tourette's or holding back a sneeze, but Skeeter just shook his head. Essentially, Skeeter was breaking the wild pony, training me to respect the simplicity and power of a groove, teaching me to refrain from gratuitous bluster. After thirty minutes, I was an entirely different drummer. This was perhaps the most valuable musical lesson of my entire life, and I am forever indebted to him for that.

The few replacements that filled his shoes on the following tours were great players, but when Skeeter offered to return it was hard to say no, even though we worried that he'd pull his disappearing act again. Things actually seemed to be looking up for the band at the time, as we had just recorded a new batch of songs that caught the attention of a fellow punk rocker turned music business insider who offered to help us find a place for it at a much bigger label. A friend of a friend, and well respected in the punk rock scene as a man of great integrity, he offered us a contract to sign that would allow him to shop our tape around and find us a deal. This could be it, we thought. Maybe this was our ticket out of the alleyways full of junkies and scabies-infested squats that we had grown accustomed to over the years. As tempting as it was to sign it right there and then, we decided to think about it before trusting our lives to a complete stranger.

It wasn't until one sweltering-hot day in Spokane months later, stranded in the parking lot of a Denny's after multiple shows across the country had been canceled, that we pulled out the contract and read it in the back of our van, thinking that we had nothing to lose. Because at this point, we truly didn't. The walls seemed to be closing in, and no matter how hard we tried, it never seemed hard enough. Without any legal representation present, we signed that contract out of sheer desperation, a reckless act of naiveté. One that eventually came back to haunt me a year later, when that "punk rock man of great integrity" sued me, a twenty-one-year-old kid, for joining Nirvana, basically claiming he owned me. This, ladies and gentlemen, was my introduction to the music industry.

At least we had Los Angeles to look forward to.

Los Angeles was always the highlight of every tour, not just because of the obvious bells and whistles that came along with a few days in hairspray heaven, but because we had family there:

Pete and Franz's sister, Sabrina. Sabrina was the most fun, bubbli-est, most beautiful woman you had ever seen, and had traded the sleepy suburbs of Virginia for the glamour of L.A. sometime in the late eighties. Whenever we were in town, we would shack up at her place, and like an eighties video vixen chaperone, she would show us around, from the bright lights of the Sunset Strip to her place of business: the Hollywood Tropicana.

Sabrina was a mud wrestler.

For those unfamiliar with this rather fringe sport, it is the act of two people wrestling in a pit of "mud," which is maybe not ac-tual mud but something else that resembles Silly String and cook-ing oil (don't ask me, I've never had the pleasure). Not necessarily sanctioned by the Olympic committee (yet), it is a very casual af-fair, usually consisting of one woman in a bikini versus a drunken businessman who blew the majority of his entertainment budget on the company card to get his ass handed to him by a five-foot-eleven supermodel in a neon swimsuit. I mean, these women glee-fully beat the living shit out of these dudes, leaving most men to be carted away holding their ruptured genitals in screaming pain as the crowds roar with the ferocity of Romans in the Colosseum. As difficult as it may have been for Pete and Franz to see their younger sister step into a slippery pit of mud with a complete stranger, we would all go down for free drinks and collapse in fits of laughter as one by one each victim was carried off. And after the merciless slaughter, we would return to the Laurel Canyon bungalow that Sabrina shared with a few other mud wrestlers and party all night. "Slumming" is not a word that comes to mind.

Los Angeles fascinated me, almost as much as the centuries of history in Europe, but in a much different way. Everything seemed so . . . unbelievable. As much as Washington, DC, could be con-sidered a transient town, with its social dynamic shifting dramatically with every new administration, L.A. seemed to change minute by minute. Like it was the world's largest Greyhound bus station, people came and went through a revolving door of opportunity and demise, leaving their filth behind for the next wave of visitors to wade through in hope that *they* would be the next big thing. There was a sadness that seemed to be masked by excess and over-indulgence, making the hangovers just a little bit harder to drink away the morning after. And nothing could be more sobering than waking up in a sleeping bag on a mud wrestler's floor, praying that your band member didn't leave you high and dry. Again.

By six P.M., there was no sign of Skeeter, so we regretfully had to call and cancel the gig that we had booked for that night. Reality started to sink in. No Skeeter meant no show. No show meant no money. No money meant no food. And no tour meant no way home, leaving me to consider the nightmarish scenario of spending the rest of my life in the dismal desperation of America's most glamorous city, wading through the filth as its latest victim. We had dug ourselves out of countless holes over the years, but this one seemed particularly deep.

The days passed, and through the charity of our mud-wrestling roommates, who came home every night emptying their purses full of dollar bills into big piles on the living room carpet, we managed to survive like the strays that we were. Food was scarce, and the hunger soon set in. Our roadie, Barry the Canadian, was having his Social Security checks sent down to help keep us from starving, but they only lasted so long. To this day, I will never use the expression "doesn't amount to a can of beans," because I remember one day finding a can of beans in that kitchen and its actually saving my fucking life. Times were surely tough, but having been conditioned to survive any challenge from years on the road, I tried my best to keep my head up. It wasn't easy.

I eventually took a job tiling a coffee shop in Costa Mesa for some spare cash, but as time went by it became more and more evident that we weren't heading home any time soon. Barry eventually went back to Canada after realizing that ours was a dead-end situation, understandably so. I was starting to feel hopeless and needed even a tiny sense of relief or rescue from our slowly sinking ship. Our gear was gathering dust in the downstairs garage of Sabrina's house, but after a week or so I noticed something else gathering dust in that little garage: a black 1985 Honda Rebel 250 cc motorcycle. Like a Fisher-Price version of a Harley-Davidson, it was a glorious little machine, only one step above a moped, but perfect for darting around town. Having always dreamed of owning a motorcycle (literally a recurring dream throughout my life), I raced upstairs and inquired about who owned this glamorized minibike. Turns out it belonged to one of Sabrina's mud-wrestling roommates, who said, "Sure, take it! Just fill it up with gas and it's all yours!"

MY LIFEBOAT WAS LOWERED.

Without a license or helmet (headgear not required in those days), I waited for the sun to go down, filled the Rebel's tiny tank with gas, and took off through the hills, avoiding any major thoroughfares for fear of getting pulled over and, well . . . because I didn't know how to ride a fucking motorcycle. I left all of my troubles behind on the floor of that cluttered living room as I wandered aimlessly through the neighborhood around Sabrina's Laurel Canyon house and spent hours driving through the winding maze of the affluent Hollywood Hills, looking down at the shimmering lights of the city below and looking up at the countless gorgeous houses nestled in the trees, dreaming of one day living in such luxury. Each one was no doubt occupied by a rock star, or a movie star, or a producer or director who had followed their dreams and somehow struck gold, and I wondered how it must feel to achieve that level of success, how it must feel to live in such comfort, and how it must feel to know where your next meal is coming from. The chasm between this fantasy and my reality was so wide, so unimaginable, it wasn't even worth pondering. So, I just drove. This was my escape. This was my temporary rescue. This was my lifeboat from the ship slowly sinking in the distance. And as I sped through the night, I took stock of all the things that had brought me to this place, retracing my steps while trying to plan the next. Night after night I followed this routine, waking up every morning in my sleeping bag on the living room floor with my eyes practically swollen shut from the dust and dirt of the canyon roads, back to the reality of being a mud wrestler's stray pet.

AND THEN I HEARD THE FIVE WORDS THAT CHANGED MY LIFE FOREVER: "HAVE YOU HEARD OF NIRVANA?"

On a phone call with an old friend who had grown up with the guys from Nirvana in the tiny town of Aberdeen, Washington, I was informed that they were in between drummers at the time and had seen Scream perform just weeks before on our ill-fated tour. Apparently, they were impressed with my playing, and I was given their phone numbers to call. Of course, I had heard Nirvana. Their debut album, *Bleach,* was a landmark record in the underground music scene, blending metal, punk, and Beatles-esque melody into an eleven-song masterpiece that would go on to change the landscape of "alternative" music (while coincidentally costing $606 to make). It had quickly become one of my favorites and stood apart from all of the other noisy, heavy punk records in my collection because it had SONGS. And that voice . . . no one had a voice like that . . .

After a few more days of frustration and starvation, I decided to roll the dice and call the bass player of Nirvana, Krist, to inquire about the drummer gig. Having never met him, I introduced myself and explained that our mutual friend had given me his number, so we chatted awhile until Krist regretfully informed me that the position of drummer was already taken by their good friend Dan Peters from Mudhoney. It had been worth a shot, I thought, but it wasn't the end of the world. I left my Los Angeles number with Krist and told him to keep in touch and give me a shout if they ever happened to come down to L.A., since it was beginning to look like the City of Angels was unfortunately now my permanent residence.

That same night, the house phone rang. It was Krist calling back. Seems he had given the matter more thought. "Maybe you should talk to Kurt," he said. Danny Peters, although an amazing drummer in his own right, had a very different style than mine, playing with a more sixties rudimental feel as opposed to my simplistic, Neanderthal disco dynamic, which seemed a bit more up Nirvana's alley. Plus, Krist and Kurt felt a bit guilty taking Danny from Mudhoney, one of their favorite bands of all time. So, I immediately called Kurt and we talked music for a while. From NWA to Neil Young, Black Flag to the Beatles, the Cramps to Creedence Clearwater Revival, we found that we had a lot in common musically and that an audition might be worth pursuing. "Well, if you can make it up here, just let us know," he nonchalantly said in a drawl the world now knows. We said goodbye, and I was now faced with one of my life's most difficult decisions.

From the day I'd joined Scream, I'd felt a part of a family. Though I was much younger than Pete, Franz, and Skeeter, they always treated me as an equal, and we became best friends, spending almost every day together, tour or no tour. I had spent the most important, formative years of my life with them, discovering music, discovering the world, and in turn discovering myself, so to move on and leave them behind in that sinking ship pained my heart in a way I had never felt, even more than saying goodbye to my own father when he disowned me for dropping out of high school. We had always been in this together, all for one and one for all, and we had overcome so much shit. But there was a finality to this new crisis that made me question my future. So, as I did whenever I questioned my future, whenever I needed a voice of reason or some words of wisdom, I called the one person who had never once in my life steered me wrong . . .

My mother.

On a collect call from the parking lot of a record store in Orange County, I tearfully explained my dilemma, and she understood entirely, because deep down she felt the same about Pete and Franz as I did. We had ALL become a family over the years, and she considered them to be much more than my bandmates; they were my brothers. To this day, I will never forget the sound of her voice giving me the advice that steered my life in its ultimate direction.

"David . . . I know that you love your friends, but sometimes you have to put *your* needs ahead of others'. You have to take care of *yourself*." Coming from a woman whose entire life was the exact opposite of that, this completely shocked me, but because she was the wisest person I knew, I hung up the phone and decided to follow her guidance, regardless of the consequences.

I packed up my duffel bag, my sleeping bag, and my drum set into a cardboard moving box and headed up to Seattle, a town I had only visited once and where I knew virtually no one, leaving one life behind to start another one. I felt a loss that I had never experienced before. I missed my home. I missed my friends. I missed my family. I was now truly on my own, back to square one, starting over. But I was still hungry. And, having never been one to let my wheels spin, I had to keep going. After all, I was also still free, and there was adventure around every corner.

I still drive past that old house, that sinking ship in Laurel Canyon, almost every day, and as the years have passed it has slowly collapsed under its own weight, disappearing under the surface in time. But the memories and lessons I learned during that period have yet to fade, and I now take my own lifeboat for a nighttime spin whenever I need to take stock, retrace my steps while trying to plan the next.

BECAUSE EVERY DAY IS STILL A BLANK PAGE, WAITING TO WRITE ITSELF.

IT'S A
FOREVER
THING

"Do you mind if we take a break? I've never done a tribal tattoo before."

Believe me, these are not the words you want to hear from a man drilling a needle full of black ink a thousand times per second into your skin as you desperately try to endure the burning pain of being permanently branded without screaming like a newborn. But the beads of sweat running down his forehead and his squinting red eyes were surely not a good sign, so with a quick and painful wipe from a paper towel, I got up from my chair and retreated outside for a quick smoke. The intricate design I had personally drawn (based on the classic John Bonham "three circles" logo) needed to be razor sharp, with straight, even lines and perfect circles intertwined to make a piece that would wrap around my right wrist like a menacing Celtic bracelet. No easy task, even for a seasoned professional, but his weary frustration was certainly none too reassuring. Nevertheless, it had to be right, and at this point there was no turning back.

AFTER ALL, IT'S A FOREVER THING.

It was the fall of 1990 in Olympia, Washington, and I had just received my first check as a paid member of Nirvana. A whopping four hundred bucks, it was by far the biggest payday of my professional life up until that point. This much-needed advance from our newly hired management company, Gold Mountain, came at a time when Nirvana was being courted by every major-label record company known to man in an all-out bidding war, yet Kurt and I were literally starving and living in complete squalor. Our apartment at 114 NE Pear Street was the back unit of a dilapidated old house built around 1914, with one bedroom, one bathroom, a small living room, and a kitchen the size of a broom closet (ironically located just across the street from the Washington State lottery building). Versailles, it was not. "Unclean" doesn't even begin to describe the carnage within. It made the Chelsea Hotel look like a Four Seasons. Whitney Houston's bathroom turned upside down. A trailer-park-tornado aftermath of ashtrays and magazines. Most people would never dare to step foot in such a disastrous cave, but it was our humble abode, and we called it home. Kurt occupied the bedroom, while I slept in my sleeping bag on an old brown couch littered with cigarette burns, which fell far short of my six-foot frame. At the end of the couch sat an old table where Kurt kept a pet turtle in a putrid terrarium. A true lover of animals, Kurt had an intriguing, perhaps metaphorical appreciation for turtles, as their shells, the thing that most protected them, were actually quite sensitive. "Like having your spine on the *outside* of your body," he once said. But as beautiful and anatomically poetic as that sentiment may have been, it eventually made no difference to me, as this goddamned reptile kept me awake every night by tapping its head against the glass for hours on end in an attempt to escape our shared den of filth. I couldn't blame the poor thing. I often felt the same.

At the time, I had figured out how to survive off a three-for-ninety-nine-cents corn dog special at the Ampm gas station across the street. The trick was to eat one for breakfast (at noon) and save the other two for a late dinner after rehearsal, holding me over until the hunger pangs set in again and I was forced to shamefully wander back into the fluorescent glow of the convenience store lights with another crumpled dollar bill in my hand. (Still to this day, I shudder at the sight of a battered frank skewered on a sharp wooden stick.) Purely sustenance, it was just enough to keep my twenty-one-year-old metabolism whirring, though sadly it lacked any real nutritional benefit. This malnourished diet, coupled with my penchant for playing the drums five nights a week with every fiber of my scrawny being, had reduced me to a virtual waiflike marionette, barely filling out the dirty old clothes that I kept in a duffel bag on the floor in the corner of the living room. It was more than enough to drive anyone back to the comforts of their mother's home cooking with their tail between their legs, but I was 2,786 miles from Springfield, Virginia. And I was free.

"I wish that I knew what I know now when I was younger," sang Ronnie Wood on the Faces' classic 1973 hit "Ooh La La." Oh, Ronnie . . . if you only knew. Truer words have never been spoken. This four-hundred-dollar advance was by far the most money I had ever seen in my life! In my mind, I was now Warren fucking Buffett! I grew up as the son of a Fairfax County public school teacher, so my childhood was far from frivolous and I learned to live well within my means, working to make ends meet as best I could while finding happiness in the simple things in life. Music, friends, and family. Never had I made such a bounty mowing lawns, painting houses, prepping furniture for delivery trucks, or manning the cash register at a Tower Records in downtown Washington, DC. As far as I was concerned, this was the big time. I had finally hit the jackpot, but rather than save and budget this grand reward in an effort to ensure survival (imagine the mountains of corn dogs!), I did what most young musicians do with their first check: I blew it on bullshit.

In hindsight, I now understand why I went straight to the Fred Meyer department store to buy a BB gun and a Nintendo console. Clearly, I was indulging in the childhood luxuries that I had fantasized about having when I was young but never received. Not to say that I was an unhappy or deprived child, but any spare money in my household was saved for more practical things like new shoes or winter jackets (there once may have been a fifty-dollar minibike, but that's another story). My tireless mother worked multiple jobs to make ends meet: schoolteacher by day; department store clerk by night; estimate writer for a carpet cleaning service, Servpro, on the weekends. As a single mother with two young mouths to feed, she did everything she possibly could to keep us happy and healthy. And we were. A genuine altruist in every sense of the word, she raised me to need very little and to give very much. Her work ethic is deeply ingrained in me, and I undoubtedly have her to thank for where I am today. The nagging feeling that I need to be productive that keeps me up at night and wakes me up in the morning can be directly traced to those long nights she would spend grading papers at the living room desk under an old lamp, only to wake before the sun to ensure that my sister and I walked out the front door bathed, dressed, and fed. Granted, my job is nothing compared to her career as an educator, but I now understand the importance of hard work, thanks to her. So, four hundred dollars for playing loud, dissonant rock and roll? Free money!

Soon, our afternoons in Olympia were spent shooting cartons of eggs from a distance in the backyard of our old house and playing Super Mario World until the sun came up (we may or may not have taken a few potshots at the lottery building across the street in the name of the revolution). Our squalid den of filth was now transformed into an adolescent recreation center from hell. To me, this *was* Versailles. However, since I had no foresight or regard for practical spending, the money quickly dwindled, and I was left with just enough cash for one last ridiculous indulgence: a tattoo. Not my first, mind you. No, that was a self-inflicted masterpiece that I gave myself with a sewing needle, some thread, and a jar of black ink at the age of fourteen. After seeing the gritty homemade-tattoo scene from Uli Edel's cinematic masterpiece, *Christiane F.*, I decided to bedazzle my left forearm in that same DIY fashion with the logo of my favorite band at the time, Black Flag. Once I had as-sembled all of the necessary elements from the cluttered junk drawers around the house, I waited until everyone was asleep, set up a makeshift tattoo studio in my bedroom, and began my nefarious operation. Just as I had seen in the movie, I sterilized the sewing needle with fire from a candle, carefully wrapped the thin thread around the tip, and dipped it into the jar of ink, watching the fibers soak up the thick black liquid. Then, with a steady hand, I began. Poke. Poke. Poke. Poke. The sting of the needle as it punctured my epidermis sent chills down my spine, over and over again, and I stopped every now and then to wipe away the excess of blurred pigment and survey the damage. Kat Von D, I was not, but I persevered, digging the needle in as deep as my pain threshold would allow to ensure this meaningful image would never fade. If you're familiar with the iconic Black Flag logo, you know that it is four thick, black vertical bars in staggered succession. A tall order for a derelict teen with his mother's rarely used sewing kit. I somehow managed to make it through three of the four bars before I said, "Fuuuuck this shit!" and stopped. Not the pièce de résistance I was hoping for, but my heart was now ripe with a feeling of finality that somehow empowered me. A forever thing.

As the years went by, I curated quite a collection of these little blurred memoirs all over my body. A little mark here, a little mark there, until I was finally blessed with the opportunity to be legitimately tattooed by an Italian artist named Andrea Ganora who lived in a legendary squat in Amsterdam by the name of Van Hall. An old two-story factory, the building had been overtaken and occupied by a small group of punk rockers from all over Europe in late 1987. Dutch, Germans, Italians—it was a tight-knit community of friends who converted the cold, cavernous building into their home, replete with a live music venue downstairs (where I coincidentally made my first live record, *SCREAM Live! at Van Hall*, in 1988). When I was eighteen years old it became a virtual home base for Scream. Andrea was the resident tattooist, and most of Van Hall's occupants proudly sported his work. He was a true artist, but unlike the sterile, laboratory-like environment of most sanctioned tattoo establishments, his studio was his bedroom, and his tattoo gun was made from an old doorbell machine. We smoked joint after joint and listened to punk and metal records as our laughter and the electric buzz of his tattoo gun filled the room. To this day, I can still vividly remember the thrill of that first "real" tattoo and am reminded of his thick Italian accent and the sweet smell of hash every time I look in the mirror at the gift he gave to me that night. Thirty-three years later, its color has yet to fade.

Before long, my *Lifestyles of the Rich and Famous* honeymoon on Pear Street was over, and I returned to rationing corn dogs and cursing the incessant tapping of the turtle terrarium night after night, head buried in the dirty cushions of that old couch. Lesson learned. The season turned dark, and homesickness began to set in. I had left my friends, my family, my sweet Virginia behind for . . . this. The cruel Pacific Northwest winter weather and lack of sunlight only deepened the feeling of depression looming in the shadows, but fortunately I still had one thing keeping me from retreating back home: the music. As dysfunctional as Nirvana could be at times, there was an unspoken focus once we put our instruments on and the amps began to glow. WE WANTED TO BE GREAT. Or, as Kurt once said to music executive and titan Donnie Ienner while being courted in his New York City high-rise office, "We want to be the biggest band in the world." (I thought he was kidding.) Our rehearsal space was a barnlike structure that had been converted into a demo studio, thirty minutes north of Olympia in a suburb of Tacoma. One small step above an old, damp basement, it had heat and a small PA system (not to mention some rather questionable shag carpeting), so it served our simple needs well. Kurt and I would excitedly make the trek five days a week in a Datsun B210 that was somehow gifted to him by an old woman, barely managing to make it up Interstate 5 without the wheels falling off (one actually did once, lug nuts scattered about the gravel driveway in the dark). Our music was the one thing that took my mind off the shortcomings of this new life I had fallen into, the one thing that made it all worthwhile. Every rehearsal began with a "noise jam," which became a sort of improvisational exercise in dynamics, ultimately honing our collective instinct and making it so that song structure didn't necessarily need to be verbally arranged; it would just happen, almost the way a flock of blackbirds gracefully ebbs and flows in a hypnotic wave over a country field in the winter. This method was instrumental in the quiet/loud dynamic that we became known for, though we hardly invented it. That credit was due to our heroes the Pixies, who were hugely influential to us. We had adopted their simple trademark in more than a few of our new songs: tight, simple verses that explode into giant, screaming choruses. A sonic juxtaposition with ferocious results, most notably "Smells Like Teen Spirit."

As the long winter turned to spring, we spent countless hours in that makeshift studio preparing songs for what would become the album now known as *Nevermind*. Unlike the bands I had been in before, Nirvana didn't play shows often, for fear of burning out the local audience, so most of our energy was directed at being ready to record once we finally decided on a label and producer. Kurt was remarkably prolific, seeming to have a new song idea almost every week, so there was always a feeling of forward motion, never being stuck or stagnant creatively. At night, after he closed his bedroom door, I would hear the quiet strumming of a guitar from his room and would wait to see his light go out from the comfort of my dirty old couch. Every day, I couldn't wait to hear whether he had something new once we arrived at rehearsal and plugged in. Whether he was writing music or entries in his now-famous journals, his need to create was astonishing, though he was practically secretive about it. His songs would sneak up on you, take you by surprise. And they were never prefaced with "Hey, I wrote something great!" They would just . . . appear.

When I joined Nirvana in September 1990, the band had already recorded a new batch of songs with their previous drummer, Chad Channing, which were intended to be their next Sub Pop release. Songs like "In Bloom," "Imodium" (which became "Breed"), "Lithium," and "Polly" had all been recorded earlier that year by a young, up-and-coming producer from Madison, Wisconsin, named Butch Vig. Showcasing Kurt's ever-evolving songwriting ability, these songs had a new, mature sense of melody and lyric; they had outgrown the previous material and promised great things to come. Simply put, Nirvana was becoming Nirvana. Paired with Butch's mega-fucking-rock sound, it was this recording that was responsible for most of the industry "buzz" around the band, eventually igniting an ensuing feeding frenzy of interest. These songs would have been an embarrassment of riches for most bands to fall back on, but Kurt kept writing, and the new songs kept coming. "Come As You Are," "Drain You," "On a Plain," "Territorial Pissings," and of course "Smells Like Teen Spirit." Usually beginning with a riff from Kurt, Krist Novoselic and I would follow his lead with our practiced intuition, serving as the engine room to his screaming vision. Hell, my job was easy! I could always tell when a chorus was coming by watching Kurt's dirty Converse sneaker as it moved closer and closer to the distortion pedal, and just before he stomped on the button, I would blast into a single-stroke snare roll with all of my might, like a fuse burning fast into the heart of a bomb, signaling the change. The subsequent eruption would often send chills up my neck, as the undeniable power of our collective sound was becoming almost too big for that tiny little space. THESE SONGS WOULDN'T BE OUR SECRET FOR LONG. They would soon sneak up on everyone and take the world by surprise.

The decision to sign with the David Geffen Company was a no-brainer. Following in the footsteps of legendary New York noise heroes Sonic Youth, we hired their manager, John Silva, and trusted that any major-label record company brave enough to endorse Sonic Youth's experimental brand of no wave was definitely a safe place for a band like us. The final piece of the puzzle was to find a producer who would do these new songs justice. Someone who could take them to the next level while retaining the same raw power that filled our rehearsal space night after night. David Briggs of Neil Young fame was considered, as we were lifelong fans of Neil's work, and David's sense for capturing the unpolished, imperfect essence of human performance was much aligned with our ragged sound. Don Dixon was also considered, having made more than a few of our favorite records with REM and the Smithereens; his catalog of song-based albums boasted an undeniable attention to songwriting, craft, and arrangement. Perfect for Kurt's ever-evolving sense of melody and lyric. But ultimately, Butch Vig was our guy. First of all, there is no easier hang than a Butch Vig hang. The word "chill" doesn't even begin to describe his Midwest Zen demeanor. Just. Fucking. Cool. How he manages to amplify every musical element tenfold without making it feel like work is beyond me, but if the magic that was captured at Smart Studios with his first Nirvana session was any indication, we were well on our way to making something that would eclipse any and all expectations, including our own.

With the help of our new partner in crime John Silva and the wonderful people at DGC, we began the process of booking a recording session. At the time, Butch was working on an album with a young band from Chicago by the name of Smashing Pumpkins, so while we waited for him to become available, it was back to the barn day after day, woodshedding our collection of material to be as prepared as possible when the call came. We wouldn't have much time (or money) to fuck around in the studio, maybe twelve days, so it was important that these songs be recorded quickly. I mean, let's face it, we weren't making a Genesis record here. And to capture the energy of the band in one take, we had to have our shit together. Which we did. As frustrating as it was to have to wait—another corn dog, another night on the couch with that fucking turtle—there was now light at the end of the tunnel.

The discussion eventually turned to choice of studio—if not the most important element, certainly a defining factor in the outcome of any album. Recording studios are like lovers. No two are the same, and not one is perfect. Some you love to hate, and others you hate to love. The trick is to find one that will bring you out of yourself. Seattle had its share of amazing studios, of course, but there was talk of a place in Van Nuys, California, that had an amazing drum room, had a classic recording console, and (most important) was cheap as fuck: Sound City. Famous for decades of legendary albums, it seemed the perfect fit with its gritty, no-nonsense, analog aesthetic. Not to mention, it was closer to the Hollywood Geffen headquarters, and I'm pretty sure they wanted to keep an eye on us to make sure we weren't pulling another great rock and roll swindle, à la the Sex Pistols (something we actually considered at one point). Can't blame them, really. The risk factor was maybe a notch higher than with our label mates Edie Brickell & New Bohemians, but little did they know, we meant business.

Once the dates were finally set (May 2–19), we began the final preparations to make our thousand-mile trek down to Los Angeles. A few more rehearsals, a few more boom box recordings of new song ideas, and we were good to go. Well, almost good to go. We needed gas money. We hastily booked a last-minute show at a small club in downtown Seattle called the OK Hotel, hoping that it would pull enough dough to fill our tanks and get us to Sound City without breaking down on the side of the highway. It was April 17, 1991, and the small room was thankfully packed with sweaty kids waiting to hear their favorite Nirvana songs. "School," "Negative Creep," "About a Girl," "Floyd the Barber"—these were all familiar to the die-hard fans who adored Nirvana's first album, *Bleach,* so we delivered them with our usual manic abandon, beating our instruments to within an inch of their lives as the crowd sang every word. Just like every other Nirvana show I had played, it was practically transcendent. But, rather than just stick with the trusted back catalog, that night we decided to try a new song that no one in that room had ever heard before. A song we had written over the winter in that cold little barn in Tacoma. Kurt approached the mike and announced, "This song is called 'Smells Like Teen Spirit.'" Crickets. He then launched into the opening riff, and as Krist and I broke into the song, the room absolutely exploded. Bodies bouncing, people on top of people, a sea of denim and wet flannel before us. Reassuring, to say the least, and certainly not the response we'd expected (though we'd certainly hoped for it). THIS WAS NO ORDINARY NEW SONG. This was something else. And maybe, just maybe, all of those months starving, freezing, longing for my friends and family back in Virginia while suffering the oppressive, gray Pacific Northwest winter in that filthy little apartment, had been a test of my own strength and perseverance, the music being my only consolation and reward. Maybe that was enough. Maybe that sea of denim and wet flannel at the lip of the stage was all I needed to survive. If it had all ended there, maybe I would have happily returned to Virginia a changed man.

As Kurt and I packed the old Datsun for the drive to Los Angeles, I knew deep down that I wouldn't be coming back. With my duffel bag over my shoulder, I took one last look at the tiny room I had called home for the past seven months, trying to burn every single detail into my mind, so as to never lose the memory or significance of this place in my life. To ensure that whatever would follow these days had been built here. And as I closed the door to leave, my heart was again bursting with a feeling of finality, like a needle digging into your skin, leaving blurred memoirs of moments that will never fade. A little mark here, a little mark there, permanent reminders of moments past.

AFTER ALL, IT'S A FOREVER THING.

WE WERE
SURROUNDED
AND THERE
WAS NO
WAY OUT

WE WERE SURROUNDED, AND THERE WAS NO WAY OUT.

With fear in his eyes, our panicked tour manager/soundman, Monty Lee Wilkes, poked his sweaty head through the dressing room door and nervously exclaimed, "There's a bunch of dudes outside that want to fucking kill you guys. So, just lock the door and stay in here until I come back, okay? When you hear my knock, open up and I'll rush you to the cab waiting in the alley."

Welcome to the fall of 1991.

Trees nightclub in the Deep Ellum district of downtown Dallas, Texas, was just another stop on the North American leg of our "Nevermind" tour, which boasted a streamlined itinerary of thirty exhausting shows in a short forty days. With a max capacity of around six hundred people, this relatively new club was similar to most of the other venues that were booked for that tour: cramped, a low stage, limited PA and lights, and a small dressing room in the back to prepare for (and recover from) another cathartic performance. As intimate as Trees may seem in hindsight, it was actually one of the bigger rooms booked for us on that trip, since we were more accustomed to playing much smaller places like the Moon in New Haven, Connecticut, where we had squeezed 100 people into its tiny, low-ceilinged room just a few weeks before, or J.C. Dobbs in Philadelphia, which was sold out with 125 paying customers a few days after that, or even the 9:30 Club in DC, where we had surely exceeded their official capacity of 199 a few days later. No strangers to a Saturday night sweatbox, these sardine-can-sized clubs were commonplace for Nirvana, so the sudden jump to much larger, 600- to 1,000-capacity venues like the Masquerade in Atlanta, St. Andrews Hall in Detroit, and now Trees in Dallas felt like slipping on a pair of Andre the Giant's tighty-whities: a bit roomy round the sensitive bits.

Traveling in our newly rented passenger van with a trailer full of gear hitched behind, the band and three crew members spent most days driving, reading, listening to music, and trying to get a little nap in here and there on our crowded bench seats, terminally exhausted from the show the night before. Fortunately, this

time there were hotel rooms along the way. Thank god. A luxurious upgrade from my days in Scream, where we either slept in the van, crashed at the house of some random stranger we had met at the gig, or sometimes resorted to laying out our sleeping bags on the beer-soaked stage we had just rocked hours before for a good night's sleep (yes, I have cuddled up to my drum set on numerous occasions). There was also a considerable pay raise. Double, actually! The jump from my $7.50-a-day Scream per diem to Nirvana's $15 made me feel rich beyond my wildest dreams. Not that I was necessarily ready to put a down a deposit on a house in the Hamptons just yet, but I had finally graduated from generic cigarettes to actual Marlboros, and that made me feel like a fucking king. At twenty-two years old, I had finally reached a much-anticipated milestone in my life, traveling the world comfortably with a band that was selling out show after show to rave reviews and quickly gaining popularity. Albeit, maybe a bit too quickly.

Nirvana's *Nevermind* was released September 24, 1991, just a few days after the first show of the tour, and within a week I had already noticed a change. Not only in the size of the crowds that we were drawing to the shows, but in the TYPE of crowds. They were no longer made up of Sub Pop fans and college radio junkies coming to hear their favorite songs from the band's first record, *Bleach*; there was suddenly an influx of people who seemed a bit more . . . mainstream. The usual uniform of Salvation Army flannels and Doc Martens was now met with designer-brand jeans and sports jerseys, similar to what suburban kids I grew up with in Springfield wore. The "Smells Like Teen Spirit" single, which was released two weeks before the album, had quickly found its way out of our native territory and into the hands of a much broader audience, driving more and more people to come see what all the fuss was about. That audience was growing at a rapid pace. There were often more people outside of the venues than inside them. THE SECRET WAS OUT.

As the keynote speaker of the South by Southwest music conference in 2013, I addressed this ethical crossroads in my speech:

> *Where do you go from there? As an artist raised in the*
> *ethically suffocating punk rock underground, conditioned*
> *to reject conformity, to resist all corporate influence and*
> *expectation, where do you go? How do you deal with that*
> *kind of success? How do you now DEFINE success? Is it still*
> *the reward of playing a song from beginning to end without*
> *making a mistake? Is it still finding that new chord or scale*
> *that makes you forget all your troubles? How do you process*
> *going from being one of "us" to one of "them"?*

I felt a certain tug-of-war within. As a little boy, I had discovered rock and roll on the AM radio in my mother's car, singing along to 1970s Top 40 music, but I was now conflicted about the idea of having a Top 40 hit myself. All of those years being a "punk rocker," renouncing mainstream music, crying "sellout" to any band that moved even slightly toward mainstream success, had turned my music-loving heart into a confused and callused lump within my cynical chest. I had become jaded and judgmental, often not knowing what was okay to "like" or "dislike" based on the rules of cool culture in the punk scene (yes, there were rules, as fucking ridiculous as that may seem in a scene that championed expressive freedom). Yet, I also rejoiced in the fact that more and more people were showing up to share this music I loved and took so much pride in making and playing. It was an ethical dilemma, one that would prove both inspiring and destructive to the band.

Much more than me, Kurt found this crossroads deeply troubling. The same guy who had exclaimed, "We want to be the biggest band in the world," to a record company executive in a New York City high-rise office was now faced with the horrifying prospect of its coming true. Of course, we never actually expected the world to change for us (because we surely weren't going to change for it), but each day it seemed more and more like it was. And that was overwhelming. Even the most stable can crumble under pressure like that.

One problem was that we were now attracting the same people who used to kick our asses in high school for being different, who called us "faggots" and "queers" for the clothes we wore and the music we listened to. Our fanbase was changing to include macho monster-truck homophobes and meathead jocks whose worlds revolved around beer and football. We had always been the outcasts. We had always been the weirdos. We were not one of them. So, how could they become one of us?

And then the video came out.

September 29, only a few days after the release of our album, the "Smells Like Teen Spirit" video was debuted on MTV's *120 Minutes*. A late-night program dedicated to alternative music, *120 Minutes* was considered the springboard for many underground bands' careers, showcasing some of our heroes, such as the Pixies, Sonic Youth, Dinosaur Jr., and Hüsker Dü. For a band like ours to be included in such lofty ranks was beyond huge. It was a turning point, not only personally but professionally, and to deny that we were delighted would be a lie. On a night off between our New York City and Pittsburgh shows, we all sat in our hotel rooms waiting for our video to be shown for the first time ever. Kurt and I shared a room on that tour, and I remember lying across from each other in our twin beds with the television on as videos from Morrissey, the Wonder Stuff, and Transvision Vamp played for what seemed like an eternity; the anticipation became painful with each passing second. The Damned, the Red Hot Chili Peppers, Nine Inch Nails, video after video, until . . . there we were! First, a short promo that we had shot backstage at the Reading Festival in England a month before, where we awkwardly said, "You're watching *120 Minutes*!" from the catering tent behind the stage, Kurt's arm still wrapped in a sling from maniacally diving into my drum set that day. I screamed from my stiff Best Western bed and was simultaneously filled with both glee *and* the feeling of tripping on too much acid (not mutually exclusive). *Holy shit!* I thought. *That's what we look like?* And then, without further ado, those familiar chords that had once echoed through our dingy little rehearsal space back in Tacoma rang through the tiny speakers of the Magnavox on the dresser. It was actually happening. I was watching MYSELF on MTV. Not Michael Jackson or the Cars. Not Madonna or Bruce Springsteen. No. It was Krist, Kurt, and me, playing a song we wrote in a fucking barn. Dalí's melted clocks had nothing on this most surreal moment.

We elatedly picked up the bedside phone and called room to room, shouting, "It's on! It's on right now!" like kids at a slumber party, the poor hotel operator pinging us back and forth, to busy signal after busy signal. Part disbelief, part celebration, part shock, this was a moment that I will never forget. From the dingy maroon carpet to the chipped wooden furniture, if I close my eyes today I can still vividly recall every detail, for this was an event that changed not only my life, but the world of music at that time.

I credit this video for the tsunami that was soon to come. Inspired by Jonathan Kaplan's 1979 film *Over the Edge*, starring Matt Dillon, the "Teen Spirit" video was a dark portrait of youthful rebellion, shot with actual fans from a show that we'd played the night before at the Roxy in Hollywood. With director Samuel Bayer, Kurt envisioned a high school pep rally turned riot, burning down the gymnasium in a blissful mosh pit of disaffected teens, tattooed cheerleaders, and young punks, leaving their angst and frustration behind in a smoldering pile of rubble and ash. THIS WAS A SENTIMENT THAT WE ALL OBVIOUSLY CONNECTED TO—BUT WE COULD NOT PREDICT THAT AN ENTIRE GENERATION WOULD FEEL THE SAME. At first, the clip was only played at night, as MTV deemed it too controversial for prime-time viewing, but before long, it made its way into the normal rotation. Once there, it spread like wildfire and proceeded to burn our whole world to the ground.

Now Nirvana was well on its way to becoming a household name. In just a matter of weeks, the buzz surrounding the band had ramped up into a frenzy, all eyes focused on the blurry mystery that was three disheveled freaks in their early twenties, armed with songs that your cool aunt and uncle could sing along to. Surprisingly, the world within the safety of our smelly little rental van had actually changed very little: duffel bags and cassette tapes, fast-food containers and empty cigarette packets. Typical for a band like us. It was the world outside of our little bubble that was changing fast: autographs and radio interviews, venues bursting at the seams, and multiple near-riots. Just days before our show at Trees, we had to abandon the stage at our Mississippi Nights show in St. Louis after the crowd rushed the stage, prompted by Kurt's frustrations with the local security's being too rough with the fans, a common occurrence for venues unfamiliar with slam dancing and stage diving. It was absolute chaos. At the time, I was using a borrowed drum set from our opening band, Urge Overkill, since Kurt and I had smashed mine to splinters in Chicago. As the waves of kids climbed over the barrier onto the tiny stage, grabbing our equipment and screaming into the microphones, I retreated to Urge Overkill's dressing room and gleefully explained, "There's a fucking riot happening out there!" to which the drummer, Blackie, replied, "Shit! My drums!"

By the time we reached Dallas, we had no idea anymore what to expect. But there was a particular electricity in the air that night, magnified by an unusually swampy humidity that further heightened the tension in the room, like a short fuse on a hand-made bomb. As we stepped onstage to play, the crowd was already spilling over the floor monitors and onto Kurt's and Krist's guitar pedals, without the band's even hitting a single note. Imagine being backed up against a wall by a mob of six hundred alcohol-fueled adrenaline junkies waiting to tear you and the entire place to shreds, multiply that by ten, and you're getting close to what it felt like to be in Nirvana that night. To make things worse, we were plagued with technical difficulties right out of the gate. So, while we waited for our gear to work properly, we stood there snarkily playing a disastrous version of "L'amour est un oiseau rebelle" as our guitar tech Nic Close frantically ran from one side of the stage to the other, doing his best to remedy this potentially hopeless situation. Finally realizing we just had to go for it, Kurt said a few words and we kicked into the first song, "Jesus Don't Want Me for a Sunbeam," a cover from one of our favorite bands, the Vaselines, from Scotland.

The place went bonkers, and the audience's psychotic, raw energy grew exponentially minute by minute. By the time we got to the song "School," six songs into the set, the waves of people spilling onto the stage had become so dangerous that Kurt couldn't sing into the microphone anymore without its getting kicked in his face and smashing into his teeth. I could sense his irritation, and I knew all too well what followed when Kurt got irritated.

SOMETHING WAS GETTING DESTROYED. Whether it would be his guitar, his amp, or my drums, I knew it was coming. The countdown began . . .

Four songs later, after a noisy, technical-difficulty-riddled version of our otherwise gentle acoustic song "Polly," Kurt snapped. Turning to his left, he took off his guitar and started smashing the monitor engineer's soundboard to pieces, chopping at it over and over, sending buttons, knobs, and shrapnel flying across the stage. Kurt had had enough. Not just of this show, but of everything that had led us to this night. The weeks and weeks of intensified chaos had finally boiled over, and Kurt's frustration was now being released in a furious display of violent rage. The crowd cheered, delighted, as if this were some form of entertainment. If they only knew. This was not an act. This was real.

All bets were now off. As I sat behind my drums watching this series of anarchic events unfold before me, all I could think was *Where's the fucking emergency exit?* This is not something that runs through the minds of most performers, but then again, we weren't like most performers. There was no playbook for what was happening to us. This was the Wild West, and the only way to survive was to follow the light at the end of each long, dark tunnel. As chaotic as my days in Scream had been, sleeping in squats, being chased by skinheads and junkies through dark alleyways, never knowing where my next meal would come from, it had nothing on the sheer size and magnitude of this. This was dangerous.

Nevertheless, we soldiered on, continuing to play as the monitor engineer hilariously placed a wood pallet over his mixing desk for fear that another thrashing was inevitable. Nothing could save him now. This speeding train was already off the fucking rails, on a collision course with everyone and everything in its path. We kicked into another cover, Shocking Blue's "Love Buzz" (the first

Nirvana single), and the chaos continued. Body after body falling to the stage, the room growing hotter with every distorted chord, every inch of skin drenched with the condensation of six hundred strangers. After the second chorus of the song, Kurt dove into the audience, guitar in hand, and soloed while crowd-surfing atop the gyrating mass of greasy hair and tattooed limbs. As he fell back to the stage, flailing in a rapturous, spasmodic dance, he landed on a gigantic security guard who had been placed there to help keep the kids offstage. Trying his best to push Kurt off him, he used his brute force on Kurt's small frame, and in a fight-or-flight moment of instant, defensive reaction, Kurt smashed the body of his guitar into the security guard's head, tearing open his flesh, drawing streams of blood that immediately started pouring down his sinister Mohawk. Taken aback, he realized that he had been cut, and as Kurt stood up, the massive security guard punched him square in the jaw, sending Kurt straight down to the floor. Without hesitation, Krist and I threw down our instruments and intervened to save our friend as the song came to an abrupt, crashing halt. Krist tried to reason with the security guy, even removing his own shirt to help stop the bleeding as chants of "BULLSHIT! BULLSHIT! BULLSHIT!" rang through the club. Kurt wandered off to the other side of the stage in a daze as I made my way toward the exit, imagining that it was all over and done.

It wasn't.

After some pleading from a club employee who feared an otherwise imminent riot, we decided to finish our set, stage still wet with blood. Kurt's guitar was viciously out of tune from the wallop he had delivered to the security guy's cranium, but hell, that had never stopped us. The dissonant, detuned sound almost accentuated the uneasy vibe in the room. Closing out the set with our fastest, most punk-rock-sounding song, "Territorial Pissings," we finally put our instruments down and headed to the dressing room, somewhat traumatized by the evening's bizarre turn of events. We were used to chaos and disorder, but this was something else. This was not fun. This was dark. At least it was over.

Little did we know, the bloodied security guard and a gang of his misfit friends were outside waiting to kill us, swift retribution for the carnage we had unknowingly brought to town. They wanted blood in return. Someone caught wind of their plan as the hundreds of patrons filed out of the venue, and it was relayed to our crew, who then quickly passed it on to us as we sat upstairs recovering in pools of our own sweat. Monty realized that we were trapped, and it was now his job to figure out an escape plan. A cab was called to the back entrance, and we ran from our dressing room to the alleyway door like rats in a kitchen, Kurt in the

lead, followed by Krist and then me. We waited for the sign, and as the door was flung open I watched Kurt duck into the back seat of the cab, then Krist. I suddenly heard someone scream, "That's them!! Let's get those motherfuckers!!" Sure enough, it was the security guy and his friends, charging down the alleyway toward the cab with fire in their eyes and murder on their minds. Someone slammed the car door shut before I could get in, and it sped away, chased into the night by the motley crew of bloodthirsty thugs, who apparently caught up with them in bumper-to-bumper Saturday night traffic on Elm Street and smashed the passenger window out with one swift punch. I wouldn't know, because I was now left alone in the club with no way back to the hotel (I may or may not have gotten a ride back with a cute girl, getting into a car accident along the way).

We all somehow managed to survive another day, and our traveling circus rolled on to the next city. With twelve days left on the tour, there was still time for the wheels to fall off, but at least we were headed in the right direction: home.

By the time we returned to Seattle for a final hometown show on Halloween, we were completely exhausted, both mentally and physically. We had left our mark and made it back with the scars to prove it. In just forty days, we had gone from three disheveled young men with nothing to lose to three disheveled young men with a gold record. Our worlds had now changed forever, and so had yours. And this was just the beginning.

WE WERE SURROUNDED. AND THERE WAS NO WAY OUT.

THE
DIVIDE

"Guess where we're swimming today," my good friend Bryan Brown excitedly said.

From the deathly hot bedroom of Pete Stahl's crowded, air conditioner–less house in the San Fernando Valley, I replied, "I dunno . . . where?"

"The house where Sharon Tate was killed by the Manson family."

I held the phone in silence as I processed this morbid invitation for a moment, then replied, "Cielo Drive? Are you fucking serious?" I knew exactly where he was talking about, having been somewhat well versed in America's most infamous and gruesome killing spree since I was a teenager immersed in the world of the macabre. I could picture the long, winding drive up the canyon hill to the gate, the driveway beside the house overlooking downtown Los Angeles, the walkway to the front door that was once desecrated with the word "PIG" written in blood, the living room where three innocent people met their horrible fate beside a fireplace under a small loft, and the kidney-shaped pool that separated the main house from the guesthouse where Abigail Folger stayed before she was ruthlessly slaughtered on the lawn. I could practically draw a blueprint of this crime scene in my head from the time I'd spent reading *Helter Skelter* and watching grainy documentaries of Charles Manson's homeless hippie "family" on Spahn Ranch. This was almost too dark of a proposition to accept.

"Let's go."

1992 began with a crippling, well-deserved hangover as I woke up in a disheveled hotel room after celebrating New Year's Eve with the Red Hot Chili Peppers, Nirvana, Pearl Jam, and sixteen thousand other people at San Francisco's Cow Palace the night before. Nirvana had finished off our tumultuous, landmark year with a short West Coast tour of arenas, all packed to the rafters with thousands of young punks, gathered to witness these three up-and-coming bands in what was quickly becoming a musical revolution. The audiences were growing exponentially, and look-

ing out from the stage every night, it was clear that a radical cul-
tural shift was imminent from the energy and aesthetic of the fans
who sang along to every word with deafening volume. This was
no longer just the sound of the underground or late-night college
radio; this was a fucking battering ram to the gates that guarded
mainstream popular culture, and our three bands were spearhead-
ing the takeover.

Beyond the changing tides of the musical landscape, life from
my tiny bedroom in West Seattle was in flux, with every day
bringing a new, outrageous development in Nirvana's chaotic little
world. I held on for dear life as the rickety carnival ride that had
once been our little group started spinning faster and faster and our
unplanned bid to change the world intensified, but it was no use.
At this point, it was out of our hands, and no matter how much
we wanted to rein it in, there was no stopping it. The album that
we had made in only twelve days at that dumpy old studio in Los
Angeles named Sound City was now selling three hundred thousand copies a week. And the news that we had knocked Michael
Jackson out of the No. 1 spot on the *Billboard* album charts came
the same day we were to play *Saturday Night Live* for the first time,
January 11, 1992.

This may have been the moment that I realized life would never
be the same. Since I was a child, *Saturday Night Live* had been my
favorite television show, hands down, and I would stay up in my
pajamas to watch it every weekend, waiting to see my heroes of
late-night TV. But I wasn't just watching to see the comedic genius
of Dan Aykroyd, Gilda Radner, John Belushi, Laraine Newman,
Bill Murray, Steve Martin, and Andy Kaufman; I was particularly
interested in the diverse range of musical guests they hosted every
weekend. As a young musician this was my education, a master

class in live performance by some of the world's most cutting-edge artists. But if there was one performance that stood out from the rest and steered my life onto a new course, it was the B-52s performing their hit "Rock Lobster" in 1980.

TO ME, THESE THREE MINUTES WEREN'T JUST A BAND PLAYING A SONG, THEY WERE A RALLYING CRY TO ALL PEOPLE SUFFOCATING IN CONVENTIONALITY, AFRAID TO LET THEIR FREAK FLAG FLY, WHO WANTED TO CELEBRATE ALL OF LIFE'S BEAUTIFUL ECCENTRICITIES. At ten years old, my thoughts weren't quite this complex; I know that now. But even then I somehow felt empowered by their pride in their weirdness. As I watched them dance their mess around in a quirky, hyperactive blur, I knew I wanted to break out too. I no longer wanted to follow the norm. I wanted to break away from the pack like the B-52s and lead a life away from the flock. There is that golden moment in any child's life when independence and identity intersect, steering you in your ultimate direction, and this was mine. I would be an outcast with a guitar who loved music and comedy. Go figure.

But the opportunity to play *SNL* came at a complicated time for Nirvana. We hadn't seen each other since finishing that West Coast tour with the Red Hot Chili Peppers and Pearl Jam, and in that time we'd all gone our separate ways, exhausted from the seventy-five shows that we had played up until that point. I had gone home to Virginia, Krist had returned to Seattle, and Kurt had gone down to his new home in Los Angeles. When we met in New York City for the show, a certain fatigue was present, most noticeably with Kurt, and what I hoped would be a triumphant reunion of the band, gathered to play the TV show that had changed my life, felt a bit . . . off. There were cracks beginning to form in our already shaky foundation, and a shaky foundation is not what you want when performing live on TV in front of millions of people waiting for their first glimpse of the band that came out of nowhere to topple the "King of Pop" from his throne.

"Ladies and gentlemen . . . Nirvana."

Kurt started strumming the intro of "Smells Like Teen Spirit," and despite the fact that I'd played it every night in packed theaters all over the world by then, my life flashed before my eyes. This was where the B-52s had stood. This was where Devo had stood. This was where Bowie had stood. This was where every living legend from Bob Dylan to Mick Jagger had stood to perform their songs for millions of young musicians like me, up way past their bedtime to see their heroes play the songs that shaped their lives. I wanted to faint. I wanted to puke. I wanted to hide. But I blasted that drum intro with all of my strength and . . . broke a stick.

Fuck.

I was now driving the song with one flat tire, coming in on three engines, one sandwich short of a picnic. I looked down at my lifelong friend Jimmy, who was acting as my drum tech for the show, and we locked eyes in horror. It was one thing for this to happen at a Scream show in front of seventy-five people; it was very different when the entire world was watching. *Just keep playing,* I told myself as I hit my drums with a lifetime's worth of purpose. In a short break between drum fills, I grabbed another stick with lightning speed and finished off the song, surging with enough adrenaline to kill a horse, but with enough pride to last a lifetime, imagining that maybe our performance was a rallying cry to a whole new generation of kids suffocating in conventionality, afraid to let their freak flag fly, finally liberated to celebrate the beautiful eccentricities of life.

Oh, and Weird Al called the dressing room that night to personally ask for permission to cover "Smells Like Teen Spirit" too. We had officially arrived.

Having powered through *Saturday Night Live,* we went our separate ways again, reconvening two weeks later in Los Angeles to shoot the "Come As You Are" video before heading down to Australia and Japan for a three-and-a-half-week tour, another unimaginable experience to add to the list of things I never thought I would live to see. Upon arrival in L.A. on the first day of the video shoot, I realized that Kurt was unwell. He seemed frail and somewhat deflated, and by the look in his eyes it was clear that he had been getting high while away from the band.

I was in Los Angeles staying with a friend in January 1991 when I first learned that Kurt was using heroin. I had never known anyone who used heroin before and knew very little about it, so I was shocked. I had joined the band only three months before and was living with Kurt in a tiny apartment, and perhaps naively, I didn't peg him as someone who would do that sort of thing. To me, heroin was a dirty street drug, used only by prostitutes and junkies in dark alleyways downtown, not by gentle, kind, beloved artists with the world at their feet. I had read the mythological tales of legendary rock stars being strung out in countless rock biographies that almost glorified that behavior as some sort of badge of honor, but I never imagined it would become a part of my world. Washington, DC, was not necessarily a heroin town. Seattle, on the other hand, was a heroin capital.

Kurt assured me that heroin wasn't something that he did all the time, just that once. "I hate needles," he said in an effort to reassure me that I hadn't just given up my life and moved across the country to live with a complete stranger who'd turned out to be a junkie. And because I knew nothing about the drug, I believed him. There was no way he would be able to keep such a secret from me, anyway. Or so I thought.

One night in Olympia while I was out drinking with friends, someone had pills. Some sort of prescription painkiller. "Take one with a few beers, and you'll be super buzzed," I was told. Even that made me nervous, so I stuck to just cocktails, but I watched Kurt take two or three with his drink. It scared me. I was always pretty timid when it came to taking anything for fear of the consequence of taking too much, but I knew friends back in Virginia who would always push the boundaries a little to see how far they could take it. I began to learn that Kurt was this way, in every way.

I EVENTUALLY FELT THE SEPARATION. There were those who did and those who didn't. And as our world expanded, that divide grew wider. Nirvana were three distinct individuals, each with his own idiosyncrasies and eccentricities that were responsible for the specific sound we made when we strapped on our instruments, but outside of the music, we lived our own lives, each very different from the others.

As we filmed the video, Kurt's fragility came as a shock to me, and I was not only concerned for his health but also concerned for the tour we were about to start, which would take us to the opposite side of the planet, far from the reach of the people we loved and needed the most. I couldn't imagine how we would survive another dizzying schedule of show after show, airport after airport, hotel after hotel, especially given his condition, but we carried on. To this day, it is still hard for me to watch "Come As You Are" knowing the state that Kurt was in at the time. Although our images are blurred by camera effects and washed-out Super 8 film projected onto raw surfaces, I see a very clear picture of three people entering what would become a period of turbulence that we would feel for years.

The warm sun of Australia's summer and the even sunnier demeanor of our Aussie hosts was a welcome and much-needed break from the dark winter—in every sense—we had left behind at home. It was the absolute right place to be at the right time, and for a moment our wheels seemed to be back on track. I had been all over North America, all over Europe, but I had absolutely no idea what to expect from this side of the world, and I took to it like a fly to barbecue. We did it all: surfed Bondi Beach, snuggled koalas, camped with kangaroos, Jet Skied, bungee jumped, and even shared the stage with the Violent Femmes, perhaps the highlight of the whole trip. Kurt was still a bit fragile but seemed to be coming out of the fog as we tore through eight ripping shows in venues that were far too small for the band's exploding popularity, something we were quickly getting used to. I started to have hope that we were going to make it. That Kurt was going to make it. By the time we headed to Japan, I thought perhaps we'd turned a corner.

If Australia was another hemisphere, Japan was another fucking planet. Every single aspect of life was a huge culture shock. I felt like I was truly a million miles from home. And I loved it. We had never seen anything like Japan before, and they had never seen anything like us. At our first show in Osaka, we performed at a venue that seemed more like the Kennedy Center than the typical beer-stained, bleach-scrubbed dive bars we had cut our teeth in. Chandeliers hung from the ceilings over rows of beautiful velvet seats, and the stage was clean as a whistle, not a blemish to be found, something I found very strange. The audience were allowed to stand at their seats but not move from them, and the aisles were lined with what looked like military police in white gloves, ready to pounce if anyone so much as took a step from their assigned place. This made us play even harder that night, trying to provoke a riotous reaction by thrashing through the songs like never before, and as I looked out from behind my drum set, I could see the audience wanting to break out, scream, explode, let their own freak flags fly. Every few songs, a fan would finally lose it and begin running to the stage, only to be intercepted by a pair of white gloves and ejected from the show. It was us versus them, I thought. I played even harder.

By the end of the night, we knew exactly what to do . . . smash the fuck out of our equipment (a signature move by now). As the audience looked on, Kurt, Krist, and I absolutely destroyed our gear, like three children having a tantrum after being told "No dessert" by Mom and Dad. Instead, we gave that crowd dessert. We left the stage in a pile of drums, toppled amplifiers, and screaming feedback, and I was approached by a young Japanese man who was shaking like a leaf, on the verge of tears. "Did you not like the drums???" he asked in a trembling whimper. "No, no, no . . . they were great!" I said, a bit confused. Most anywhere else in the world, this performance would have been considered triumphant! But we were in Japan, a country that is rooted in a culture of respect and civility, and ours was a brazen act of rebellion uncommon there. Plus, this dude was the Tama drums representative and was terrified that I didn't like the set they had prepared for me, so I sat him down and explained that our rebellion had nothing to do with the beautiful drum set I was so honored to play; it was an act of celebration.

Before heading home, we made one last stop in Hawaii for a show at a small club in Honolulu called Pink's Garage, another venue that was far too small for the band, now at the peak of our popularity. Knowing that this show would be the end of our tour before a long break at home, I planned to stay for a week afterward, renting a ridiculous ocean-blue Mazda Miata convertible to buzz around from beach to beach like an annoying tourist (which I was), reaping the rewards of the most insane year of my entire life. Seeing this chapter of the band come to a close felt bittersweet, as I had almost fallen in love with the everyday chaos that surrounded us wherever we went. Plus, it felt good to go out on such a high. We had seen the cracks start to form, but we had patched them over just by playing our hearts out the way we had always done. Of course, I was also tired, so it was time to return, reset, and remind myself of the things that are the most important to survival: family, friends, and home. I needed to take a breath and actually figure out what had just happened to me.

"Mr. Grohl, there's a package for you."

As soon as we checked into our Honolulu hotel, the delightful woman at the front desk in the colorful tropical dress handed me a FedEx envelope, and I curiously tore into it, surprised that anyone one would send me anything on the road, much less locate my whereabouts as we zigzagged around the planet on our never-ending tour. A letter from my mother? A congratulatory note from my manager? A summons for petty crimes committed along the way? No. Even better.

My first credit card.

At twenty-three years old, I had never owned a credit card or an ATM card, or even had a bank account with more than a hundred dollars in it (thank you, Grandma), so this was a game changer. For the past four years, I had been surviving on measly per diems that would disappear by the end of each day, spent on cigarettes, junk food, and beer. This was too good to be true! Though the band had already sold well over a million records, I had yet to spend a penny of the money I had made, oblivious to how much that might be. I was about to find out.

I looked to the left of the front desk and saw a gift shop. Itching to test this fresh slice of Monopoly money, I sprinted across the lobby, lei flapping in the wind, and went straight to the sunglasses rack, where I gleefully picked a pair of mirrored blue shades (to match the Miata, of course). I nervously took them to the cashier, and seconds felt like hours as she swiped the card and awaited approval, but as she tore the receipt from the cash register roll to hand to me for my signature, I felt a sea change. No more cans of cold beans. No more three-for-a-dollar corn dogs. No more "shit on a shingle" dinners. (Canned tuna, pepper, flour, and toast. Kurt's specialty.) With new shades proudly resting on the bridge of my soon-to-be-sunburned nose, I looked across the parking lot to the Benihana restaurant down the street.

Awwww shit, I thought. *We're gonna feast tonight . . .*

The rest, as they say, is history.

Tan, fed, and happy, I flew straight back to Virginia after my week with Mr. Roarke and Tattoo on Fantasy Island, my first "vacation" since I was a kid, but with this newfound fiscal freedom came newfound responsibilities. The unimaginable had finally happened. I had money. After a lifetime of watching my mother juggle multiple jobs, count every penny, there could be comfort. Still unaware of the magnitude of what would come, I remained relatively frugal, as my father (who had gotten over the disowning) soon warned me, "You know this isn't going to last, right? You need to treat every check like it's the last one you will ever make." This is, perhaps, the best piece of advice he or anyone has ever given me still to this day. Though that didn't stop me from going straight to the motorcycle dealership and buying Jimmy and me matching Yamaha V-Maxes, it did instill a fear of bankruptcy right out of the gate, so in the grand scheme of things, my life stayed relatively the same.

As was our norm, we scattered in our different directions. Krist headed back to Seattle and purchased a warm, comfortable home in the Green Lake area north of the city. Kurt went to Los Angeles and rented a nice little apartment in an old building in Hollywood. Since I was not yet ready to commit to living full-time in Seattle, I bought a house just blocks from the beach in Corolla, North Carolina. Only a few hours from Northern Virginia, the Outer Banks was the perfect place for me to invest in property, not only because of its raw natural beauty, with high dunes and wild horses running along the wide beaches, but also because of its proximity to home, meaning that I could share my rewards with my mother and sister.

BUT "IDLE HANDS ARE THE DEVIL'S PLAYGROUND," OR SO I'VE HEARD.

As we all settled into our new lives, the divide appeared again. No longer crushed together in crowded vans or shared hotel rooms for months on end, we were now free to experience the lives we had always dreamed of, for better or worse. We had watched the world change around us, a blur of flashbulbs and near-riots at every turn, but with that hurricane of madness gone, we were now left to create our own realities, however we pleased. Being the faceless drummer of the band, I was lucky to walk through life practically unrecognized, rarely stopped in public, usually only to be asked, "Are you Dave Navarro?" It was almost as if I were on the outside looking in, watching this all happen to someone else from a distance, enjoying the benefits of "making it" without having to answer for it. That certainly could not be said for Kurt, whose face was now on the cover of every magazine, in every *MTV News* episode, his voice echoing from every FM radio station coast to coast, a life sentence that most are not prepared to navigate. We retreated to our corners, licked our wounds, and turned the page on the year that punk broke.

With nothing but time to spare until Nirvana's next tour, I bounced from surfing the warm waters of North Carolina, to revisiting my old DC haunts with lifelong friends, to recording my primitive songs in the basement with Barrett Jones in Seattle, to flying down to L.A. to reconnect with my old friends Pete and Franz from Scream, who had stayed there since the day I left to join Nirvana, starting new lives (and a new band, Wool) after the demise of Scream. What was meant to be a week on the floor of their little house in the Valley turned into at least a month, waking every morning in the scorching summer heat. Without air-conditioning, the house was a red-hot pizza oven by noon, so the only thing to do to escape the desert heat was to find a pool and spend the afternoon swimming in someone else's oasis, and this was my buddy Bryan Brown's specialty.

As we drove up to the house on Cielo Drive, my anticipation was laced with trepidation, as I realized that the morbid fascination I'd once had with this house was now about to be met with the eerie reality of standing within its cursed walls. We rang the bell on the gate, pulled into the driveway, stepped out of the car, and there it was, exactly as it looked in every crime scene photo I had ever laid my young, curious eyes on. Chills ran down my spine. We walked to the front door—THAT front door—and knocked. We were led inside, but I needed no guide to show me the layout of this house; it was almost as if I had been there before. I turned the corner into the living room and was hit with a shock wave of terror. The stone fireplace, the wooden beams, the small loft . . . it was all exactly the same as it had been that horrific night of August 9, 1969. Except for one thing: there was a large recording console in the middle of the room.

Nine Inch Nails were making a record here.

I didn't know Nine Inch Nails personally but had seen them perform live. I was a fan of industrial music, with Throbbing Gristle, Psychic TV, Einstürzende Neubauten, and Current 93 all part of my teenage soundtrack. I'd enjoyed the first NIN album, *Pretty Hate Machine,* quite a lot. With the band's aggressive electro-tension and dark lyrical themes, it only made sense that they would choose the Manson house to make their next album. As fucked up as it was, it was a perfect fit, and some of their most powerful songs were recorded there—"March of the Pigs," "Hurt," and "Closer." I have always been a firm believer in the idea that the environment in which you record dictates the outcome of the music, and every time I hear one of these songs, I am convinced it's true. There is a pain and desperation within these tracks that was surely infused by some kind of spiritual osmosis. Or Trent Reznor's pain and desperation. I didn't know him well, but I found him to be a brilliant artist and a kind man. Similar to another kind, brilliant artist that I knew, using his music to identify the demons that haunted his soul.

After a while, the pervading vibe of the house certainly cast a pall over the energy of the environment, one that I could not connect or jibe with at all. I was all too familiar with the feeling of darkness, fragility, and pain, so I hit the pool, not only to escape the heat, but to wash myself of that feeling I felt standing in that living room.

The darker side of music was something I was always attracted to sonically, but I began to realize that it wasn't who I was as a person. Music had always represented light and life to me. Joy, even. I wanted to celebrate that we had found a way out of the tunnel. I wanted to let my freak flag fly. I didn't want to hide away. I could understand how others might veer in the opposite direction, per-

haps revisiting past unresolved traumas, but I finally felt emanci-
pated from mine, and that felt good. Whether in the sand dunes
of North Carolina or the tranquility of Virginia's sleepy suburbs, I
needed to find peace, and with this newfound freedom that success
had afforded me, I was going to spend my time looking for it.

The rest of my days in Los Angeles were passed bouncing
around town in a rented white Volkswagen Cabriolet convertible (yes, I had a thing for convertibles at the time), swimming
in strangers' pools, jamming with friends, and calling the airlines
every few days to change my return ticket to Seattle, extending my
stay on Pete's scorching-hot floor for a little more summer and a
little more distance before heading back to the gray skies up north.
I think, deep down, I knew what was waiting for me there.

Finally, at the very last minute, I decided it was time to go and
threw all of my belongings into the back of the Cabriolet with no
time to spare, racing to LAX in the hope I would make my flight on
time. I knew basically nothing about the tangled web of busy highways that crisscrossed the massive city, so I blindly started racing
through the Valley at a dangerous speed, hoping that I was moving
in the general direction of at least one entrance ramp. As I came
screaming around a corner, I saw one only meters ahead of me, so
I cranked the wheel to the right as hard as I could and . . . BAM!

I slammed head-on into a tall curb at forty-five miles per hour,
which not only dragged the front axle out from beneath the car
but also triggered the airbag (which I didn't know it had), which
exploded ten inches from my face like a stick of dynamite. I spilled
out of the car, bruised and battered, coughing from the smoky
powder that shot out as it hit me in the face like a canvas bat, and
called a tow truck. (Don't be fooled by those safety commercials,
ladies and gentlemen. An airbag, although a lifesaver, is not a soft
silky pillow. That shit will fuck you up like a right uppercut from

Mike Tyson.) After the truck arrived and the driver surveyed the damage, the welt on my left eye began to swell like a giant balloon, and he declared the car totaled.

I called a cab and slithered back to Pete's house with a black eye and my tail between my legs for another week's stay, having completely destroyed a perfectly good Cabriolet convertible that cost only $12 a day. The extra week in Los Angeles gave me time to nurse my black eye but also time to think about what lay ahead. That divide between the three of us, and whether we could close it this time. The world had opened its ears to Nirvana. We were the unconventional freaks that the world was now watching. Could we survive?

News came that Kurt was in a rehab facility in Los Angeles. Though concerned, I was not surprised. I took this as a good sign. As I was on the other side of town reconnecting with my old friends, maybe he was finding some light and peace of his own. Having never known anyone who had been to rehab, I naively imagined it to be a quick fix, like an appendectomy or having your tonsils removed. Outside of my father's struggles with alcohol, I didn't understand the true nature of addiction. I didn't know the depths of Kurt's, to be sure. I had yet to realize that the healing required to free yourself from the grips of this kind of sickness is a lifetime of repair—if you can hang on and stay out of the darkness.

THERE WAS STILL SO MUCH TO LOOK FORWARD TO. WE HAD ONLY JUST BEGUN.

PART THREE

THE MOMENT

HE'S
GONE

"He's gone, Dave."

My knees gave out and I dropped the phone as I fell to my bedroom floor, covering my face with my hands as I began to cry. He was gone. The shy young man who had offered me an apple upon our first introduction at the Seattle airport was gone. My quiet, introverted roommate who I'd shared a tiny little apartment with in Olympia was gone. The loving father who played with his beautiful baby daughter backstage every night before each show was gone.

I was overcome with a more profound sadness than I had ever imagined. I couldn't speak. I couldn't think. I couldn't stand. I couldn't breathe. I could only picture his face, knowing that I would never see him again. I would never see his strange, flat fingers, or his skinny elbows, or his piercing blue eyes. Because he was gone. Forever.

Moments later, the phone rang again. Still on the floor, I answered, barely able to speak through the tears and hyperventilation.

"Hold on . . . he's not dead. He's still alive . . ."

I jumped up from the soft carpet with my heart racing wildly. "Wait . . . are you sure??" I asked frantically.

"Yes . . . he's still in the hospital, but he's gonna make it, Dave! He's gonna make it."

In the course of five minutes I had gone from the darkest day of my entire life to feeling born again. I hung up the phone. I was in shock. I was numb. I wanted to laugh, or cry, or have a complete nervous breakdown. I was in a state of emotional limbo. I didn't know what to feel.

This was my first brush with death, and I was left utterly confused. I now knew the shattering pain of loss, but only for a brief moment before it was pushed aside like a hideous prank. My process of mourning was forever changed. From that day forward, losing someone close to me became a complicated exercise in waiting for that call to tell me that it was all just a mistake, that everything was fine, and then begging the pain to come to the surface when the phone never rang.

You cannot predict a person's sudden passing, but there are certain people in life that you prepare yourself to lose, for whatever reason. You foolishly try to protect yourself by building a wall around your heart as a sort of preemptive defense mechanism so that when you get that call, you are prepared somehow. Like being emotionally vaccinated, you have already built up an immunity to their inevitable passing.

But this never works.

It was March 3, 1994, when I woke up that morning in Seattle to the news that Kurt had overdosed in a hotel room in Rome. I immediately turned on the news and saw images of him strapped to a gurney as he was being rushed to the hospital in an ambulance, so I frantically began calling everyone on our team to see what was going on, praying that it was just another accidental overdose, something that had happened before. There was confusion and conflicting reports; some were painfully dire, some were encouraging, but no matter how much I wanted to be there, I was five thousand miles away feeling totally helpless. After all, I had just seen Kurt two nights before in Munich, playing what would tragically become the last Nirvana show.

From that day forward, I built my walls higher.

And thirty-six days later, they closed in.

News of Kurt's death came early in the morning on April 8. Though, this time it was real. He was gone. There was no second phone call to right the wrong. To turn the tragedy around. It was final. I hung up the phone and waited for that same shattering pain to bring me to my knees again . . . but it didn't come. It was stuck somewhere deep within me, blocked by the trauma from a month before when I had been left in a state of conflicted emotional confusion. I don't remember much of that day other than turning on the news and hearing his name over and over again. Kurt Cobain. Kurt Cobain. Kurt Cobain. Each time his name was said, it slowly chipped away at the armor that I had designed to guard my heart. Kurt Cobain. Kurt Cobain. Kurt Cobain. I waited for the armor to be pierced, sending me to the floor one more time, but I wouldn't let it. I fought back, too afraid to feel that pain again. Kurt was more than just a name to me; he was a friend, he was a father, he was a son, he was an artist, he was a human being, and over time he became the center of our universe, the point that our entire world orbited, but he was still just a young man with so much to look forward to. WE had so much to look forward to.

That night, we all joined together at his home to somehow try to comfort each other, but that comfort was hard to find, because no matter how many brushes with death he may have had, no one had imagined it would be like this. At least not me. There was shock, followed by despair, followed by remembrance, returning to shock. I looked around the living room full of people, all the different lives that he'd touched, each in a different way. Family members, lifelong friends, and more recent acquaintances, all mourning in their own ways. Life would never be the same for any of us, and we were now all forever bonded by this devastating event, a wound that would certainly scar. For years, I couldn't drive within a mile of that house on Lake Washington without being shaken by crippling anxiety, remembering the sound of those cries.

The next day, I woke up, walked to my kitchen, began to make coffee, and it hit me. *He's not coming back. He's gone. But . . . I am still here. I get to wake and live another day, no matter how good or bad.* It made no sense. How could someone just . . . disappear? It seemed unreal. And unfair.

Life soon became a long series of firsts. My first cup of coffee since he disappeared. My first meal since he disappeared. My first phone call. My first drive, and so on and so forth. It seemed that every step I took was a step away from a time when he was alive, a succession of moments in which I had to relearn everything. I HAD TO LEARN TO LIVE AGAIN.

"Empathy!" Kurt wrote in his suicide note, and there were times where I would beg my heart to feel the pain he must have felt. Ask for it to break. I would try to wring the tears from my eyes as I cursed those fucking walls I had built so high, because they kept me from the feelings I desperately needed to feel. I cursed that voice on the phone that had told me he had died prematurely, leaving me in this state of emotional confusion without a way of accessing the reservoir of sadness I needed to purge. I was held down by the weight of it, knowing that grief was eating me alive, even if it was buried deeper than I could reach. I was anesthetized when all I wanted was to feel the surgery required to cure me.

I felt ashamed at times that I could not feel, but eventually I accepted that there is no right or wrong way to grieve. There is no textbook, no manual to refer to when in need of emotional guidance. It is a process that cannot be controlled, and you are hopelessly at the mercy of its grip, so you must surrender to it when it rears its ugly head, no matter the fear. Over the years, I have come to terms with this. To this day I am often overcome with that same profound sadness that sent me to the floor the first time I was told Kurt had died.

Is it time that dictates the depth of your grief when losing someone? Is the emotional relevance simply determined by the number of days that you spent together? Those three and a half years that I knew Kurt, a relatively small window of time in the chronology of my life, shaped and in some ways still define who I am today. I will always be "that guy from Nirvana," and I am proud of it.

But without my childhood best friend Jimmy Swanson, I never would have even made it to Seattle, and his passing bored a hole in my life that is entirely different.

I learned of Jimmy's death from the bedside phone in my Oklahoma City hotel room on the morning of July 18, 2008. He had passed in his sleep in the same North Springfield house where we had discovered the world of music together as kids, on the same couch where we would watch MTV for hours, dreaming of someday experiencing the lives of the famous musicians we admired.

I hung up the phone, opened the shades in my room, looked into the sky, and spoke to him. Where we'd once passed notes to each other in the high school hallways between classes, we now were left to communicate through spirit and prayer.

A part of me died with Jimmy. He was more than just a person to me, he was my home, and though I could never let go of him, I had to let go of who I was with him when he died. And so began another process of firsts, but this time they proved to be more difficult, because Jimmy and I had shared so many of life's firsts together. As if we were two conjoined twins separated after sharing a body for years, it was like I was alone, questioning who I was now that I was on my own. I looked up to him, followed him, and envied his ability to live life exactly as he wanted, fully as himself. Jimmy was loved by everyone, because there was no one on earth like him. We both discovered individuality, together, but embraced it in our own ways. As much as we both loved music— and Jimmy tried his hand at playing too—he was never inspired to follow through like me, preferring to stay in the background, cheering from the sidelines.

I felt Jimmy's absence to my core. At the time of Kurt's passing, I was only twenty-five years old, not yet equipped to handle the challenges that followed. But Jimmy died when I was thirty-nine, and by then I had a much broader understanding of life, which in turn gave me a better understanding of death. By that time, I had become a husband, a father, and the leader of a new band, accepting all of the countless responsibilities that came with those roles. I was no longer just a skinny little boy hiding behind a mane of hair and a giant drum set. As my emotions became more mature, they also became more focused, more intense. I could no longer just push everything down, not allowing myself to feel. I knew there were no magic phone calls coming. I knew that death was final. I knew that grief was a long road, and an unpredictable one. IN A WAY, LOSING KURT PREPARED ME FOR LOSING JIMMY FOURTEEN YEARS LATER. Though two entirely different relationships, they were almost equally formative, and both made me the person that I am today.

Though Kurt and Jimmy were not "family," I invited them to be, and that invitation can sometimes be even more intimate than the connection to any blood relative. There was no biological obligation here; we were bonded for other reasons: our parallel spirits, our love of music, and our mutual appreciation. You cannot choose family, and when you lose family, there is a biological imperative that implies a built-in type of mourning. But with friends, you design your own relationship, which in turn designs your grief, which can be felt even deeper when they are gone. THOSE CAN BE ROOTS THAT ARE MUCH HARDER TO PULL.

These deaths still resonate like a long echo throughout my life, and not a day goes by when I don't think of Kurt and Jimmy. There are simple reminders: A song on the radio that Jimmy would air-drum to while driving his old, beat-up Renault car. The pink strawberry milk that Kurt would sometimes buy at the gas station as a treat for himself. The smell of the cheap Brut cologne that Jimmy would douse himself in each morning, for no one to enjoy but himself. The Elmer Fudd hat that Kurt would often wear to hide his face from the public, and the white-framed Jackie O glasses that became his trademark. It seems that everywhere I turn there is a reminder to be found, and I have come to a place where they no longer break my heart; they make me smile.

But it's when I sit down at a drum set that I feel Kurt the most. It's not often that I play the songs that we played together, but when I sit on that stool, I can still picture him in front of me, wrestling with his guitar as he screamed his lungs raw into the microphone. Just like staring at the sun will burn a spot into your retinas, his image will forever be burned in mine when I look past my drums to the audience before me. He will always be there.

And every time I return to Virginia, I *feel* Jimmy. He is in the trees that we climbed as children, within the cracks of the sidewalks that we followed to elementary school every morning and every fence that we jumped to take shortcuts through the neighborhood. There are times when I speak and they are his words, though it's my voice. And when I see him in my dreams, he hasn't changed a bit. He is still my best friend.

Though they're no longer with us, I still carry these people wherever I go.

And the walls are finally gone.

THE HEART-BREAKER

"Dave, there's a phone call for you."

The studio engineer passed me the handset at the end of the long, curly cord, and to my surprise it was none other than Ron Stone calling, an associate of my manager we would always refer to as "Old School" from his days of working with legendary artists like Bonnie Raitt and Neil Young. We technically had never worked together, so it was unusual for him to call me directly, but even more unusual was the news he'd called to share.

"Tom Petty wants to know if you'll play drums for him on *Saturday Night Live . . .*"

Bewildered, I replied, "Wait, what? Why me? The man could have any drummer in the world, and he's calling me?" I mean, this is Tom Petty we're talking about, America's favorite Floridian, the embodiment of grassroots, working-class cool, the voice behind decades of classic rock hits, like "Breakdown," "American Girl," "Refugee," and "Free Fallin'."

His music was the soundtrack to a thousand hickeys, songs that oozed with feel and groove, and he was calling the guy who only knew how to play the drums one of two ways: on or off? It made absolutely no sense.

At the time, Tom was gearing up to release what would become one of his most celebrated solo records, *Wildflowers,* and had recently parted ways with original Heartbreakers drummer Stan Lynch, so he needed someone to fill the drum stool for a promotional *Saturday Night Live* performance. Any invitation to visit the fabled television studios of *SNL,* my favorite show, was an honor (fun fact: as of this writing I have been on fourteen times, more than any other musician), but still, I didn't quite get it. Petty was one of my favorite artists ever, a musical hero to millions of young suburban misfits like me, so the fact that he even knew my name was a lot to take in. Not to mention I had barely touched a drum set, much less played live, since Nirvana had ended. I hemmed and hawed, taken aback by such a flattering request, and politely asked for a day or two to think about it. My head was in a much different place at the time, to say the least. I DID NEED TO THINK THINGS THROUGH.

I had always known the day would come where I would be asked to cross this bridge, to move on with life after a year of mourning, but I wasn't prepared for the catalyst to be something like this. I hung up the phone in the studio control room where I was standing with a guitar around my neck and got back to what I had been busy doing when the call came in: recording what would, unknowingly, become the first Foo Fighters record.

After Kurt's death, I was lost. We all were. With our world pulled out from under us in such a sudden, traumatic manner, it was hard to find any direction or beacon that would help guide us through the fog of tremendous sadness and loss. And the fact that Kurt, Krist, and I were all connected by music made any music seem bittersweet. What was once my life's greatest joy had now become my life's greatest sorrow, and not only did I put my instruments away, I turned off the radio, for fear that even the slightest melody would trigger paralyzing grief. It was the first time in my life that I rejected music. I just couldn't afford to let it break my heart again.

In those months after his passing, I felt like a fish trapped in a tiny bowl, desperately swimming back and forth all day long but never really going anywhere. I was just twenty-five years old with a whole life ahead of me, but in many ways I felt like my life had ended too. The thought of putting my drum set onstage behind just another face was more than unappealing, it was downright depressing. I was too young to fade away but too old to start again. Sure, I could just go out and join another band, but I would forever be known as "that guy from Nirvana," and I knew deep down that nothing would ever compare to what Nirvana had gifted to the world. That sort of thing only happens once in a lifetime.

After months and months of spinning my wheels in suffocating bouts of introspection, I decided that I needed to get away from Seattle and clear my head, so I traveled to a corner of the earth that I have always adored, a place of serenity and natural beauty where I hoped to find some healing from my broken life at home: the Ring of Kerry. A gorgeous, remote area in southwestern Ireland, the Ring of Kerry is a return to what the earth must have been thousands of years ago, before man carved it into concrete lots and crowded thoroughfares. With miles of the greenest fields over-looking coastal landscapes and seaside villages, there is a calm and tranquility there that I so desperately needed to reassess my life and start over. I had been there once before, spending a week with my mother and sister driving from Dublin to Dingle before Nirvana's 1992 Reading Festival show (our last performance in the UK), and connected to that landscape in a way I had with no other part of the world. Maybe it was my mother's Irish heritage, or maybe it was the pace of life, which was similar to that of the rural areas of Virginia where I would go hunting as a kid, but whatever it was, I felt at home in its quiet and isolation. I craved that now.

One day, as I was navigating my rental car around the pot-holes and deep ruts of a faraway country road, I noticed a young hitchhiker in the distance. With his long, greasy hair and over-sized parka, I could tell this kid was a rocker and, being miles from the nearest town, desperately needed a ride to his destination. As I grew nearer, I decided that I would kindly pick him up and give him a lift, until I saw something that immediately made me change my mind.

He was wearing a Kurt Cobain T-shirt.

A wave of anxiety hit me like a jolt from an electric chair, and I sped past with my head down, praying that he didn't recognize me. My hands were shaking, and I felt like I was going to be physi-cally sick, dizzy in the grips of a crippling panic attack. Here I was, desperately trying to disappear in the most remote area I could find and sort out a life that had been turned upside down only months before, and there was Kurt's face staring back at me, almost as a reminder that no matter how far I ran, I could never escape the past.

This was the moment that changed everything.

I flew back to the States and decided that it was time to get back to work. Without a band or any real master plan, I retreated to the place where I always felt most comfortable: recording songs by myself. I learned to do this by default when I was twelve years old with the help of two cassette recorders, an old guitar, and some pots and pans. My method was simple: record a guitar part on one cassette, eject that tape and put it in cassette player number two, hit Play, record myself playing "drums" along with the guitar part on another cassette, and so on, and so on. I was essentially multi-tracking without even realizing it. I would write ridiculous songs about my dog, my school, and Ronald Reagan, but I was fascinated with the process, so I did it quite often. The best part? No one ever knew, because I was deathly afraid of letting anyone hear the shriek of my prepubescent voice.

By the time I started hanging out and recording with my friend Barrett Jones on the eight-track machine in his Virginia basement studio, I was familiar with the concept of laying down all of the instruments myself, systematically layering guitars, drums, and vocals as I had done as a child, though now the RadioShack cassette players were replaced with Barrett's professional reel-to-reel equipment. I never wanted to impose (and never had any money to pay him for engineering), so I would wait until the end of someone else's session and shyly ask, "Is there any extra tape at the end of the reel? I want to try something . . ." Knowing that this was a big ask (and I had already smoked most of his weed), I would race from one instrument to the next as fast as I could, doing only one take on the drums, one take on guitar, and one take on bass so as not to waste any more of Barrett's time or generosity. Then I would go home and listen to my little experiment over and over, imagining what I could do if I had more than fifteen minutes to record a song.

Once Barrett moved out to Seattle and we found a house together, his studio was in MY basement, so I took advantage of its proximity and started writing songs that, although still primitive and not yet ready for the world to hear, were a bit more evolved. "Alone and Easy Target," "Floaty," "Weenie Beenie," "Exhausted," and "I'll Stick Around" were just a few of the dozens of songs that we recorded in our little basement on rainy days, and I was slowly banking what would eventually become the Foo Fighters' repertoire. Nirvana were in full swing at the time, and god knows we didn't need any help in the songwriting department, so I kept the songs to myself, remembering that old drummer joke, "What was the last thing the drummer said before getting kicked out of the band? 'Hey, guys, I wrote a song I think we should play!!'"

With nothing to lose, nowhere left to run, I returned from Ireland and decided to book six days at a twenty-four-track studio down the street from my house in Richmond Beach, Robert Lang Studios, a state-of-the art facility built into the side of an enormous hill overlooking the Puget Sound. I had recorded there before, including Nirvana's last session, where we'd tracked our final song, "You Know You're Right," earlier that year. The studio's eclectic, oddball owner, Robert Lang, had decided to build a recording facility underneath his house in the early seventies and spent fifteen years digging deeper and deeper into the hill, hauling thousands of dump trucks' worth of dirt away and creating what can only be described as a gigantic concrete bunker with a great collection of vintage microphones. But the biggest difference from other studios was the materials he chose to use in the tracking rooms: marble and stone. Rather than the warm absorption of natural wood and acoustically treated baffling, his rooms had the unforgiving reflection of hard stone, which lent a much more "live" sound. It was actually the dark green Chinese marble that made Nirvana choose to record there, as upon our first tour around the studio, Bob showed us a small slab that he was convinced held a vision of a saintlike figure, a halo, a dove, and of the resurrection descending. That was enough for Krist Novoselic and me to say, "Oh, we're DEFI-NITELY recording here . . . this guy is WILD." Not to mention, it was so close to my home, I could drive there on my lawn-mower-powered go-kart.

I booked October 17 to 22, 1994, and started to prepare. I chose the fifteen songs that I considered the best of countless recordings Barrett and I had made over the years, assembled the gear, and made a plan: four songs a day for four days, and the last two days for vocals and mixing. If I recorded at the pace I always had, running from instrument to instrument, doing only one or two takes before moving on to the next, I could actually pull it off. I made a calendar, deciding which songs to record on which days, and rehearsed like crazy, knowing there was little time to spare. Six days in the studio seemed like an eternity to me, but I needed to prove that I could meet the challenge I had set for myself, the entire reason for this new project.

Barrett and I loaded in the gear that Monday morning, made coffee, got sounds, and were ready to hit Record by noon. A new song named "This Is a Call" was first up, and I blasted through the drums in one take, immediately strapped on the guitar, and finished that quickly before moving on to the bass for one pass. Within forty-five minutes, the instrumental was done. Next up was "I'll Stick Around." Same drill: drums, guitar, bass, and done in forty-five minutes. Then "Big Me," then "Alone and Easy

Target" . . . by the end of the first day, we had met our four-song quota with time to spare, and my lofty challenge didn't seem so challenging anymore. I actually felt . . . good.

This was more than just a recording session to me—it was deeply therapeutic. A continuation of life. This was what I needed to defibrillate my heart and return it to its normal rhythm, an electric pulse to restore my love and faith in music. Beyond just picking up an instrument and feeling productive or prolific, once again I could see through the windshield rather than look in the rearview mirror.

By the end of the week, I had not only achieved my goal of finishing the fifteen songs (actually recording them in the sequence of the eventual album), but I had also agreed to play with Tom Petty on *Saturday Night Live*, which was a leap back into my former life but something I was no longer afraid to do. There was light at the end of the tunnel now. Neither of these things was considered as any permanent life direction, they were just small steps forward. There was no vision for what came next. Not just yet.

I took the master tape of Barrett's rough mixes to a tape duplication place in downtown Seattle, where I decided to make a hundred cassette copies of my new project, imagining that I would give them to friends, family, and anyone who had any interest in what "that guy from Nirvana" had been up to since the band ended. I had kept my songs secret for most of my life, but now I was ready to share them with the world because I was proud of them, more so than anything I had ever recorded before. It wasn't just the sonic element of Barrett's amazing production skills; it was more the emotional gratification. I had finally come to the surface with the exaggerated gasp of someone held underwater too long.

Even though I had played every instrument on that cassette (minus one guitar track played by my friend Greg Dulli from the

Afghan Whigs, who I handed a guitar to while he was visiting the studio one day), I was horrified at the idea of considering it a "solo" project. I couldn't imagine "the Dave Grohl Experience" was a name that would have people running to the record stores, and quite honestly, I knew that the connection to Nirvana would certainly outweigh any listener's objectivity. So, I decided to follow a more anonymous route, taking inspiration from Stewart Copeland, the drummer of the Police, and his 1980 "solo" project Klark Kent. At the time, the Police were an emerging band, so as not to disrupt the band's career, Stewart decided to record under the pseudonym Klark Kent, playing all of the instruments himself, just as I had done. I loved the mystery of that. Having been a UFO fanatic my entire life, I took a simple phrase from a book I was reading at the time, *Above Top Secret*, which was a collection of UFO sighting reports and accounts from the military dating back to the early forties. In a chapter about unidentified craft over Europe and the Pacific during World War II, I found a term that the military used as a nickname for these unexplained glowing balls of light and thought it was just mysterious enough for me. Not only did it sound like a group of people, it almost sounded like a gang: Foo Fighters.

I designed the simple cassette insert that would be stuffed inside the case with each tape, choosing the font and paper color, writing the credits and song titles, and left the tape duplication place feeling ten feet tall, knowing that my prize would be ready by the end of the week. I was walking on air. The reward was simple: I had done this myself.

While I waited, I prepared to fly down to Los Angeles for my rehearsal with Tom Petty. I had been sent the two songs to be performed on the show, "You Don't Know How It Feels" and "Honey Bee," and was listening to them on repeat, trying to memorize all of Steve Ferrone's sublime drum licks and lock into his perfect feel.

My style was worlds away from his relaxed groove, so I focused on finding some sort of Zen to calm my usual anarchic method. But it wasn't just the music that I was nervous about. I was about to meet the one and only Tom Petty.

When I arrived at the massive rehearsal space in the San Fernando Valley just outside of Hollywood, a temple of paisley and incense with a massive totem pole at one end of the room, I was met with the most down-to-earth, genuine, and kind welcome by the band and crew. The Heartbreakers were the epitome of cool, with their relaxed swagger and faint Southern accents; they made me feel at home and appreciated, doing their best to disarm any nerves that they undoubtedly sensed I was experiencing. They were legitimate rock stars, after all, and I'm sure they had this effect on most everyone, but with their kindness and empathy they wanted to make me feel comfortable. I set up my drum set on the riser as we chatted, and gave my kick drum a strong WHACK, which made the entire room jump from its sheer volume, and they turned to each other and laughed, almost as if to say, "Holy shit, what have we gotten ourselves into?"

And then, there was Tom. He was just as I had imagined him to be, totally laid-back and effortlessly cool, and when he said hello, that voice of a thousand high school dances flowed from his mouth like thick molasses. Within a few minutes, any nerves that I had from this rock and roll fantasy camp daydream had faded, and we began to play. I could hardly contain my excitement, so I think I was probably giving it a little more muscle than I normally would, because the band were practically wincing from the cannon-level volume of my drums. We spent the afternoon jamming, hanging out, and casually getting to know each other in between takes, and by the end of the day they made me feel like an honorary Heartbreaker. I felt like we were a band. And that was a feeling I hadn't felt in a long, long time.

We met a week later at the *Saturday Night Live* studios for soundcheck day, which is usually Thursday. This is when the *SNL* team gets the sound levels correct and does the camera blocking as well. First, you soundcheck and rehearse, playing each song two or three times to get the stage monitors dialed in and everything sounding right in the control room, then you break for lunch and return an hour later for camera blocking, where the director rehearses his camera angles and moves for when they go live. This is typically a simple affair, just a few takes, and they nail it with ease, having decades of experience behind them.

But after the first take of camera blocking, the stage director walked up to my massive drum set and said, "Ummm, Dave . . . is there any way to move that rack tom just a few inches to the left? We're having a hard time seeing your face." Terrified and embarrassed in front of these heroes, I wasn't sure how to respond. I didn't want to rock the boat, as I was just a humble guest along for this most excellent ride, so why the fuck did they care about seeing me? This was a Tom Petty show! I looked over at Tom for guidance, and he gave me an expression that said, "Don't let them tell you what to do, kid. Stand your ground," so I nervously replied, "Ummm . . . no, that's where it goes, I'd rather not." Within seconds, a stagehand appeared with a smaller microphone for the drum, hoping that maybe that would give a clearer shot for the cameras. We ran through the song one more time, and the stage director appeared again, but this time he approached Tom. "Excuse me, Mr. Petty, is there any way we can move you just a few feet to the right?" Now, this was sheer audacity. The balls on this guy. You could have heard a fucking pin drop on that legendary stage, a stage that Tom was certainly familiar with, having graced it four times before. "No, man, we worked all day to get it to sound good, and it finally sounds good. If you move anything it's gonna fuck it all up." The stage director begged and pleaded until Tom finally threw his hands up in the air and relented, saying, "Fine. But I'm telling you, it's gonna fuck it all up . . ."

They moved Tom's monitors and microphone a few feet to the right, and we counted into the next take. As Tom approached the microphone to sing the first line, there was an ear-piercing squeal of feedback that was so loud it made us all immediately stop playing and plug our ears. *Oh fuck . . .* , I thought, *here it comes.*

Tom was pissed, but in a way that only Tom Petty could be. He never for one moment lost his cool, he just looked at the stage director and said, "You. Come here." The poor guy slinked up to the stage, knowing that he had perhaps made a career-defining mistake, and in his signature Southern drawl, Tom said, "What did I just tell you?" The director apologized and said he would immediately put the gear back in its original position, but Tom continued, "No, I want you to tell me what I just told you." The director then proceeded to repeat Tom's warning word for word, to which Tom then said, "That's right, now put it back." To me, it wasn't a scolding, and it wasn't a shaming, it was a man who had fought his whole life for what he believed in, facing countless adversities and demoralizing industry bullshit, letting the world know that you couldn't fuck with him. I was proud to be his drummer in that moment—not the guy from Nirvana, but Tom Petty's drummer. And as if I hadn't already respected the guy enough, I now looked up to him even more.

The show was great. We rocked both songs with groove and intensity, and in the short week and a half that we had known each other, I was starting to feel surprisingly comfortable within the band's laid-back dynamic, something that I had never even gotten close to feeling in the three and a half years I was in Nirvana. The awkward dysfunction of Nirvana definitely made for quite a noise, but the sense of family and community in the Heartbreakers' camp seemed so much healthier and less chaotic. This was exactly what I needed to soothe my past traumas, and a great reminder that music does represent joy and life and celebration. This was a perfect one-off to get me back on my feet, I thought.

And then Tom asked if I would consider doing it again.

Now, this was a game changer. An unexpected turn of fate that made the experience both more rewarding and ultimately confusing. How on earth could I say no to such an opportunity? Never in my wildest dreams had I thought I was worthy or capable of such an offer, but goddamn, it felt good to be asked. As we stood in the narrow hallway outside of the tiny dressing room after our performance, he asked me to think about it, and I thanked him profusely, still blown away that I was even speaking with the man who wrote the classic "Runnin' Down a Dream," a song about following life's crooked path with all of its twists and turns, never knowing where it may take you.

I returned home and picked up my box of one hundred cassettes, neatly stuffed in a cardboard box that I proceeded to load into my truck as if I were bringing a newborn home from the hospital for the first time. Had I left my heart in New York City with Tom Petty? Or was it somewhere in that cardboard box full of fresh cassettes?

I WAS AT A CROSSROADS.

The feeling that I experienced with the Heartbreakers was so rewarding, so comforting, so needed at that moment, but deep down I knew that I would never really be a Heartbreaker. They were connected by decades of history, and as lovely and welcoming and hospitable as they were, I would forever be "that guy from Nirvana," something I was obviously honored to be, but with that title came some extremely heavy baggage.

I loved Tom's music so much, and I would have had the time of my life playing his songs night after night, but . . . they weren't mine. We spoke on the phone one more time, and Tom explained that they toured very comfortably. I would have my own bus, and the schedules were super relaxed, not the grueling van runs that I was used to doing. It all sounded so perfect. Almost too perfect. I was twenty-five years old and still hungry, not ready to relax into a "sure thing." I still had the restless energy of a teenager, driven to thrive in the unknown even if it was frightening at times.

So, I politely declined and decided that the cardboard box in the back of my truck was my key to a new life. It was definitely not a sure thing, but nothing ever is.

Yeah, I'm runnin' down a dream
That never would come to me
Workin' on a mystery
Goin' wherever it leads
Runnin' down a dream

RIP Tom Petty 1950–2017

SWEET
VIRGINIA

"I'm going to need some privacy, so . . . nothing under four hundred acres," I said confidently.

"Wow!" my real estate agent, Connie, replied in shock. "Okay! Well, let me get on that and I'll circle back with some listings ASAP!" I was a bit taken off guard by the surprise in her voice, to be honest. This didn't seem like such an unreasonable request to me, considering that I was looking for a house to live in, a guesthouse for the band, and a barn to convert into a recording studio so that I could ride off into the sunset, living out my dream of being completely self-sufficient in a sleepy Virginia town.

Then again, I had no idea how big an acre was.

After seven years in Seattle, my life there had finally run its course. I had arrived a total stranger, lived in squalid desolation and emotional isolation, found my groove with a new group that became the biggest band in the world, had it all ripped out from under me, and started over again. A lifetime in itself. As much as I loved the city and the friends I had made there over the years, I had left my heart in Virginia, my forever home. Growing up among the rolling hills and tall oak trees of its suburbs, I never believed that I would live anywhere else, no matter how badly I wanted to break out of its quiet monotony and predictability as a kid. I'd always figured that I would end up right where I started.

As we began recording the Foo Fighters' second album, *The Colour and the Shape* (our most popular record to this day), in the fall of 1996 at a studio outside of Seattle named Bear Creek, I sensed that my time in the Pacific Northwest was coming to a close. Not only had I always felt like a visitor, just another transplant in a city fiercely protective of its precious roots, but the death rattle of my first marriage was in its final throes, casting a shadow over our recording sessions in the deep woods as the darkest winter months lay ahead (themes that are evident throughout the lyrics of that album). The fire that Seattle had built in my heart was going out, and no matter how hard I fanned the embers, I could never reignite what once was. *It's time to move on,* I thought. *I don't belong here anymore.*

Or, as Pat Smear once said, "Too many ghosts."

But, before moving back east to the place I felt most at home, I decided to make a twelve-month pit stop in Los Angeles (my version of *The Lost Weekend*), getting a feel for my newfound emancipation just blocks away from that sinking ship full of mud wrestlers I had once managed to barely escape. No longer surviving on dollar-bill handouts and cans of baked beans, I could now afford the luxury of my own place (and food). I rented a comfortable little two-bedroom house just down the street from the Sunset Strip, which I proceeded to take advantage of with reckless abandon, no longer tied to anywhere or anyone. The Foo Fighters had now become more than an off-the-cuff side project, we had become a band, although the making of our second album left us on shaky ground (original drummer William Goldsmith quit after I rerecorded his drum tracks, but was thankfully replaced by the overly qualified Taylor Hawkins, and Pat Smear temporarily left soon after). After making it through the challenges of recording our second album, I needed to blow off some steam.

I felt liberated in a way that made me want to indulge in all the things I had been holding back from all those years. And hold back, I did not. After years of swilling pitchers of heavy Hefeweizen and the sophisticated microbrews of the Pacific Northwest, I was introduced to the much less pretentious and far more lethal combination of Coors Light and tequila by my new partner in crime, Taylor Hawkins. Any timidity that I'd once had when it came to letting my hair down was now gone, left in a wake of Patrón bottles and chewed-up lime wedges. At the time, former Scream vocalist Pete Stahl had taken a job working at the Viper Room, a hedonistic den of vice conveniently located down the street from my house. This became my nightly haunt, usually ending with a bungalow full of derelicts after last call, drinking until the sun came up. That year was, to say the least, a good time. But after twelve months of gluttonous debauchery, I realized that this was not the sunset I was meant to ride off into. I set my sights on another, more wholesome horizon: the paradise of rural Virginia.

I flew back east to meet Connie, and we began our house hunt in the quaint little town of Leesburg, only an hour from the cosmopolitan buzz of Washington, DC, and built in 1740, with beautiful historic buildings on every corner and stone walls lining miles of winding horse country. This was a return to my youth, as I had spent many summers walking these fields when I was a boy, looking for Civil War bullets while dove hunting in the sweltering heat, and winters placing goose decoys in the hardened, icy mud before sunrise, waiting for the flocks to arrive from a pit dug into the cold earth, hoping to bring home dinner. Those memories washed over me as we drove to our first listing, but as we arrived, Connie offered one disclaimer: "Now, this first property is a bit smaller than what you were looking for, but the house itself is gorgeous, and it has the guesthouse and barn you were looking for." A bit disappointed, I asked, "How much smaller?" "It's about one hundred acres," she replied. *One hundred acres? That's nothing!* I thought. How could I possibly disappear and play music into the wee hours with my band on only a hundred acres? "Well . . . ," I said, "we're here. I guess we should at least go check it out . . ."

As I stood on the front porch of this immaculate, two-hundred-year-old mansion that was once a foxhunting lodge, I was dwarfed by the huge columns that towered overhead, and as I looked out at the expanse of lush green fields below, I realized why my real estate agent was in shock on that first call. A hundred acres was a goddamned farm. And four hundred acres? That was an entire fucking county. A surveyor, I was not, and I was mortified by my agricul-

tural ignorance, but also humbled by the awe-inspiring beauty of the property that stretched before me, its perimeter lined with trees as a natural border, running down to a small river in the distance. *Holy fuck!* I thought. *What have I gotten myself into?*

After walking through the main residence (which was a bit too similar to the White House, somewhere I *know* I'll never live), we headed over to the guesthouse, where it suddenly dawned on me that this was all wrong. Here I was, just thirty years old, about to literally "buy the farm," as they say, as if I were done with my blessed life of music and adventure, ready to ride off into the sunset, never to be seen or heard from again. Not to mention, the fucking guesthouse was twice the size of the tiny home I grew up in just an hour away, a house that my mother, sister, and I were more than comfortable sharing our entire lives. The barn was tempting, though. I could totally imagine its becoming a world-class recording facility, with its high ceilings and its immense square footage, more than enough room to fit an entire orchestra. But I wasn't ready to get so comfortable just yet. THERE WAS STILL MORE WORK TO BE DONE.

Connie drove me to a few more listings, all in the two-hundred-fifty-to-four-hundred-acre range. ("Wanna walk the property line?" she would ask. *Um, no thanks*), but it was no use; my mind was made up. This pipe dream would have to wait. Maybe someday when life slowed down, and I had a beautiful family to share it with, I would embrace this domestic, rural Americana thing. But not yet.

I eventually settled for a more reasonable house on one and a half acres outside of historic Old Town Alexandria, only miles from my old neighborhood, and began construction on what would become the basement recording studio where the Foo Fighters would work for years to come. We had recently been freed from our contract with Capitol Records on account of a "key man clause" that stated if Capitol Records president Gary Gersh (an old friend who was also the man who'd signed Nirvana to Geffen years before) were to leave, we had the option to go as well, a provision that was written and accepted because of our long history together. His departure was an unprecedented stroke of luck, and we opted to follow him, now making us completely independent, something that most bands never have the luxury of experiencing after being locked into a deal for multiple albums.

The beauty of this was that we weren't *obligated* to be a band anymore. We didn't have to do it, we wanted to do it, proving our intention to be pure. It had been a rough few years since our first album, touring relentlessly, trying to find our legs, pushing through the sophomore slump, and losing a few members along the way, but we always persevered out of our genuine love of playing together. The only time I ever seriously considered giving up was the time Nate quit for twenty-four hours in the spring of 1998. While I was at home at my mother's house in Virginia, Nate called to inform me that his heart wasn't in it anymore and that he felt more at home with his former band Sunny Day Real Estate, which was planning a reunion. This one got me. William was never really cut out for the band's intensity and drive, Pat was just "over it" when he left, Franz was a dear old friend but it never really clicked, but Nate? The guy I had put this whole thing together with? I'd finally had it and angrily replied, "Okay, well I'm sick of teaching people these fucking songs, so when I find a guy YOU have to teach them." We said goodbye, but deep down I knew that without Nate, the Foo Fighters was over. I couldn't handle one more resignation, and it was beginning to feel suspiciously like the solo project I never wanted it to be.

That night I went out drinking at my favorite low-rent barbecue joint, Ribsters, with my best friend Jimmy and proceeded to get blackout drunk, crying in my Jack and Cokes, defeated by another blow to my life's greatest passion. Returning home, I passed out in my childhood bedroom, head spinning like a top, and was awakened the next morning by the sound of my mother's voice whispering gently outside my door, "David? Nate is on the phone . . ." Confused, I grabbed the giant cordless phone, extended the long antenna, and growled, "Helloooo . . ." Nate proceeded to apologize, explained that he'd had a momentary lapse of reason and that he didn't want to quit the band after all. To say that I was relieved is a gross understatement; I was practically born again. We cried, said "I love you, man" to each other, and hung up the phone, and then I crawled back into bed, realizing that I had pissed it the night before.

As my new house was being prepared, Taylor and I plotted a cross-country trek from Los Angeles to Virginia, just two young men in a black Chevy Tahoe listening to classic rock at dangerous volumes, speeding down the highway on a crazy coast-to-coast odyssey. Taylor and I had become practically inseparable since he had joined the band the year before, becoming devious partners in crime from day one. During his stint as Alanis Morissette's drummer, long before he became a Foo Fighter, we would bump into each other backstage at festivals all over the world, and our chemistry was so obvious that even Alanis herself once asked him, "What are you going to do when Dave asks you to be his drummer?" Part Beavis and Butthead, part Dumb and Dumber, we were a hyperactive blur of Parliament Lights and air drumming wherever we went, so there was no one I would rather have shared this psychopathic safari with than Taylor. We mapped out the trip to make a few stops along the way, visiting Taylor's grandmother and Pantera's strip club (the latter being top priority), but for the most part it was a straight 2,600-mile shot back to my hometown. (Upon arrival, Taylor broke into his best Bruce Springsteen impression, serenading me with the Boss's classic anthem of the same name. The only thing funnier was the time he played the theme from *Cheers* on a piano in the middle of a crowded Costco.) I hosted one last going-away party in my little canyon bungalow, packed up my meager belongings into a stack of U-Haul boxes, threw everything on a moving truck, and said goodbye once again to the excess and desperation of America's most glamorous city. As Taylor and I began our journey, I was more than happy to see Los Angeles disappear in my rearview mirror, leaving another chapter behind, one that still remains a bit blurrier than the rest.

We had met the almighty Pantera (the undisputed kings of metal) earlier that year at an Ozzfest concert in the UK where we were asked to fill in for Korn at the last minute, a most terrifying request. Don't get me wrong, I was a lifelong, card-carrying, diehard metal fan. A back-patch-wearing, cassette-collecting, fanzine-subscribing, stage-diving lifer at heart. But Ozzfest? The Foo Fighters? We were the rock and roll equivalent of *Revenge of the Nerds* compared to the bludgeoning metal of all the other acts. Some of us even had hair ABOVE our collars at the time, so this made little sense to me. This was perhaps the greatest mismatch of all time. Disaster waiting to happen . . .

To make matters worse, we were booked to go on *after* Pantera. The absolute heaviest, tightest, grooviest, most badass metal band of all time. The kings of Cro-Magnon carnage. The motherfucking COWBOYS FROM HELL. "There'll be nothing left once they play their final chord, believe me," I told my manager. Stage, gone. Minds and PA blown. Nothing but a muddy field of shattered eardrums and melted brains. But, never being one to say no to a bad idea, we agreed, and set our sights on Milton Keynes.

The National Bowl in Milton Keynes is no stranger to rock and roll spectacles. From Michael Jackson to Metallica, Queen to Green Day, Status Quo to the Prodigy, the venue had hosted decades of massive shows within its natural surroundings (apparently a former clay pit for brick making). With a capacity of sixty-five thousand, and only fifty miles northwest of London, it was the ideal place for a glorious, sunny Saturday of doom. And the lineup was ridiculously strong. Sabbath, Slayer, Soulfly, and . . . ahem . . . us. The day was primed to be a mammoth metal showdown of gigantic proportions.

Pulling into the backstage area, I peered out of the tour bus window to see if I could catch a glimpse of some of my heroes. Tom Araya! Scott Ian! Tony Iommi! Max Cavalera! There they were, wandering about like us mere mortals. And in the light of day, no less! I had always imagined (hoped) that these dark figures only came out at night after hanging upside down like bats in their mausoleums, nocturnal creatures refusing the sun, just waiting to terrorize us all with their evil anthems beneath a full moon. To my dismay, I think I saw a few of them in shorts holding soda pops, but whatever. Metal lives.

I hid in our dressing room, for fear that I would get eaten alive. Plus, I couldn't bear to walk to the stage and take a frightened glimpse of the certain fate that awaited us in that undulating mosh pit of leather and spikes. I sat there nervously, trying to concoct a set list that was a little more Motörhead, a little less 10cc, scouring our back catalog for anything without the word "love" or a George Harrison–style slide guitar solo. More than wanting to impress the audience, I wanted to impress my hard rock heroes, hoping that they would recognize that I too was a metalhead in my heart.

Finally working up the courage to venture out of my sweaty porta-cabin, I stepped to the side of the stage and witnessed what can only be described as the most awesome, most brutal, most vulgar display of power known to man, Pantera. Just as I had imagined, they were absolutely *destroying* the stage. Vinnie Paul, the master, the legend, beating the ever-living shit out of his thunderous mountain of drums. Phil Anselmo screaming bloody murder like a man possessed by every evil spirit from every single exorcist movie ever made. Rex Brown stalking the stage, carrying his bass like a massive flamethrower aimed at the crowd. And Dimebag Darrell . . . god's gift to guitar, stealing the show with such ease, such swagger, such cool, leaving jaws dragging in the summer dirt. It was a Valhalla of volume. At one point, I looked behind the drums and saw a deranged, shirtless fan, breaking bottles and moshing alone, singing along to every word as if his life depended on it. THIS was a true Pantera fan. Not unlike like the 64,999 others out there in that bowl, mind you, but this dude was going totally mental literally within a few feet of the drum set. He then leaned down to the drums to fix a cymbal stand that had shifted from Vinnie Paul's merciless bashing. *How strange,* I thought. Turns out this deranged, shirtless, slam-dancing fan was Vinnie's drum tech, Kat. Let me tell you, never ever ever in my years of touring had I seen something so badass. This wasn't a road crew. It was a gang of hoodlums. And this wasn't a band. It was a force of fucking nature.

For a moment, I forgot that we were even on the bill that day. I was so lost in the music, I forgot that I would soon have to follow this historic performance with my version of post-grunge alternative rock (cue fingers ramming down throat). Some people meditate, some people go to church, some people lick little frogs in the desert to find this feeling. All I needed that day was Pantera. Unfortunately, that euphoric feeling immediately disappeared the second they finished and the crowd ferociously roared. We were dead meat.

I don't remember much about our set (sometimes traumatic memories can be suppressed and pushed down to the darkest depths of your psyche, only to be unlocked by years of difficult therapy), but I do recall a few guys from the other bands watching us while we played. That, at least, made me feel a bit less like a fish out of water. I felt validated to see these heavy metal heroes singing along to our songs word for word. Thankfully we managed to make it through the gig without any bottles of piss being hurled at our faces, so I considered it an incredible success. That roaring, angry mob was not so roaring as before, but we made it back to our little room without losing any limbs. Phew.

Afterward, we had the honor of meeting and hanging out with Pantera, and anyone who's ever had the chance to hang out with Pantera knows that it is not for the faint of heart. First of all, there was never a band more welcoming, more hospitable, more down-to-earth than Pantera. It didn't matter who you were, what you did, where you were from, they would welcome you in, stuff a beer in your hand and a shot in your mouth, and make you laugh harder than you'd ever laughed before. We got along like a house on fire, and as we said our drunken goodbyes, Vinnie gave me a business card. "Dude, next time you're in Dallas, you gotta come by the Clubhouse." I looked at the card, and to my amazement (but not surprise) they had THEIR OWN STRIP CLUB. Some rock stars have expensive cars. Some have castles. Some even have exotic animals. But a fucking strip club? That takes the cake. That's like me owning a Starbucks. Danger.

Months later, as Taylor and I looked at our old, dog-eared road atlas to prepare our trip back to Virginia, we realized that this was our big chance to witness Pantera's wild world firsthand, so we routed the entire trip around visiting the Clubhouse. It was time. Our first day on the road we stopped at a gas station in Barstow to empty our bladders and fill up on gas. Windows down, speakers distorted from blasting classic rock at ninety miles per hour, just two best friend/drummer dudes racing down the highway without a care in the world. All sunglasses and hair, cigs hanging from big smiles, risking our lives air drumming while speeding past eighteen-wheelers blowing like sails in the desert wind. I called and left our Texan friends excited messages from my Flavor Flav–sized cell phone: "Be ready, we're on our way."

Walking up to the counter at a roadside motel in Phoenix, I slapped my back pocket as I would always do before pulling out my favorite green Velcro-and-vinyl wallet (Fort Knox, as it was jokingly referred to). Though, this time it didn't make that familiar thump. My pocket was empty. My wallet was gone. Must have been in the truck. I checked the cup holders. The center console. Under the seats. The glove compartment. Nothing. Zilch. Gone. The only place we'd stopped that day was that gas station in Barstow . . . FUCK. Where else could I have left it? And that was 372.9 miles in the opposite direction! Everything I had was in that old wallet. License, credit cards, cig money, Dimebag Darrell guitar pick . . . I was entirely screwed.

Fortunately, Taylor saved the day and threw down for our room, while I phoned my accountant in Seattle and made a plan to ship some replacement cards to our next roadside motel. Alas, we soldiered on. Nothing, and I mean NOTHING, was going to stop us from getting to the Clubhouse . . .

Anyone familiar with American geography knows that Dallas isn't necessarily "on the way" to Virginia from L.A. No. It's a proper two-hundred-mile detour if you're planning on taking I-40 across. But the heart wants what the heart wants, so what's an extra couple hundred miles compared to the stories we'd have to tell when I got back to my old neighborhood friends in Springfield? Stories that would make David Lee Roth's toes curl . . . tales of mischief that would make Keith Richards cover his ears in disgust . . . hell, even Lemmy might crack a smile . . .

After dinner with some of Taylor's relatives at an authentic Texas roadside steakhouse, we were cleared for takeoff. We jumped in the Tahoe and drove the short distance outside of town to the Clubhouse. Actually, we may have floated there on a rainbow wave of cotton candy unicorn glitter, but maybe that's just my romantic revisionism kicking in (it does that sometimes). Regardless, it was really happening. Months and months of waking every day, counting the minutes until we walked into the neon/black light of Pantera's palace, enveloped by the aroma of Coors Light and peach body wash, DJ blasting old-school Scorpions, to find a booth full of Pantera just waiting to greet us with a big, Pearl Jam–style high five. I had the whole thing dialed into my mind. It was the *Goodfellas* kitchen scene on acid. And it was about to go down.

"ID, please."

The doorman stood there with his glow-in-the-dark hand stamp ready to go, waiting for me to do that old familiar slap on the back pocket everyone does before whipping out their own trusty Fort Knox. I looked at Taylor, eyes wide in shock. He returned my panicked expression. All the blood rushed from my face, tears welled up in my eyes, and I began to tremble with fear. I stuttered the only words I could muster, "B-B-B-B-B-B-Barstow . . . I lost my wallet in Barstow, sir." Silence. Then, the words I most dreaded, more than the grim reaper himself, spilled from the doorman's sneer: "Sorry, bud. Can't let you in without ID." Taylor jumped in and pleaded, "But, but, but . . . we're friends with Pantera!" The man looked up with his cold, dead eyes and growled, "*Everyone's* friends with Pantera. Sorry."

And . . . that was that. Three days, fourteen hundred miles, and a dream, stomped out like a dirty old Parliament Light in the parking lot of an industrial complex outside of Dallas. No candy coating here; it fucking crushed my soul. A few more unanswered calls from the Flavor Flav phone, a few more cigs in the parking lot, and we slowly climbed back into the Tahoe, heads down, hearts broken, totally dejected. No hanging out with our besties Pantera. I knew Taylor would never let me live this down.

THEN AGAIN, I WAS ON MY WAY HOME.

Ten years later in Oxnard, California, I was at a local surf shop in the harbor buying some sunglasses with my baby daughter Violet, and as we walked up to the cash register, the nice girl behind the counter greeted me with a hello and began to ring up my purchase. She looked up, paused a moment, squinted, and asked, "Are you Dave Grohl?" "Yes," I said with a smile. Still squinting, she said, "Did you lose your wallet in Barstow in 1998?"

No. Fucking. Way.

"YES!!!!!!!!!!" I replied in amazement. She laughed and said, "That was my parents' gas station. They still have your fucking wallet, dude."

I stopped trying to understand fate and destiny a long time ago, but dumb luck seems to be my specialty. Astonishingly, my wallet was returned to me not long after that, completely intact, and just like a time capsule buried for years, it was still filled with sweet memorabilia from that glorious period in my life, when I was young, free, and ready to start again.

And yes, even my old driver's license was inside.

When we arrived in Virginia a week later, ears ringing from days of classic rock and in great need of long showers, I walked into my new house and immediately felt at home, only blocks from my father's old apartment that I would walk to every Tuesday and Thursday after Catholic school, and just a short drive from my mother's. This was a return to the place that made me who I am, and unlike Seattle or Los Angeles, I felt like I belonged. No longer a drifter crashing on a stranger's couch or a temporary visitor, I had returned to my forever home. It was almost as if I had never left, even more so because I was now sharing the house with my oldest friend, Jimmy Swanson.

Jimmy and I had been inseparable since sixth grade. Like Siamese twins, we walked through life beside each other, every formative experience mirrored in a parallel trajectory. Like brothers, we discovered everything together, and not a day would go by without our seeing each other. Jimmy was a year older than me, tall with a Scandinavian build, his blue eyes hidden behind his perfectly feathered dirty blond hair, which was always kept in check by a plastic comb he had permanently stuffed in his back pocket. A total rocker. A lifelong rebel. He was a picture of heavy metal parking-lot cool, but without a hint of irony. He was the real fucking deal. Wherever Jimmy led, I followed, because deep down I wanted to be just like him. He and I were never cut out to be valedictorian homecoming kings, so we created our own little world as outcasts, huddled in front of the boom box in his bedroom, discovering metal, punk rock, and weed together, becoming so close that we barely needed words to communicate, we could just rely on our own ESP. This was most important because Jimmy had a very heavy stutter, something that affected him socially throughout his life, so he kept within a very tight circle of friends. Always very kind, always very polite, he was a knight in weathered denim, and he was as much my home as the home I grew up in. So, since we had shared everything together our entire lives, it only made sense that I would share this new house with him, as well. Though we had never lost our connection (Jimmy had toured with both Nirvana and Foo Fighters over the years), it had been ages since we could say, "Hey, man, I'll be over in five minutes . . . ," and spend the day together in our little world, so returning to him felt like a return to myself, a much needed reunion.

Having had absolutely no experience in building a recording studio, I began to research equipment, design, and materials, and reached out to a few of my brilliant engineer and producer friends for advice on how to turn my crummy little basement into the next Abbey Road. One of them was Adam Kasper, a killer producer and friend from Seattle with whom I had worked before, most notably on Nirvana's final session in January 1994. Along with a wicked sense of humor, Adam had a very easygoing, analog style of recording, so he seemed the perfect person to not only help assemble a simple basement studio but produce our next record as well. The making of *The Colour and the Shape,* which had been produced by Gil Norton, the man responsible for the Pixies' classic hits, was a long, arduous, hyper-technical affair that took its toll on the band over those difficult months in the woods outside of Seattle. Gil was a notorious taskmaster, and his meticulous attention to detail ultimately paid off, but not before breaking our spirit after thirty to forty takes of each song. We swore we would never put ourselves through that painful process again, so the idea of moving back to Virginia and building a simple little studio with Adam Kasper in a house sounded much more appealing. One twenty-four-track machine, one vintage mixing console, a few microphones, and a few compressors were all we needed, and we began to hunt down the gear as we converted my basement into a soundproofed chamber of rock.

My mother would often come by to visit and inspect the progress, and I would take her on a tour from room to room, doing my best to explain the science behind the precise acoustic design required to make a studio (something I knew absolutely nothing about, but since I'm a seasoned bullshit artist, she bought it hook, line, and sinker). Mostly, after years away, I think Mom was just happy to be able to stop by and see me whenever she wanted.

On one of her weekly inspections, we heard the sound of a tiny kitten coming from somewhere in the piles of rubble scattered throughout the room, quietly meowing tiny cries for rescue. Startled, we began frantically searching every corner of the studio to find it, but it seemed to be moving. "It's over here!" I said, and my mother ran to my side of the studio. Silence. "No, it's over here!" my mother replied, and I ran to her side of the room. Silence again. Back and forth we went as the minutes passed, perplexed by the kitten's ability to throw its little voice in every direction. We stood perfectly still, doing our best to not scare it away. I quietly whispered to my mom, "Maybe it's inside a wall," and proceeded to get on my knees and slowly crawl across the dirty floor, putting my ear to the freshly painted drywall, hoping to locate this helpless animal. My mother slowly walked up beside me and I heard a faint meow. "Shhhh!" I said. She took one step closer. *Meow.* It was closer, I thought. Standing just beside me, my mother leaned in to listen, and . . . *meow.* I looked down at my mother's sandals and said, "Hey, Mom . . . will you shift your weight on your right foot for a second?"

Meow.

The kitten that we had been chasing all over the studio for the past forty-five minutes happened to be my mother's right sandal, "meowing" every time she took a step. We both fell on the floor in fits of laughter, barely able to breathe, thankful that no one else was there to witness the two of us in this most ridiculous moment, one we still laugh about to this day.

With the completion of the studio came spring, my favorite of all Virginia seasons. After months of cold, dead leaves, and barren trees, the sun arrived and nature was soon in full bloom, a rebirth that somewhat poetically coincided with our newfound independence as a band, and we opened all the windows to welcome the new chapter in. What I once imagined as a state-of-the-art recording facility turned out to be a very bare-bones, no-frills arrangement, with packing foam, pillows, and sleeping bags haphazardly nailed to the walls for sound treatment. This was the definition of DIY to me, an ethos that I had learned and had always tried to follow since my days in the Washington, DC, punk rock scene, where we all did everything ourselves, from booking shows to starting our own record labels to releasing our simple recordings on vinyl. I found that the reward was always much sweeter when you did things yourself. And here we were, years later, figuring it out as we went along, step by step, in the most unsophisticated and blissfully naive fashion, but most important, we were hidden away from any expectation of the industry, left to our own devices to discover who we really were as a band.

Our daily routine was simple. Since the band had moved into the house with Jimmy and me, my day would always begin with a little housekeeping: emptying overflowing ashtrays; disposing of warm, half-empty Coors Light cans; and mopping the hardwood floors like a haggard maid from hell in dirty sweatpants. One by one, each member would appear and stare at the coffeepot like a crackhead waiting for the pipe as it slowly brewed. Taylor would complain about the "ducks" outside his window (crows) and we would slowly wake, planning the day at the kitchen table. Maybe a few rounds of hoops in the driveway before lunch, and then we would head down into the basement for a review of last night's recordings. We would work all day, finish with a few beers and a barbecue out back as the fireflies danced around the grill, and pass out in the living room watching TV with Jimmy as he took bong hit after bong hit from his favorite chair. This was our routine, day after day, and it was exactly this relaxed nature that made these recordings the most natural-sounding album of our entire catalog. Coupled with the restrictions imposed on us by the minimal technical capability of the studio, it made for a simple, raw, and honest recording. Not to mention, I was obsessed with AM Gold music at the time (soft rock hits from the seventies), perhaps revisiting that magical era because it reminded me of growing up listening to the radio as I drove the same streets that I had returned to. Andrew Gold, Gerry Rafferty, Peter Frampton, Helen Reddy, Phoebe Snow—those rich, melancholy melodies were making their way into our new songs. Popular rock music at the time had turned its focus to a new genre, nu metal, which I appreciated but wanted to be the antithesis of, so I intentionally moved in the opposite direction. There was a glaring absence of melody in most nu metal songs, and it was my love of melody (inspired by the Beatles from an early age) that led me to write from a much gentler place. That, coupled with the overwhelming feeling of rebirth that the Virginia spring ushered in, gave way to songs like "Ain't It the Life," "Learn to Fly," "Aurora," and "Generator," all great examples of a man finally comfortable in his surroundings, no longer wandering but somewhere he belonged. By the end of our sessions in June, we had made what I still to this day consider to be our best album, the aptly titled *There Is Nothing Left to Lose.*

And our new studio, which would serve us well for years to come, was now given a name: Studio 606.

As I stood at the Grammys podium to accept the Best Rock Album award a year and a half later, I looked out at the audience of musicians and industry players, all dripping in diamonds and dressed in the latest fashion, and felt a huge sense of pride that we had created this all on our own, away from the glitter and shiny lights of Hollywood, making the reward for our very first Grammy even sweeter. If ever there was a time when I felt that we had actually earned a trophy, it was then. From our little ramshackle basement studio nestled in the trees I once climbed as a child, we had not only captured the sound of rebirth and renewal brought upon us by the majestic Virginia spring, but we had found a return to who we once were. After years of pushing through adversity after adversity, death, divorce, and a revolving door of band members, I had persevered and come out the other end stronger, not yet ready to buy the farm. There was still more work to be done. And with this new trophy that represented our revival of spirit, one thing was clear:

WE DIDN'T HAVE TO DO THIS ANYMORE. WE WANTED TO DO THIS FOREVER.

THIS IS
WHAT I
WANTED

"Mom . . . we're having a girl."

I heard my mother's voice crack as she began to cry. "Oh, David . . . ," she whispered. "Oh my goodness . . ." There was a long pause as she put down the phone to mop the tears of pride from her face, and as I stood in my backyard trying to process the words that had just come out of my mouth, it suddenly hit me. I was going to have a daughter. My mother was overjoyed. I was in shock.

I had always known that someday I would be a father, but in my mind, it would be long after this life of touring and traveling was over. As my father had said years before, "You know this isn't going to last, right?" I had imagined that the music would some-how just stop, and I would begin a new life of domestic anonymity. I had seen others try to raise a family on the road (preach, Steve Perry!) but because of my traditional upbringing, I found that idea to be too rickety, without stability. The sight of a Pack 'n Play next to a table full of beer and Jägermeister always gave me the creeps.

It wasn't until the Foo Fighters were invited to play at Neil Young's Bridge School Benefit in 2000 that I realized these two worlds could coexist. The Bridge School Benefit was an annual weekend-long concert organized by Neil and Pegi Young to raise money for the Bridge School, a nonprofit organization that Pegi started to find a place for their son Ben, who has cerebral palsy, and other children with severe speech and physical impairments to help them with language and communication needs. Each year the concert was held at the Shoreline Amphitheatre just outside of San Francisco, with incredible lineups including Springsteen, Dylan, McCartney, Petty, the Beach Boys, Pearl Jam, and Metallica (just to name a few), all playing acoustic sets as the students sat behind them onstage. These shows raised millions of dollars, and the feeling of love and joy at those events was beyond anything I had ever felt. Every single human being in attendance was there for the children, and I was convinced that the communal energy of that much positivity in one place had a healing power of its own.

The weekend always began with a barbecue at Neil's house on Broken Arrow Ranch, a sprawling, rustic 140-acre paradise in Redwood City that he purchased in 1970, where he would invite all of the performers for a dinner the night before the concert. As

we drove down the winding mountain roads deep in the redwoods toward his home, I pictured a formally catered event, tables lined with rock and roll royalty rattling their shiny silverware, laps lined with linen napkins, as they shared mythical folklore of yesteryear. That couldn't have been further from the truth. When we arrived at the gate, there was a hand-painted sign that said DON'T SPOOK THE HORSE hanging from the dilapidated fence, and upon entering the property, there was still another ten-minute drive through winding hills before we saw the little house, lit up like a Christmas tree in the distance. Part *Harry Potter,* part *Swiss Family Robinson,* it looked like the work of a mad survivalist with a penchant for tree houses, complete with a bellower and a tall teepee in the yard. No valet parking, no reception, you just . . . walked right in.

As I shyly entered the kitchen, I was greeted with a warm hug from Pegi, who had been cutting vegetables by the sink. She offered me a coat from the mudroom in case it got cold outside but warned me to "check the pockets for mice." David Crosby was sitting by the fireplace. Brian Wilson was wandering around lost, looking for his wife. Tom Petty's band was on the porch, and Neil's kids were hanging out with all of us. This was not a formal rock and roll event at all. This was a home. This was a family.

THIS WAS WHAT I WANTED, AND NOW I SAW THAT IT COULD BE POSSIBLE.

As my mother regained a bit of composure after hearing the news that she would have a granddaughter, I explained to her that, although I'd always known I would be a parent someday, I'd never for one second imagined having a girl. By no means am I a cigar-chomping, NASCAR-watching, Sunday-afternoon-armchair-quarterback kind of guy, but what could I ever offer a daughter? How to tune a kick drum and catalog her Slayer bootlegs? I was at a loss. And then, as she had always done, my mother imparted a little

bit of her well-earned wisdom that has since proven to be one of my life's most indisputable truths: "The relationship between a father and daughter can be one of the most special relationships in any girl's life." She knew this because of the relationship she had with her father, a military man of charm and wit who everyone loved dearly before his early passing when she was in her twenties. I never had the pleasure of meeting him, but from all that I've heard, he was a good man and indeed had that special connection to my mother. Though still terrified, I was slightly reassured. Maybe cataloging Slayer bootlegs together could be fun.

As the months flew by, Jordyn and I began to prepare for the new baby, readying her room, shopping for all the necessary gear, and eventually settling on the name Violet (after my mother's mother, Violet Hanlon). I was given a library of books to study with subjects ranging from sleep training (which is a farce because ultimately they sleep-train you, making it impossible to sleep past six A.M. for the rest of your life) to swaddling (I'm bad enough at rolling joints; how could I successfully roll a child?) to how to change a diaper (something I may hold a land speed record in by this point). I was taking a crash course in fatherhood, or at least the logistical side of it.

One day toward the end of Jordyn's pregnancy, my manager called and asked, "Hey, you wanna write songs with John Fogerty?" As it would be for any rock and roll lover who grew up in the seventies, the answer was an excited "Duh." I was told to meet John at his house up in the hills for a songwriting session a few days later. As he opened the door to his home studio, I was face-to-face with the legend himself, exactly as you would imagine him to be: flannel shirt, jeans, and work boots. We talked awhile, trading jokes and telling horror stories of our rocky pasts, and when the guitars finally came out, he started singing lyrics off the top of his head based on the intimate conversation we'd just had. His trademark voice, so raw and soulful, was right in front of my face, but so powerful it sounded like it was coming straight out of a stadium PA. It was a beautiful moment that made me realize why he is considered such an American treasure: because he is real.

After jamming awhile, we walked down to his kitchen for bowls of minestrone and SunChips (if John Fogerty hadn't been sitting there, I would have sworn I was home sick from school), but I watched the clock intently, knowing that I only had until four thirty before I had to leave. After lunch he asked, "Welp . . . wanna jam a little more?" but I regretfully told him that I couldn't stay because I had an appointment I had to go to with my expecting wife. "Where you goin'?" he asked. "Breast-feeding class," I said with a hint of embarrassment in my voice, to which he smiled and said, "Can I come?"

Night after night I would speak to Violet in the womb (no matter how strange that may seem to some people) because I was looking forward to the day when I would hold her in my arms, no longer just talking to my wife's pajamas like a fucking lunatic. When the day finally came, I was nervously packing up the car to go to the hospital when I noticed a huge rainbow overhead, something that happens maybe once every thousand years in Los Angeles. I was immediately calmed. Yes, it sounds nauseatingly romantic, but yes, it's true, and I took it as a sign.

After a long and difficult labor, Violet was born to the sound of the Beatles in the background, and she arrived screaming with a predetermined vocal capacity that made the Foo Fighters sound like the Carpenters. Once she was cleaned up and put under the little Arby's heat-lamp bed, I put my face close to hers, stared into her gigantic blue eyes, and said, "Hey, Violet, it's Dad." She immediately stopped screaming and her eyes locked with mine. She recognized my voice. We stared at each other in silence, our first introduction, and I smiled and talked to her as if I had known her my whole life. I am happy to say that, still to this day, when we lock eyes it's the same feeling.

This was a love I had never experienced before. There is an inevitable insecurity that comes along with being a famous musician that makes you question love. Do they love me? Or do they love "it"? You are showered with superficial love and adoration on a regular basis, giving you something similar to a sugar high, but your heart crashes once the rush dies off. Is it possible for someone to see a musician without the instrument being a part of their identity? Or is that a part of the identity that the other loves? Regardless, it's a dangerous and slippery slope to question love, but one thing is for certain: there is nothing purer than the unconditional love between a parent and their child.

Once the delivery was over and we were led to our hospital room for the night, Jordyn was famished, so I went down to the cafeteria to find her something to eat. I scoured for something that she might actually be able to stomach but retreated back to our room empty-handed, opting to perhaps order from the Jerry's Deli across the street. I walked across the hall to the nurse station, where there was one nurse on duty, a large woman with Hulk Hogan's build who barked at me in a thick eastern European accent, "CAN I HELP YOU?" "Yes . . . um, can you tell me if Jerry's Deli delivers here?" She stared at me with her ice-cold eyes and growled, "I AM NOT AT LIBERTY TO DISCLOSE ANY INFORMATION ABOUT WHO IS DELIVERED HERE." I smiled, realizing that she'd misunderstood my question, and said, "Hahaha . . . no . . . does JERRY'S DELI deliver here?" Looking like she was about to leap over her computer and strangle me with her giant, professional-wrestling hands, she raised her volume and repeated, "I TOLD YOU! I AM NOT AT LIBERTY TO DISCLOSE ANY INFORMATION ABOUT WHO IS DELIVERED HERE!!!" I scurried away in fear, walked across the street, and ordered a sandwich for Jordyn while standing next to Jennifer Lopez.

Another night in Los Angeles.

My mother was right, being a father to a daughter was indeed the most special relationship of my life. I was soon well versed in the art of a smudgeless pedicure, how to tie the perfect ponytail, and how to identify every Disney princess just by the color of her dress. This was easy, I thought.

THEN CAME THE HARD PART: BALANCING THE NEW LIFE WITH THE OLD.

I remember the first time I had to leave Violet behind for tour. I stood above her crib as she slept, and I began to cry. How could I possibly leave this little miracle behind? I had to tear myself away, and so began a lifetime of leaving half of my heart at home. At this point, all of the band members were procreating like rabbits, and our tour itineraries were now dictated by people who couldn't even chew solid food yet, so what had been six-week tours were whittled down to two weeks at the most. As much as touring in a rock band is hands-down the best fucking job on earth, it can be exhausting, but the minute you set foot back in your house after a few weeks away, you are handed a screaming baby and are officially on daddy duty 24/7. This, of course, is partly to relieve your wife of the maternal duties that she was overwhelmed with from sunrise to sunset while you were out shotgunning beers with your best friends (cue slight resentment) but more so because you feel the need to overcompensate for your absence. You are forever haunted by the fear that the time away from your child will leave them with lifelong psychological repercussions, so when you're home, you are HOME. Tour, home, tour, home, tour, home . . . after a few years of that, you begin to find the balance, and you realize that the two worlds CAN coexist. So why not do it again?

This time, it'll be a boy, I thought.

Having already mastered the role of "dad who knows every word to every *Little Mermaid* song," I was now ready to try my hand at raising a son. And I already had the name picked out: Harper Bonebrake Grohl, named after my father's uncle, Harper Bonebrake (we called him Uncle Buzz).

The Bonebrake family tree can be traced all the way back to Johann Christian Beinbrech, who was baptized in Switzerland on February 9, 1642, eventually immigrating to Germany and fathering eleven children. It was his grandson Daniel Beinbrech who bravely traveled to America by ship and settled in a wilderness called Pigeon Hills around York, Pennsylvania, in September 1762.

Numerous offspring and various spellings followed (Pinebreck, Bonbright) until the most awesome "Bonebrake" moniker was landed on with Daniel's son Peter, who was an American Revolutionary soldier who had nine children of his own. By 1768, the name was set in stone and carried all the way to the birth of my uncle Buzz and my grandmother Ruth Viola Bonebrake in 1909, to their parents Harper and Emma. In turn, my father was named James Harper Grohl, so in keeping with tradition, I decided to name my son Harper as well. (We proudly have a Civil War Congressional Medal of Honor recipient, Henry G. Bonebrake, and the drummer of Los Angeles punk legends X, D. J. Bonebrake, in the family tree as well.)

"Mom . . . we're having another girl."

To be clear, I truly never had any gender preference, but I did *really* want to name a child Harper Bonebrake Grohl. So, we named her Harper (never got the Bonebrake past the goalie) and she was born only two days after Violet's third birthday. The feeling of overwhelming paternal love was renewed, and now I had two daughters to fawn over, Violet walking and talking at a level far beyond her age, and Harper (my spitting image) cooing in my lap, never without a smile. This was a home. This was a family. This is what I wanted.

As I watched every step of their development, it was hard not to think about my parents doing the same. I have very few memories of these years in my life, most of them with my mother, who showered me with unconditional love, and not so much with my father. My parents divorced when I was only six years old, leaving me to be raised by my mother, and I had a hard time grasping this separation now as a father myself. How could he not want to spend every waking minute bouncing me on his lap, pushing me on the swing, or reading me stories every night before bed? Was it that he didn't want to? Or that he didn't know how? Perhaps this was the crux of my fear of being an absent parent, my overcompensation every time I returned home after being away. As lucky as I was to be raised by my amazing mother, I was seeing how the broken relationship with my father and his absence in my childhood had some lifelong psychological repercussions, and that I was desperate to not create those for my own children.

We began to travel the world with our daughters, and I no longer felt strange about a backstage full of children (though they were in their own dressing room so they wouldn't be playing next to

the beer and Jägermeister), because no matter where on the planet we were, if we were together, it was home. The life that my father warned would never last had blossomed into what I had witnessed that night at Neil Young's house: music and family intertwined. It was possible after all.

So, why not do it one more time?

This time, I didn't even question that it was going to be a girl. By the time news came that we were having another child, I was already singing every line to *Frozen* and had assumed the role of concierge, bodyguard, therapist, line cook, and personal stylist. What on earth would I do with a boy? I wouldn't know where to start. Though, number three was different. Jordyn and I were officially outnumbered. Shit was getting real.

Ophelia was born just down the hall from where I once ran for my life from that Slovakian Hulk Hogan in Crocs and baby-blue scrubs, and a few days after we brought her home, we invited Paul McCartney and his wife Nancy over to the house to see the baby. This was a monumental occasion for more than a million reasons, but I did notice one thing that will stick with me forever. Violet and Harper obviously knew that Paul was a musician in a band called the Beatles but at their tender ages had no idea what that meant in the pantheon of music history. To them, Paul was just our musician friend Paul, and I saw that when those mythical preconceptions are taken away, there is a purity of spirit, an unconditional love. I, of course, spent the hour before his arrival hiding the mountains of Beatles stuff I had in the house (you never know how much Beatles memorabilia you have until a Beatle comes to visit), but the kids were without any inflated sense of who he really was.

As they were leaving and we were saying our goodbyes, Paul noticed the piano down the hall and couldn't resist. He sat down and started playing "Lady Madonna" as I stood in shock, hearing a voice the world adores echo throughout my own house, now filled with my own family. Harper disappeared for a moment and returned with a coffee cup that she had filled with spare change and placed it on the piano as a tip jar for Sir Paul. We fell about the room laughing, and he invited her to sit on the bench next to him for a piano lesson, her first. He showed her the keys, and which note each one was, and they began to play together while Paul sang, *We're playing a song . . . we're playing a song . . .*

The next morning as I was making breakfast in the kitchen, I heard the piano again, that same melody that Paul and Harper had played the night before. I peeked around the corner and saw Harper by herself on the bench, her tiny hands playing those same chords in perfect time, and I knew exactly what she was feeling: inspired by Paul. Because I once had felt the same. Though, the difference was that the sound of his voice was coming from the tiny turntable on my bedroom floor, not right beside me on the piano bench as I played along with him.

THE CIRCLE WAS COMPLETE.

This was a home. This was a family. This is what I wanted.

A few days later, my father passed. We had lost touch in the last year of his life, but upon hearing news of his illness the month before Ophelia's birth, I flew to visit him, knowing it would be the last time we would ever meet. In the same Warren, Ohio, hospital where I was born, we sat and chatted, trading updates on life as I complimented him on his long white hair and beard, which had almost outgrown mine. I told him that I was to become a father again soon, and he congratulated me, wishing me the best of luck. When it was time for me to go, I kissed his hand and said, "Okay, Dad. I'll see you later. I love you."

He smiled and said, "I love you too, David."

PART FOUR

CRUISING

CROSSING
THE
BRIDGE TO
WASHINGTON

"I'll see you down there, dude!"

Paralyzed, with my back against the wall of a long hallway downstairs in the White House, I couldn't believe my ears.

The president of the United States of America, George W. Bush, had just called me "dude."

Frozen in shock, I politely waved as he was whisked away by Secret Service agents, and then continued on my mission to find the coatroom to get my very pregnant wife's winter jacket so that we could head down to the Kennedy Center Honors, where I would be performing the classic "Who Are You" for a star-studded tribute to the Who, which President Bush would be watching from his center seat in the balcony.

HOW ON EARTH DID I GET HERE?

Since 1978, the Kennedy Center Honors has been considered America's most prestigious performing arts awards ceremony, celebrating those in music, dance, theater, opera, motion pictures, and television for their lifetime of contributions to American culture. To be included in any capacity is an honor in itself, to say the least. The event, a virtual who's who of Washington, DC's most recognizable faces, is actually a weekend of multiple gatherings, from dinner at the State Department the night before to an awards presentation in the East Room of the White House the afternoon of the show, but the festivities always kicked off with the Chairman's Luncheon at a hotel. Not unlike a brunch buffet at your cousin's wedding, it's a relatively informal affair, except instead of sharing the salad tongs with your crazy uncle, you're passing them like a baton to former secretary of state Madeleine Albright. The absurdity of this most surreal experience was hard to ignore, and I found myself trying to keep a straight face while surrounded by the people who made the planet's most important decisions as they fumbled with the smoked salmon sliding off their bagels. At most of the award ceremonies I attend, I tend to feel like I'm crashing the party, usually only one drink away from being escorted out to the parking lot by security. But I've never been afraid of striking up conversations with the most unlikely people no matter how out of my element I may be.

For security reasons, all performers are required to be shuttled to and from the Kennedy Center on one of those large buses that tourists usually fill to visit Washington's most popular attractions, except instead of gangs of blue-haired seniors from the Midwest, the bus is filled with America's most recognizable artists, usually breaking into a roaring version of "99 Bottles of Beer on the Wall" (take it from me, the song really acquires a whole new life when sung by Steven Tyler, Herbie Hancock, and the Jonas Brothers). It's never a long drive to the gig, but just long enough to get to know these familiar faces and become fast friends, sharing stories of fabled careers and getting hearing aid advice from the best of them (thank you, Herbie).

Rehearsals for the performances are held in one of the many rooms off to the side of the main stage, which undoubtedly have seen their share of history over the years. Growing up just over the bridge in Virginia, I was no stranger to the Kennedy Center, of course, having seen many performances there and taken more than a few school field trips to experience the gorgeous display of modern architecture overlooking the Potomac River, but the backstage was new to me. As I walked through the hallways behind the stage, I tried to imagine all of the voices that have filled these hallowed rooms since its opening in 1971, asking myself once again, "How on earth did I get here?" This building was reserved for America's most prestigious performers, not former DC punk rock thugs.

As much as it's considered a nonpolitical event, a rare chance for people from both sides of the aisle to put down their differences and pick up a drink in the name of culture and the arts, there is an inevitable tension that permeates the proceedings, as if all the attendees are little kids who've been told to play nice on the school playground. I surely didn't agree with all of the policies and principles that some of these people spent their days bickering about, so I took my mother's advice and avoided the three topics that we were always told not to bring up at any dinner table: money, politics, and religion. This was a weekend where everyone could recognize each other as something more than Democrat or Republican. We were all human beings, first and foremost, and nothing can bring human beings together better than music and art.

For some crazy reason, I was tapped to make a toast to the Who for their award at the ultra-formal State Department dinner the night before the show. Not the type of blathering, slurred rant that you would give from a barstool in your local dive, this was meant to be a formal speech, commending the recipient of this highest honor for all of their achievements. And to a room full of orators, no less. Not to be taken lightly. I was assigned a speechwriter who kindly met me backstage at rehearsal and did a quick interview with me to come up with material for my speech. After a brief conversation, she thanked me and said she'd have my speech ready before the dinner that night. I would have preferred to write my own, but not wanting to rock the boat, I left it up to the professionals.

Later on, as I was squeezing into my penguin suit back at the hotel, my speech arrived, and to my horror it was written in a primitive form of "dude-speak" so as to seem like I had written it myself (I suppose). *Oh my god,* I thought. *I can't fucking read this!* As the son of a former Capitol Hill speechwriter and prominent journalist, I would forever stain my father's legacy as a man of intelligence, wit, and Washington charm. I also felt obligated to go with the program and deliver these words to the people in a selfless gesture of comic relief. FUCK, I THOUGHT. MADELEINE ALBRIGHT IS GOING TO THINK I'M A MORON.

Filing through the receiving line, I was already dreading my time at the podium as I shook hands with current secretary of state Condoleezza Rice, another on the list of things I never in my wildest dreams imagined happening. Looking around at the room full of scholars and intellectual titans, my deep childhood insecurity about being thought of as stupid kicked in, and I began to second-guess myself. All of the pomp and circumstance on display in the ballroom was certainly entertaining to watch, and I've never been one to shy away from the opportunity to embarrass myself for a mortified laugh, but this was being thrown to the goddamned lions. Cocktail, please.

As I sat at my table with various senators and cabinet members, I held that dreaded speech in my hands like a string of prayer beads, counting the minutes until my most gruesome public execution. I sat and watched as each speaker, one by one, gave a long, eloquent disquisition worthy of any inaugural or State of the Union address . . . knowing that soon I would be the one jackass in the room to use the word "dude."

As Bob Schieffer, one of America's most treasured television journalists and debate moderators, toasted the legendary country artist George Jones, I sat in front of my uneaten dinner, stunned by his ability to be outrageously funny, deeply emotional, perfectly informative, and brilliantly poetic all at once off-the-cuff, speaking with a relaxed and confident tone and commanding the room with no prepared speech to refer to. *Okay. Fuck this.* There was no way in hell I was going to read the speech that had been written for me. Not after Bob Schieffer!

It was time to think of something and think of something fast.

With only minutes to spare, I came up with a concept: The unique reversal of musical roles in the Who was what set them apart from other bands. Keith Moon's lyrical drumming made him more like the vocalist, Pete Townshend's solid rhythm guitar made him more like the drummer, John Entwistle's unconventional bass soloing made him more like the lead guitarist, and Roger Daltrey's muscular vocals pulled it all together like a conductor for an orchestra of fire. *This could work!* I thought. Either way, I had nothing to lose, as it was already miles above the crumpled speech currently clenched in my sweaty hand. I had built an entire career on abiding by one very simple rule: you fake it till you make it. My name was called; I stood up; I left the crumpled speech next to my cold, untouched coq au vin; and I headed to the stage.

I must say, I was no Bob Schieffer that night, but I did manage to pull it off without any rotten tomatoes being thrown my way, and without a single "dude." I may have even gotten a smile from Madeleine Albright.

The next afternoon at the White House reception, we all sat in the East Room as President Bush presented the honorees with their colorful medals. Of course, I had only been to the White House as a tourist before, so this was another huge moment for me. Let me tell you something, though: considering the hundreds of years of history that have shaped our world from within those walls . . . it's really not that big a joint. Crammed in like commuters on the morning bus, we all sat quietly in our little folding chairs as the president draped the rainbow-ribboned medals over the necks of that year's recipients: Morgan Freeman, George Jones, Barbra Streisand, Twyla Tharp, and the Who. I FELT LIKE I WAS WITNESSING HISTORY, WHICH MADE ME ASK MYSELF AGAIN, HOW ON EARTH DID I GET HERE?

At this point, the only thing left to do before finally heading to the gig was to get a picture with the president and First Lady in front of the White House Christmas tree. This was a decision that took more than a moment to ponder. To put it mildly, my personal politics did not align with those of the current administration, so I felt a bit conflicted about joining in on a picture with the president. Even though this weekend was supposed to be free of any political division, a chance to come together and celebrate the arts, it was difficult to put all of my politics aside, even if just for a snapshot in front of a bedazzled Christmas tree. The questioning in my heart rose up again. *What am I doing here?*

I thought of my father. What would he do? As a staunch Republican, he had spent decades establishing lifelong relationships with people on both sides of the aisle and could share a generous cocktail with almost anyone. On our weekends together, he would sometimes take me to a corner saloon in Georgetown called Nathan's, where scores of seersucker barflies would come to drink, laugh, and debate—but most important, to coexist. I would sit at the bar nursing my ginger ale while listening to the booming voices of these Beltway news junkies, agreeing to disagree on current events, saving any real debate for when the House was in session Monday morning. This was the Washington, DC, I was raised to know, a place where people with opposing ideas could engage in civilized discourse without it turning into a barroom brawl. A place that has now sadly vanished.

Jordyn and I decided to get in line for the picture. Surrounded by marines in their dress uniforms, we were eventually called into the room where the president and First Lady were standing like cardboard cutouts in front of a towering Christmas tree, and we greeted them with smiles and firm handshakes. First impressions? The president was taller than I'd expected, and the First Lady had the most beautiful blue eyes. "Where are you from???" the president shouted in my face with the fervor of a military drill instructor. Stunned, I replied, "Uhhh . . . uhhhh . . . just over that bridge right there!" as I pointed out to the South Lawn. I told him I was there to perform a Who song at the Kennedy Center, he smiled, the picture was snapped, and we were shuttled out the door faster than you can say "We won't get fooled again."

I can only imagine that he recognized me in that downstairs hallway later on that evening because I was the only person in attendance with hair below my collar, but I had to laugh, as he proudly called me the one word that I had gone to so much trouble not to say the night before. *If only Nathan's bar in Georgetown were still open,* I thought, *I bet the two of us would have a rather eventful Sunday afternoon.*

In 2010, President Obama was giving Paul McCartney a Library of Congress Gershwin Prize, which is an award given to only one recipient a year for their lifetime contribution to popular music. It's basically the American equivalent of being knighted, and perhaps the highest of all honors for musicians. There was a performance planned in the East Room of the White House (I guess I was becoming a regular), and having made friends with Paul, I was invited to come perform "Band on the Run" with him on a tiny stage in that small room full of people. Of course, I jumped at any opportunity to play with Paul, not only because he will forever be the reason I became a musician, but because he's really fucking fun to jam with.

When I arrived for rehearsals at Lisner Auditorium (just across the street from the Tower Records where I once had a part-time job), I was greeted onstage by his lovely band and crew, and after a bit of catching up, the musical director approached to introduce himself. I was somewhat prepared, I thought, but figured that Paul and his band would most likely do all the heavy lifting anyway, so in the event that I forgot a lyric or chord, I probably wouldn't even be in the PA. "Okay, Dave, this is your microphone right here," he said as he pointed to the mike stand center stage. *That's odd*, I thought. "Ummmm, where's Paul going to stand?" I asked. He laughed and replied, "Paul will be sitting directly in front of

you with the president. You'll be singing the entire song yourself!"
Panic disguised by manufactured enthusiasm swept over me.

AGAIN, YOU FAKE IT TILL YOU MAKE IT.

We ran through a few versions, we got it "good enough for
grunge" (a ridiculous saying that's floated around the Foo Fighters
for years), and I retreated back to my hotel room to practice the
song on repeat until I felt comfortable playing it to the two most
important people on earth, who would be sitting shoulder to shoulder six feet in front of me. This was a big one, and it was no ragtag
side-stage lineup by any means. Stevie Wonder, Elvis Costello, Jack
White, Emmylou Harris, and Faith Hill were all performing Paul's
classics for the event, so I felt dwarfed by the level of talent on display. It was without a doubt the most nervous I had ever been, for
good reason.

At soundcheck the afternoon of the show, all of the performers were milling around the White House, rooting each other on
and marveling at the size of the minuscule stage, which was about
two feet high and barely big enough to fit Paul's band. When it
was finished, I was free to roam around the White House, admir-
ing the historic portraits and browsing through books in the small
library downstairs. My favorite find? A complete anthology of Bob
Dylan lyrics. I'm not sure how much time it spent off the shelf, but
knowing it was there gave me a little hope for the future. At one
point, I asked an official-looking White House employee if there
was any catering or a craft service table for the performers, as I was
fucking starving for lunch. He offered to go check for me, asking if
I had any preferences, but I am quite literally the least picky eater
on earth (ask anyone I know), so I just said, "Whatever!" After a
few minutes, he returned with some SunChips and a sandwich on a
plate that had been made in the kitchen downstairs, and I thanked
him profusely. *What a nice guy!* I thought.

I later found out he was the admiral of the Coast Guard.

The night of the show, all performers were standing in an adjoining room waiting their turn to play, like a line of paratroopers waiting to leap out of an aircraft and into the sky. One by one they were introduced and walked through the tightly packed crowd to that tiny little stage where they would greet Paul and the president and then perform their song. *I can't be the only one who's nervous here,* I thought. Without the Foo Fighters' wall of sound behind me, I felt practically naked. Naked in front of Paul McCartney and President Obama. My pulse started to speed up, my stomach started to turn, and I began to imagine the worst-case scenario: a crippling anxiety attack that required not only medical attention but a lifetime of living it down.

And then, something came over me . . .

I DECIDED NOT TO WASTE THIS MOMENT. I decided to stop asking "How did I get here?" I was there. I told myself that I was not going to spend a second being scared or wishing I were somewhere else. The long journey from my childhood in Springfield, Virginia; to cutting my teeth as a musician in the Washington, DC, music scene; to performing in the White House for a Beatle and a president made this in every way the most full-circle moment of my life, but rather than get lost in complicated introspection, I just smiled.

A calm came over me, and just then my name was called. I walked to the stage with my head held high and stood before Paul and the president with pride, feeling like the luckiest person on earth to have made it to this very moment, past and present, right and left, bridged together in music.

DOWN
UNDER
DUI

"Asseyez-vous, s'il vous plaît . . ."

Confused, I turned to my French-speaking girlfriend, who was acting as translator, for some much needed assistance, and she said, "She wants you to sit down." I nodded and folded into the chair across the table from the older woman, smiling nervously as she inspected my every move. I had good reason to feel ambivalent about this unexpected meeting. I had never been to a psychic before.

It was January 2000, and Foo Fighters were Down Under for Australia's biggest annual tour, the Big Day Out, a festival that began in 1992 with a Sydney-only show that saw Nirvana playing alongside the Violent Femmes, and eventually grew to a massive three-week, six-city extravaganza hosting up to a hundred bands each year. Set in the scorching heat of the glorious Aussie summer, it was the highlight of any touring band's itinerary, given the easy pace of six shows in three weeks, making it more of a vacation in the sun than the usual grueling pace we were all used to. "The Big Day Off," we called it, and we took advantage of every moment offstage.

My girlfriend had flown down from the States for a quick visit, and her heart was set on visiting a renowned French psychic who lived in an apartment complex outside of Sydney. Apparently, she had visited her before on another trip to Australia with her own band years ago, and according to people familiar with this phenomenon, this lady was the real deal. Our old friend/promoter Stephen Pavlovic had taken other mystical musicians to her over the years as well, all returning home with glowing reviews of her intuitive powers.

I myself had never seen a true psychic, for no other reason than I had no interest whatsoever. Other than one silly card reading in a New Orleans souvenir shop during the peak of Nirvana's success where I was told by a woman with a bone in her nose, "Don't give up, someday you'll make it!," I had managed to steer clear of any contrived psychic introspection. Not that I didn't believe in the idea that some people have the ability to read your mind and see the future, I just didn't care to know what they saw. In a way, I preferred to keep the future a mystery for fear that I would alter it by following someone's faulty prediction. I thought that life should take its natural course, a journey with no road map to refer to in the event that you get lost.

This woman's method was simple: you were asked to bring a photograph of yourself, any photograph, and she would quietly inspect it as she traced her fingers along your figure, receiving some kind of otherworldly information with her touch before revealing her psychic opinion. You have to remember, this was not an appointment I had made for myself, but rather for my girlfriend, who had prepared for this meeting by bringing her own portfolio of pictures, including one of me. Steve and I were just acting as chaperones/chauffeurs to deliver her to this woman's apartment for the session, so we ran out to grab a coffee while they made contact with the other side.

Upon our return, my girlfriend looked a bit exhausted from her reading, and the psychic quickly turned her focus on me, as I unfortunately must have been a difficult topic of discussion while we were away. The fact that she spoke very little English and needed translation made for quite an awkward dynamic between my girlfriend and me, as I relied upon her (a Montreal native) to translate the psychic's most intimate revelations, no matter how uncomfortable they may have been for her to hear.

After inspecting my photograph for a few minutes, the psychic reached out and took my hands, holding them gently as she surveyed the lines and calluses from years of abuse.

"*Tu as beaucoup d'énergie . . . ,*" she said.

I turned to my girlfriend for translation, and she replied, "She says you have a lot of energy."

Ah! She's off to a good start! "Yes, I'm kind of hyperactive," I replied in English, hoping that she understood, which she did with a little help from my girlfriend.

"*Non, tu as beaucoup d'énergie psychique . . .*"

For this I did not need a translator. She was telling me that I had psychic energy. I lit up with great surprise. This was getting good.

"*Tes mains brillent . . . ils ont une aura . . . c'est bleue . . . tres puissante . . .*"

According to my new, clairvoyant best friend, my hands glowed with a powerful blue aura. Whether I believed her or not, I was overjoyed, and dare I say flattered, by this psychic declaration. *How could I not have known this?* I thought. *I could have been using my powerful blue aura all this time!* Then she looked up at me and asked if I saw ghosts.

This was a difficult question to answer. Had I ever been visited by the stereotypical floating apparition, crossed over from the other side to stake a claim to its former territory in a cliché haunting? No. Had I experienced a series of unexplainable events where I felt I was in the presence of something that was neither alive nor dead? Yes.

At the height of Nirvana's success, I was still living in a tiny room with only a dresser, a night table, and a futon mattress on the floor, as the band became so huge so fast that I didn't have time to assimilate into this new life of rock stardom. In reality, I felt no desire to go out and take advantage of my expanding bank account because I felt perfectly comfortable with the way things were. I never had much, so I never needed much, and this living arrangement felt perfectly natural. But, beyond anything, it was fun. Sitting around watching MTV while eating Totino's Party Pizzas together with my friends on a rainy afternoon was my idea of "making it," so why change anything?

It was my father (my default financial adviser) who eventually told me it was time to invest in a house of my own in Seattle for the sake of equity (and to keep me from blowing all of my money on Slim Jims and cigarettes), so he flew out and we started the search together. A local real estate agent had gathered some listings around town, and we spent a few days walking through houses, looking for the perfect fit. Most were either too old, too weird, or too far away from amenities, but there was one that stood out from the rest, a newly built home in a northern suburb of Seattle called Richmond Beach. Just blocks from the beautiful Puget Sound, it was nestled in tall pines at the end of a dead-end street, a rather modest and inconspicuous house at first glance. Upon entry, however, you were met with an architectural masterpiece. Multiple levels of landings and rooms framed in gorgeous wood, all flooded in natural light from the skylights built into the tall ceilings and huge windows that overlooked the thick forest outside. Because the house stood at the top of a hill, it looked like only one level from the driveway, but the back of the house was carefully built down the terraced property behind, with decks and landings that faced the giant evergreens out back. It was hard to imagine living alone in such a cavernous space, but I was drawn to its warmth and design, snatching it up quickly and moving my dresser, my night table, and my futon in with ease.

The first night in the house, I was watching my new television (true rock and roll excess!) as I sat on my old futon with my back against the bedroom wall. The rain was coming down in sheets, and I was feeling a bit tense about being alone in this massive residence, when all of a sudden the house shook with a huge BANG! It wasn't lightning or thunder, and it wasn't an explosion from somewhere outside. This sounded like an eighteen-wheeler had crashed into the wall that I was propped up against, jolting my body forward as if I had been rear-ended. I immediately hit the mute button on the remote and sat perfectly still, rendered motionless in absolute terror. Eventually, I gathered the courage to step outside my bedroom and look down from the small landing into the empty living room, scanning the dark space for any moving shadows or signs of an intruder. I had goose bumps up and down my body from fear as I tiptoed quietly from one room to the next, expecting some evidence of a break-in, but I found absolutely nothing. Returning to bed, I kept the TV on mute and slept with one eye open the rest of the night.

After a few months in the house, I realized that it was the downstairs where things felt a bit . . . off. Walking through the winding hallways that snaked through the lower levels, I always sensed that there was someone behind me, like I was always being closely followed. The skin on my neck and back would warm from the proximity to this invisible force, sending the tiny hairs on my spine straight up, and I would race to my destination as fast as I possibly could before running back upstairs to the safety of my kitchen. I had never experienced this feeling before and convinced myself that it was only my wild imagination—that is, until I found that I was not the only one to experience this frequent and most frightening occurrence.

Eventually, I settled in and began to fill the house with modest furnishings, at least enough to invite some friends over for a Halloween dinner at my new dining room table. After dinner, we decided to tell ghost stories over cocktails, some firsthand, some not, but I kept my suspicions of this brand-new house to myself. But when one friend said, "You know . . . it's weird . . . whenever I'm downstairs in your house, I feel like someone is right behind me, following me from room to room, so much that I have to announce myself whenever I'm down there to let whatever it is know that I'm coming . . . ," I practically choked on my drink. As much as I was relieved to hear that I wasn't the only one to have this feeling, that maybe I wasn't crazy after all, I took this as confirmation that this amazing first house I'd bought was fucking haunted. I wasn't moving out anytime soon, and though I hadn't minded sharing a house with my old friend Barrett, sharing a house with a ghost was not what I had signed up for.

The feeling grew stronger and stronger over time, so much that I started to avoid the downstairs at any cost. And before too long the feeling crept upstairs, too. At night, I would fall asleep with my face at the edge of the bed (something I have always done, as I hate the claustrophobic feeling of my own breath on my face) and I would sense someone else's face only inches from mine, staring at me with glaring eyes as I clenched my eyelids tightly shut, terrified of what I might see if I opened them. It became a recurring visitation, happening night after night as I lay paralyzed with fear, making it impossible to sleep.

And then the dreams began.

It was always the same woman, dressed in an old, tattered gray sweater with a dark blue wool skirt. Disheveled and covered in stains from soil, her brown, wiry hair was knotted and unkempt, and she just stood there barefoot, never saying a word, staring at me with her piercing eyes and an expression of deep sorrow. In the first dream, I walked out of my bedroom onto the landing above the stairs and looked down into the living room, where she was standing motionless, looking up at me from a distance. I woke up in a cold sweat. The following dreams were just as horrifying but took place in other areas of the house, which signaled to me that maybe this house wasn't mine after all. Maybe it was hers.

A Ouija board came out a few weeks later on Thanksgiving night, which coincidentally was my first time meeting Mr. Nathan Gregory Mendel, future Foo Fighters bassist, who had come to dinner with a mutual friend. Let's just say that, whether you believe in that shit or not, I came to the conclusion that my dream house was now more along the lines of the Amityville Horror. But I continued to live there for years and gradually got used to the sound of footsteps on the hardwood kitchen floor, the motion detectors going off for no reason, and the occasional door opening by itself. Friends sent me piles of sage to cleanse the house of unwanted spirits, but it remained untouched, as I wasn't falling down that rabbit hole, and frankly, it smells like cat piss.

To make things simple, I told the psychic that I did not necessarily "see" ghosts.

She then asked if I saw UFOs. Now, *this* was something I was obviously fascinated with. After all, I had named my band the Foo Fighters after the World War II slang term for unidentified flying objects; our record label imprint is named Roswell Records after the 1947 UFO crash in Roswell, New Mexico; and my publishing company moniker is MJ Twelve Music, a reference to the alleged secret committee of scientists, military leaders, and government officials assembled by Harry S. Truman to recover and investigate alien spacecraft. So I was well versed in the world of UFO conspiracy, though I had sadly never witnessed one myself.

"No," I said. "But I dream about them quite often."

She looked me in the eyes and with a warm smile said, *"Ce ne sont pas des rêves."*

I TURNED TO MY GIRLFRIEND FOR TRANSLATION, AND SHE INFORMED ME, "THOSE ARE NOT DREAMS."

I immediately flashed back to the countless vivid dreams I'd had since I was a child of being visited by extraterrestrials, which I can still clearly remember to this day. From an early age, I would dream that I was floating through my neighborhood, looking down at the rows of tiny houses below from the window of a small craft, silently hovering and shooting through the air at unimaginable speeds with ease, undetectable to the human eye. In one, I was lying in the wet grass of my front yard, staring up at the night sky filled with stars, desperately trying to summon a UFO to take me away to another world. As I stared into space, I suddenly realized that I was actually staring back at the reflection of myself in the grass, mirrored by the smooth metal underbelly of a saucer-shaped craft hovering only meters above my head. And then I woke up.

But there is one dream that I will never forget, a dream so intense and deeply involved that I still can't shake the feeling of it.

It was a beautiful early evening in a coastal town in southern Europe, and the sky was a perfect shade of cerulean blue in the twilight hour between sunset and full night. I was casually walking a steep, grassy knoll, taking in the warm summer air while looking down at the harbor below filled with cafés and people in white clothing strolling hand in hand along the promenade. The stars were just barely visible, becoming brighter with each moment as the sun fell behind the ocean, when all of a sudden the sky imploded in a blinding flash, knocking me to the ground. I looked up and saw that the stars were now replaced with thousands of UFOs darting across the sky, different sizes, different shapes, different colors, and I sat there in shock, taking in this incredible event while looking around at the incredulous faces of thousands of others doing the exact same thing. Time stood still.

A booming voice came thundering into my head by some form of telepathy. "THE EVOLUTION OF MAN," the voice sounded as animated diagrams were projected into the sky, explaining how our species was helped along by beings from a distant corner of the universe. Leonardo da Vinci's drawing *Vitruvian Man* was projected on the left side of the sky, and to the right, a map of the world with all of our borders and territories redrawn, while the voice declared this event to be the "DAWN OF A NEW ERA."

I woke up knowing this was more than just another dream but continued on with my life, not letting it sink in enough to send me down the unfortunate and common rabbit hole that some UFO conspiracists never recover from, spending the rest of their days waiting for "full disclosure." I was definitely moved, but the most traction this dream ever got in my life was as the inspiration behind the Foo Fighters' video for our song "The Sky Is a Neighborhood," which I directed and which features my two daughters Violet and Harper. A wonderful dream, I thought, but just a dream. Until now. According to the psychic, this was no longer my imagination, this was real.

After a few more favorable revelations, including the specific dimension I'm from, she then proceeded to tell me things that absolutely no one on earth could have known. This wasn't spitballing; she told me things about my life that were so detailed, so intimate, and so right on that I was entirely converted. I was now a believer. Whether she had "postcognition" (the ability to supernaturally perceive past events) or an advanced form of intuition, I was totally convinced that this woman was the real deal.

We finished my session, said goodbye, and left her tiny apartment for the long drive back to Sydney. I felt emboldened by these revelations, wondering if this power was something I had been born with, and thinking of all the moments where I could have called on my psychic ability to help me.

Including the week before, in the Gold Coast.

The Gold Coast, a coastal town in Queensland just forty-five minutes south of Brisbane, is Australia's equivalent to Fort Lauderdale, Florida. Beach bars overflowing with flaming, neon-colored drinks, blond-haired surfers with their wetsuits half off at every turn, and yes, a Sea World theme park for the more family-oriented vacationers. Any visit to this resort paradise was always an adventure, so we milked every second in this bronzed wonderland for every last drop of mischief we could find, and since we were down to play the Big Day Off tour, we had plenty of time to take advantage of its juvenile trappings. Upon arrival, Taylor and I decided to rent scooters so that we could buzz around town during the day, beach to beach, for the three days before our massive show at the Gold Coast Parklands, a greyhound racing track only a few miles from the city. Our hotel, the Sheraton Grand Mirage, had become one of our favorites over the years, with its totally eighties cocaine-white motif and its gluttonous dinner buffets that overlooked chlorinated pools full of displaced swans. If Tony Montana from *Scarface* were ever to take a vacation, it would undoubtedly be here. It was like walking through a Nagel painting in flip-flops.

Fortunately, the hotel was just a few miles from the gig, a straight shot down the Smith Street Motorway, so rather than take the overcrowded shuttle to the show with the other bands, Taylor and I thought we would drive ourselves on our ridiculous little scooters, getting in as much *Easy Rider* action as we could before we had to return them and leave the next day. With no helmets (or licenses), we set off on our little trek, laughing at the absurdity of two famous musicians about to play for fifty thousand people zipping down the road on battered minibikes. Just as most days were back then, it was pure comedy.

We arrived at the entrance, and the local security guards looked at us suspiciously, like we were two sunburned American tourists who had somehow stolen backstage passes from the actual Foo Fighters. After much cajoling and unintelligible walkie-talkie chatter, we were finally rescued by our tour manager, Gus, and sped through the backstage compound, weaving around the picnic tables full of bands, who pointed and laughed at us as we flew past. Other than Blink-182, we were without a doubt the nerdiest, goofiest, most annoying band on the bill. I mean, there were real heavyweights on this one—Red Hot Chili Peppers, Nine Inch Nails, Primal Scream, just to name a few—and I can safely say that none of those dudes would ever be caught dead riding around on those dork-mobiles in broad daylight.

As we prepared for the show, I came up with another ridiculous idea: I was going to drive my scooter onstage during our show and rev the engine like Rob Halford from Judas Priest had always done, though with a massive Harley-Davidson motorcycle, to pay tribute to the heavy metal god himself. As I sat and wrote the set list over a few beers, I found the perfect spot in the show where I could come bounding onstage like Evel Knievel, wind out the puny 50cc engine in a cloud of smoke, and continue playing while the audience doubled over. *Anything for a laugh,* I thought, and my plan was put into action. It went off without a hitch.

After the show, I retreated back to the dressing room and looked at the schedule of performers that was taped to the wall. I noticed that one of my favorite bands, the Hellacopters, from Sweden, were playing on a side stage in the distance, so I grabbed a few beers, I threw Bobby Gillespie from Primal Scream on the back of my now-famous scooter, and we putted over in the dark to see them play. A hard rock barrage of classic riffs and classic hair, the Hellacopters never failed to put on a great show, and I was fortunate enough to see more than a few, having toured extensively with them over the years.

While I sat on the side of the stage headbanging and sipping my beers, I noticed that it had started to rain. Not a torrential tropical downpour, but enough to make me think that it was time to drive back to the hotel before it really started coming down. These scooters weren't necessarily roadworthy, and even a light drizzle could turn the highway into a slick would-be disaster, but it was just a few miles away, so I didn't think much of it. I gathered Taylor for the ride back to our DeLorean-themed castle in the sand and put on my hoodie, and we set off.

Within a mile or so, traffic had come to a complete halt on the busy two-lane highway. It was late, and there was basically only one road for all of the other 49,999 folks who had been to the concert to get back into town, so our quick trip home had become a virtual heavy metal parking lot. *There must be an accident,* I thought, and we moved at a snail's pace for what seemed like an eternity. And then I saw what was really slowing traffic.

A sobriety checkpoint.

Now, I must stop here to try to rationalize why I didn't just jump off that stupid fucking scooter, park it on the side of the road, and call Gus to come pick me up in the rain. First . . . it was a goddamned scooter. This thing was about as much of a motor vehicle as a riding lawn mower. I couldn't imagine that a policeman would even think twice about waving me past, most likely snickering at how silly I looked trying to keep up with traffic in my rain-soaked hoodie and camouflage shorts. Second, I truly didn't feel the least bit impaired from the drinking I had done over the course of the last five hours. Not to toot my own horn, but it takes more than a few tins of malted beverages and a few shots of whiskey to put me down. I honestly didn't feel the least bit drunk. So, I was in the clear, right?

Wrong.

"Blow in this, mate," the policeman said as I pulled up to the checkpoint. Shocked, I happily obliged as I saw Taylor whiz past, free as a bird (apparently he had abstained from alcohol that night, preferring to indulge in other party favors instead), blowing as hard as I could into the tiny straw at the end of the copper's little device. He took one look at it, looked at me, and in the thickest, most Crocodile Dundee Australian accent said, "Step off the bike, you're over the limit . . ." I couldn't fucking believe it. All of those years getting away with doing the most jackass shit you could possibly imagine and never getting caught, and here I was being arrested in Australia for drunk driving on a fucking moped. "Pull over and take it out of gear!" he said. I had to laugh. *Gears?* This thing had no gears. You practically had to use your feet like Fred Flintstone to get the damn thing moving. I put it on its kickstand, and the officer asked me for my ID. Now, this was a problem. I never, ever carry my passport around while on tour, as I would lose it in a hot New York minute. (Yes, I'm that guy who loses everything in my pockets at least once an afternoon.) Gus has always held on to it for me, only letting me touch it when crossing a border or checking into a flight, and then immediately demanding I give it back. All I had was the Big Day Out tour laminate that was draped around

my neck, which fortunately had my name, picture, and band affiliation on it, so I said, "Oh, man, my tour manager has my passport,
but I do have this," and I handed it over in hopes that, by some slim
chance, he would be a huge fan and let me go.

MAYBE, FOR ONCE, THIS ROCK STAR NAME-DROP
WOULD ACTUALLY WORK. NOPE.

"Musician, huh?" he said with a bit of newfound swagger. I
explained that we were on the Big Day Out tour and that we had
been here for a few days, enjoying his marvelous city, hence the
ridiculous scooter. "Ah . . . ," he said. "When's the next show?"
"Tomorrow in Sydney," I replied with a glimmer of hope. "Sorry,
mate, you're gonna miss that one. I have to take you to jail." Panic
set in. I explained that I could practically see the hotel from where
we were standing, and that I could very well just park this piece
of shit and walk the rest of the way. "Sorry, mate" was all I got in
return. I was indeed fucked.

Just then, Taylor, who had successfully made his way through the checkpoint and doubled back to make sure that I was okay, pulled up to us and said, "Dude, what's going on???" I explained that I was on my way to jail, and that he should race back to the hotel and get Gus to prepare my bail. Taylor sped off ("sped" being a generous term) and I was left standing there alone as row after row of cars passed with people from the show sticking their heads out the window, screaming, "Fuck yeah, Dave! Good on ya, mate! Nice show!" I could only smile and wave. What a dunce.

I was soon handcuffed, placed in the back of the police car, and driven to a mobile police station across the street, where I was interrogated by detectives as if I were Ted Bundy. "What's your home address? What's your mother's home address? What's your mother's work address?" It went on for ages, and if I did indeed have any buzz going, it was wearing off quickly with the tedious and totally irrelevant questioning that I was being subjected to. *Just throw me in the goddamned cell,* I thought after what felt like hours. And that they did.

Once I arrived at the jail, I was again cheered on by all of the other criminals from the show as I was formally booked at the front desk and placed in a cell with a passed-out punter in a Primus T-shirt who snored so loudly, I thought I might have to hang myself with my shoelaces. I retreated to my concrete slab of a bed and did my best to drape the stiff complimentary canvas blanket they had given me around my body, shivering from the cold wet clothes I had been wearing all night in the rain. Since the cell door was plexiglass, the room fell completely silent once it was closed, like an acoustically treated vocal booth in a recording studio, so I just lay there listening to my ears ring from the triumphant show I had performed just hours before, wondering how on earth my weekend in paradise had come to this.

Within a few hours, my hero and savior Gus arrived, and as he looked up at the security monitors full of prisoners, he pointed at my shivering figure on the screen and announced to the officers, "That one is mine." I was sprung, and the ride back to our hotel was a chorus of laughter as I soberly recounted all of the juvenile events that had brought me to this incredibly absurd fate. We got in a few hours' sleep and flew down to Sydney the next morning for a show that night.

But my life of crime wasn't behind me. I was required by law to return to the Gold Coast for my court date a week later. If convicted, I would not only have to pay a fine but could quite possibly face actual jail time, not to mention fuck up my chances of ever being allowed in their beautiful country again, which was the most heartbreaking prospect as Australia had become my favorite place to tour over the years. If I lost that opportunity to a few beers and a cheap scooter, I would never be able to forgive myself, and neither would my band. I began to take this all very seriously, so seriously that Gus and I went to a department store and blew $700 on a suit so that I wouldn't look like a complete dirtbag when face-to-face with the law. Nothing is as pathetic as two grown men strolling through racks and racks of clothes in a department store, making fashion decisions based on the objectivity of a stuffy judge, saying things like "Too conservative?" and "Too disco?" We decided on something dapper but not too rakish, and prepared for our trip back north. The next day, as we were leaving the hotel in Melbourne to fly back up to Queensland, I bumped into the guitarist of Primal Scream in the lobby, who quipped, "What do you call a Foo Fighter in a suit? GUILTY!!!" This did not help.

We met my lawyer, or "barrister" as they call them, at a Burger King down the road from the court building and discussed my defense over some greasy cheeseburgers and stale fries. There wasn't much to say, really. I blew over the limit on a motor vehicle. Case closed. There were no dubious technicalities that I could fall back on to nullify my charge, so it was basically up to the judge to decide the severity of my punishment (and the wisdom of suit choice). I fixed my cheap tie and we headed over to the gallows for judgment day. This shit was getting real.

Before we even set foot in the building, I was ambushed by a local news crew, microphone prodding my face as I walked and delivered "No comment" from behind my new sunglasses. I must say, if there's any good that came from this whole experience, it's that I now know what it feels like to be Johnnie Cochran. Thank god it's only happened once (and thank god I'm not Johnnie Cochran). *At least I look good in this suit,* I thought. We stepped inside and crossed our fingers for an unlikely "not guilty" verdict.

The judge threw the book at me. I thankfully managed to escape any jail time or community service, but technically it was a conviction, so I paid my fine (less than the suit!) and am now forever considered a criminal in Australia, which means still to this day, when entering their country, I have to check the little box that says, "HAVE YOU EVER BEEN CONVICTED OF A CRIME IN AUSTRALIA?" And every time I hand an immigration officer my form, they flip a small switch under their desk that illuminates a red light, signaling their supervisor to come assist them. And every time I explain my crime to said supervisor, they laugh and say, "Oh, right! I remember that!"

I GOT OFF EASY, I SUPPOSE. MY REAL SENTENCE? A LIFETIME OF RIDICULE.

If only I had harnessed my psychic ability that night on the rainy highway, shivering in my hoodie as I inched toward the sobriety checkpoint, I wouldn't have to answer for this embarrassing crime for years to come. Mine is a small price to pay. . . . But ever since that meeting with the psychic in Sydney, I sometimes look down to find the powerful blue aura that apparently radiates from my callused hands and wonder if it will ever help me out. Though, with all of my supposed superpowers, I will still always choose to let life take its natural course, a journey with no road map to refer to in the event that you get lost.

LIFE WAS
PICKING UP
SPEED

"How old are you?" the doctor asked, seeming somewhat puzzled.

"I'm forty," I nervously replied.

"And why are you here?" he inquired.

"Because I'm having chest pains and I think I'm going to fucking die!" I shot back in a panic.

As we sat in front of the CT scan monitors at Cedars-Sinai hospital in Los Angeles, where I had just been subjected to lying perfectly still in a claustrophobic tube for half an hour, he flipped through the blurry digital images on the screen, checking for any clogging or decay in the arteries and chambers of my strained heart. I sat beside him, wringing my sweaty hands while anxiously awaiting my fatal diagnosis as he examined the seemingly indistinguishable black-and-white pictures closely for a minute or two, and then he sat back in his chair.

"Hmmmm . . . not really seeing anything here . . . are you under any stress?"

If he only knew, I thought. I almost fell out of my chair laughing at this slow-pitch of a question, but I respectfully answered him without making it seem so blatantly obvious.

"Ummm, yeah . . . little bit," I said with a smirk.

"Do you get much sleep?"

"Maybe three to four hours a night?" I sheepishly replied, which, to be fair, was a rather generous estimate at the time.

He took one more swing and asked, "Do you drink a lot of coffee?"

Bingo!

"Define *a lot* of coffee . . . ," I said, knowing that my caffeine consumption would probably make Juan Valdez pack up his donkey and run for the hills of Colombia. I was almost embarrassed to admit the amount of coffee I would drink in one day, for fear that he would 5150 me and send me off in a straitjacket to the nearest Caffeine Anonymous meeting. I had recently come to terms with this addiction, realizing that maybe five pots of coffee a day was slightly overdoing it, but I hadn't accepted the dire consequences until now. Unfortunately, I'm THAT guy. Give me one, I want ten. There is a reason why I still to this day have never done cocaine, because deep down I know that if I did coke the same way I drink coffee, I'd be sucking dicks at the bus stop every morning for an eight ball.

Coffee. Just writing the word makes me want some. Hot, cold, gourmet, gas station, fresh brewed, bottom of the pot, instant, French press . . . let's just say that I'm no connoisseur, I just need the fix. I'm the furthest thing from a coffee snob (a pretentious cult that I loathe intensely), so I'll drink anything within reach. From Dunkin' Donuts to the world's most expensive bean that is plucked from the dung of wild civets in Southeast Asia, I've had it all, and I drink it for one reason and one reason only: to get high.

But it wasn't just the coffee that sent me to the hospital that day. Life was picking up speed.

2009 was a banner year. It began with my fortieth-birthday party, held at that bastion of class, the Medieval Times theme restaurant in Anaheim, California, a gigantic equestrian arena where you watch fake knights with fake English accents joust as you eat greasy turkey legs with your bare hands and drink Coors Light from BeDazzled chalices. Forever memorialized in Jim Carrey's greatest movie, *The Cable Guy,* it is the most absurd, hilarious, downright embarrassing dining experience known to man, and apparently not somewhere a grown man would typically celebrate another trip around the sun, which I didn't realize until the fake king's voice came booming over the PA with a few announcements. "Ladies and gentlemen, we have a few birthdays tonight! Eddie is turning seven! Tommy is turning ten! And Dave is turning . . . forty???"

As with most things in my life, I revel in the absurdity of it all and take advantage of every bizarre moment, so what better place to assemble 150 of my closest friends, all seated in the "Blue Knight" section of the arena, drunkenly cheering on our noble chevalier with bloodthirsty abandon, praying for a kill. And what better moment to start a band, for this was the night that I introduced Led Zeppelin's bassist, John Paul Jones, to my old friend Josh Homme to begin our new, top secret project, Them Crooked Vultures.

I had met Josh in the early nineties while he was playing guitar in one of my favorite bands of all time, Kyuss, and we had subsequently toured the world together over the years with his band Queens of the Stone Age, which I had even joined for a short time, recording their album *Songs for the Deaf* and playing some of the most incendiary shows of my entire life. Josh has "the thing," an indefinable, unspoken, magical ability that is truly one in a million, and whenever we played together, the result was always like the hypnotic wave of a murmuration of starlings, the music effortlessly flowing from one direction to the next with grace, never losing its tight pattern. Our onstage improvisation was that of two old friends finishing each other's sentences, often laughing hysterically behind the audience's back at our musical inside jokes. In essence, it was a match made in heaven, and any opportunity to join forces, we would take.

We talked about a side project from time to time, usually when we were exhausted from the responsibilities and obligations of our day jobs, and when our bands crossed paths on tour. We would sit around fantasizing about something weird, loose, and fun over cartons of cigarettes and gallons of backstage cocktails. Josh was a drummer too, so he and I could easily flip back and forth, swapping instruments while trying to get as far away from the sound of

Queens and the Foos as we possibly could. But beyond any musical prediction, we knew we would have a blast, and after a year and a half on the road playing "Learn to Fly" every fucking night, the promise of something fun was much needed to keep me from quitting music altogether and finally becoming the mediocre roofer I was destined to be.

Around the same time, I was asked to present a *GQ* Outstanding Achievement Award to the members of Led Zeppelin (let the painfully obvious sentiment of that colossal understatement sink in for a moment), so I called Josh and asked if I should mention the idea of our secret project to John Paul Jones, the greatest, grooviest bassist in the history of rock and roll. "You *know* John Paul Jones?" he said. Turns out I did, having recorded with him once for the Foo Fighters' album *In Your Honor* in 2004. He also conducted the orchestra for a Foos Grammys performance. I found him to be not only pleasant and down-to-earth, but a blinding musical genius. Plus, he had manned the boards as a producer for fringe artists like the awesome Butthole Surfers and Diamanda Galás. The guy was not afraid to get weird, to say the least, so there was hope that he might consent to our freaky scheme. If the magic that Josh and I had together was coupled with the almighty John Paul Jones, we would surely have ourselves a "supergroup" (a ridiculous term that we shunned). Josh and I figured, what the hell, it was worth a shot, and before long I was standing face-to-face with John at the award ceremony, timidly putting the idea in his ear. He didn't say yes, but he didn't say no either, so we decided to keep in touch via email and see if we could work something out. I flew home giddy at the prospect of actually playing drums with a man who once played alongside the drummer who had inspired me most. I could only hope that he would accept our offer but didn't hold my breath, because, well, he was John Paul Jones.

Lo and behold, John decided to make the trek out to Los Angeles and test the waters to see if we indeed had the chemistry that I imagined we would, and his arrival just so happened to coincide with my fantastically juvenile birthday party, so I invited him along for a medieval festival of greasy fast-food delights. Poor guy, he was unknowingly about to be thrown into a nauseating, Americanized version of the Middle Ages while his host and future bandmate proceeded to get cross-eyed drunk, smoking joints in the men's room like a high school delinquent between choreographed jousting tournaments. If he could survive this night of lowbrow theater and teenage hijinks without running straight back to LAX, then we might have a chance at something special. Bless his heart, he kindly suffered my immaturity with a glacier's patience, and we met a few days later at Josh's studio, Pink Duck, for our first jam.

I sat down behind my kit and made small adjustments while John was warming up his fingers on the bass, ripping the most uncanny phrases with ease, and then I joined in with his groove, locking in so perfectly, so seamlessly, I thought to myself, *WOW! I'm fucking killing it right now!!* But what I quickly realized was that it wasn't me making the drums sound good, it was John. His ability to lock into the drums and adhere to your every beat was amazing, making the groove flow so much smoother, so much stronger than anything I had ever experienced with another bassist. It was in that moment that I knew this experiment was going to work. Once Josh joined in, it was only a matter of seconds before we all realized this was meant to be. There was no turning back now.

We jammed for a few days, getting to know each other while ordering out from another medieval-themed restaurant across the street, Kids Castle (or, as we kindly referred to it, Kids Asshole), feeling each other out and writing a few riffs, eventually coming up with a master plan to pursue this new musical union: we would meet in L.A. for two weeks to write and record, disperse and retreat to our corners for a small break, and then reconvene and continue to build an arsenal of our psych-rock boogie to someday unleash upon the world. It was official.

LIFE WAS PICKING UP SPEED.

Meanwhile, my day job beckoned. After a long hard year and a half on the road, the Foo Fighters were releasing a greatest hits collection and were asked to write and record a new song to include in the track list to help promote it (otherwise known as "the song on the greatest hits record that is neither great nor a hit"). Discussions of how, when, and with whom we would record it began, and now that I was technically in two bands, this scheduling required a bit of logistical massaging. I wasn't sure how or when we could do it, but I did know who I wanted to do it with: my old friend Butch Vig.

Butch and I had a fabled history between us and had always been close, but we hadn't worked together since the recording of Nirvana's *Nevermind* in 1991. For years, I was reluctant to work with Butch again for fear that the long shadow that Nirvana had cast over me after Kurt's death would negate any of the validity of my own music. Whatever we recorded together would only be compared to what we had done in the past, which is a cross that I have had to bear ever since the day we met. As much as I loved Butch, and even though he is one of the greatest producers of all time, and the drummer of alt-rock heroes Garbage, I just didn't want that weight to impact what should have been nothing more than a beautiful reunion. Butch's technique is simple: get big sounds, play big riffs, and make a big song. That's it. It was sometimes hard to tell if he was even working, because the guy is so laid-back, so chill, you forget you're on the clock. With his thick Wisconsin accent and gentle studio demeanor, it was also easy to forget that he had made some of the biggest rock albums of all time with Nirvana, Smashing Pumpkins, and Green Day, just to name a few. But, after some serious soul searching, I decided to forget about what the critics would say and give Butch a call. *Life is just too damn short to let someone else's opinion steer the wheel,* I thought.

The calendars came out, and as hard as we tried to find free time, the Foos sessions unfortunately had to overlap with previously scheduled Them Crooked Vultures sessions. We figured if I recorded with the Foos from eleven A.M. to six P.M. and then raced to the Vultures' studio from seven P.M. to midnight, I could pull it off. *No sweat!* I thought. *I'll sleep when I'm dead!* After all, this was nothing a few extra pots of java a day couldn't solve! So, soon I began to up my intake of that muddy, black daily grind to injurious levels in order to accomplish this crazy objective.

Oh, and I had another kid.

Harper Willow Grohl was brought into this world April 17, 2009. She was a screaming bundle of joy from day one, so perfect, so adorable. My notion of love expanded tenfold upon her arrival, and I was once again a proud father. I always had a great appreciation for life, but my new baby made me love it all even more, waking excitedly every morning to see her beautiful face, no matter how sleep deprived I may have been. As any parent can attest, the miracle of a newborn overrides every other facet of your life, and you forget about your own survival because you are completely focused on theirs, an ethos that was certainly demonstrated by my mother in my childhood years. I was overjoyed to now have two beautiful daughters and would run to any opportunity to be with them, day or night, regardless of how exhausted I was from my demented schedule of speeding from one studio to the next all day long, drinking coffee like it was an Olympic competition.

LIFE WAS PICKING UP SPEED.

As if this all weren't enough to send me to an early grave (HERE LIES DAVID ERIC GROHL. HE SHOULD HAVE SWITCHED TO SANKA), the Foo Fighters had been asked to perform at the White House for a July 4 barbecue that newly elected President Obama was hosting for our military families. Set on the manicured South Lawn overlooking the monuments of the National Mall, it was an opportunity that I could not resist, for a myriad of personal reasons. This was my hometown, after all, and I had spent countless Fourth of Julys on the other side of that White House fence, watching the magnificent fireworks display above from a blanket in the grass as the Beach Boys played on a festival stage in the distance, or attending punk rock concerts at the base of the Lincoln Memorial as an angry teenager, exercising my right to protest on the day where it perhaps meant the most. But this was different. This was a personal invitation to join our first African American president in his backyard to celebrate the men and women who defend our right to have the freedom to celebrate, or protest, or elect our leaders by democratic process. This wasn't just a barbecue; this was an honor.

Oh, and I was also remodeling my house.

With my ever-expanding family, my once-spacious house began to feel not so spacious. So plans had been made to convert formerly unimportant rooms into something a bit more kid-friendly (and . . . ahem . . . a studio for myself where we would one day record our album *Wasting Light*). Violet was three years old at this point, and Harper only three months, so there needed to be some reconfiguration to accommodate them, which required some serious construction. Loud construction. With a driveway that looked like the valet parking at a Dodge truck convention and scores of workers wielding power tools that raised the decibel level to Motörhead-worthy numbers, there is only one way to describe it: fucking chaos.

LIFE WAS PICKING UP SPEED.

For weeks, my new routine went something like this: Wake at the crack of dawn to a newborn and a three-year-old demanding my undivided attention while buzz saws and jackhammers roar in the distance. Make a pot of coffee. Drink said pot of coffee and speed over to the Foo Fighters' studio. Make another pot of coffee. Start working. Drink that pot of coffee, but also drink strong brewed iced tea between pots, thinking that this is hydration. Make another pot of coffee so that I have some to drink on the way to the next studio (road soda). Arrive at the Vultures' studio, put on another pot, and drink that over the course of the next four hours as I bash the living shit out of my drums, desperately trying to impress John Paul Jones. Drive home shaking like a leaf from

the approximately four thousand milligrams of caffeine that I have just ingested in the course of eighteen hours and unsuccessfully try to get in at least four hours of sleep before waking and doing it all again. Et cetera, et cetera, ad nauseam, on repeat.

LIFE WAS PICKING UP SPEED.

This unflattering period of my mounting crisis is best understood by watching the now-infamous YouTube clip "Fresh Pots," a two-minute short film that was put together by our old friend and comrade Liam Lynch, who was present during the making of the Vultures record. There to capture the creative process of our secret project, he witnessed my breakdown and compiled my most psychotic moments into a hilarious (and embarrassing) video with the intention of showing it only to the band. When the first Vultures single was eventually released, the band had no music video to promote the song, so my manager asked if we could release the "Fresh Pots" clip instead. I figured that, although it was mortifying, I would take one for the team and allow the world to see a man in the throes of a full-on caffeine binge, acting like a complete maniac. *No one will ever see it,* I thought. I was wrong. The day after its release, I was in the checkout line at the grocery store and the kid bagging my groceries looked up at me and said, "Hey, man . . . want a cup of coffee?" Fuck. As of this writing it has over seven million views.

I remember the first pain. It was the day before we were to leave for the White House and I was in my hallway at home, stressing about the deafening renovation that shook the house like falling bombs, and it hit me like a knife in my rib cage. The pain was sharp, and I stopped and raised my hand to my chest, terrified that I was having a heart attack but praying it was just a pulled muscle from all of the drumming I had been doing with the Vultures. But something told me that this was no pulled muscle. I had pulled them all before. This was coming from somewhere deeper. I took a few deep breaths to see if it would pass, to no avail. It lingered. Without wanting to raise any alarm and start running around the house screaming, "THIS IS THE BIG ONE!!" like Fred Sanford, I calmly opened up my laptop and foolishly searched "symptoms of a heart attack." (I now know better than to self-diagnose with the help of some random blogger's homemade website.) I didn't necessarily have ALL of the symptoms, but I was definitely experiencing something serious, so I looked up heart attack prevention tips and decided to keep it under wraps. After all, I wasn't missing this White House gig for the world. Not even a heart attack was keeping me from flying home and playing for the president.

I put two aspirin in my wallet and never said a word.

LIFE WAS PICKING UP SPEED.

When I arrived at the White House, the pain in my chest was almost soothed by the sweet humidity of DC's muggy summer weather, and as we prepared to soundcheck on the lawn, I looked out over the fence to the monuments I had once taken for granted. The Washington Monument, towering in the distance like a maypole for the city to perform its complicated dance around. The Jefferson Memorial, adorned by rows of cherry blossoms in the annual rebirth of spring. And the Lincoln Memorial, the site of many of the Fourth of July concerts I attended when I was a young punk rocker. These were not the Beach Boys; these were musical protests. Dubbed the "Rock Against Reagan" concert, it was held every year on the Fourth of July during his administration, a gathering of punks from far and wide who came to sing along with their favorite bands in unified opposition to the president's ultraconservative policies. I was no poli-sci major by any means, but I did join along and lend my voice to fighting for the freedom to express myself however I pleased. Once Reagan left office, the concert was renamed "Rock Against Racism" and I attended each of those shows with the same fervor and intention. This particular memory resonated with me that day, as not only was I on the other side of the fence this Fourth of July, but so was President Obama.

LIFE WAS PICKING UP SPEED.

Our road crew did their best to look formal, opting for black cargo shorts instead of black sweatpants, and as the stage was being readied, we all made friends with the kind White House staff of security guards and electricians. The one bit of sage advice I remember: "If you guys need to use the restrooms, there's one over there and one over there. Whatever you do, don't go pee in the bushes. There are people in the bushes." Noted.

After a quick run-through of the songs, we were led up to the house to meet Barack Obama for the first time, and as we walked into the Blue Room, overlooking the barbecue below, we were greeted by the president and First Lady with a very down-to-earth, personable, and warm welcome. The casual nature of the day's ceremony defused the stately tension that usually surrounded most political events, so we chatted and laughed in a relaxed manner, almost forgetting that we were actually standing with the president and First Lady, Michelle (who, to be honest, seemed more presidential than the president himself). As we stood there talking and taking pictures, I noticed that Pat wasn't his normal, carefree self. He seemed quiet, which was unlike him. When we returned to the South Lawn, he shared with me the reason why. This was Pat's first time in the White House, a place where his great-grandfather, a former enslaved person, once stood in line to meet and shake hands with Abraham Lincoln.

Our trip to the White House had now taken on a whole new meaning.

That night, as we watched the fireworks overhead, I looked up at the First Family standing on the balcony, and I was filled with emotion. History was being made. And as I saw the illuminated faces of my wife, my children, and my mother staring up at the sky, I was filled with not only nostalgia but pride, honored to share this historic moment with them. And for Pat, my most trusted and faithful friend, I was filled with love. We had all made it over the fence together.

LIFE WAS PICKING UP SPEED.

I returned to Los Angeles and immediately called my doctor. "Dude, I've been having chest pains," I told him. "Are you having them right now??" he said, sounding more concerned than usual (and that's pretty concerned). "Ummm . . . kinda . . . ," I replied. He told me to jump in the car and get to his office immediately, so I sped out the door and split traffic like Moses. I burst into his office and within moments was lying on a table, poked and prodded and wired up like a vintage synthesizer. He watched the paper readout from the EKG as it spilled onto the floor and said, "Hmmmm . . . not seeing anything here . . . let's get you on the treadmill and then we'll do an ultrasound . . ." I was taken to another floor where I was again covered in little electro-patches, and told to jog on a treadmill like the Six Million Dollar Man. Then I jumped onto a table where they covered me in gel and watched my heart throb via the wand of an ultrasound. "Hmmmm . . . not seeing anything here . . . let's get you over to Cedars for a CT scan . . ." I was starting to feel like the little girl from *The Exorcist,* being subjected to test after test, when really it was just a simple demonic possession. Maybe I needed a priest?

After sitting with the doctor at Cedars and finding no signs of real danger, he explained to me that I needed to take it easy. As much as I felt indestructible, I was no superman, and I had to take care of myself in order to take care of the ones I love. My passion for life could be a bit much sometimes, so much that I pushed myself a bit too far, but if I wanted to stick around awhile, I needed to be a bit more mindful of my mortal limits. His prescription? "Play drums only three times a week, have a glass of wine before bed, and lay off the coffee."

TWO OUT OF THREE AIN'T BAD. DECAF BLOWS.

And life is still picking up speed.

SWING
DANCING
WITH
AC/DC

"Do you mind if AC/DC comes to dinner?"

This text from my wife, Jordyn, will forever go down as the most surreal, ridiculous, and painfully obvious question that I have ever been asked in my entire life. Dinner with AC/DC? The band that practically walks in the shadows, never to be seen in public, only to appear on giant stages adorned with massive exploding cannons and giant amplifiers stacked to the rafters? The band that has personified fist-pumping, headbanging, foot-stomping bad-boy boogie with an outlaw's grin and a devilish wink for over forty deafening years? Not to mention selling over two hundred million albums and inspiring generations of young rockers to devote their lives to three chords and a pair of ripped jeans?

I should know. I was one of them.

It was 1980 when AC/DC unleashed their monumental concert film *Let There Be Rock* on the unsuspecting world of overly glamorized pop music, and it quickly made the rounds to all of the hip movie theaters across the country that showed midnight movies on the weekends. (A long-lost phenomenon that most people my age remember as a stoner rite of passage. *The Rocky Horror Picture Show, The Wall,* and *Heavy Metal* were some of my favorites.) A live performance filmed in Paris only a few months before the passing of their original lead singer, Bon Scott, the film is a tour de force, with the world's grittiest, grooviest no-bullshit hard rock band serving up a megadose of sweat, denim, and high-voltage rock and roll. If you were a wannabe student of all things rock, this was a master class in how to kick fucking ass and take fucking names.

At eleven years old, I was already familiar with AC/DC, as their albums *Dirty Deeds Done Dirt Cheap* and *Highway to Hell* were two of the most cherished records in my growing collection, so this movie was something I had to see. The *Washington Post* listed that the film was playing at the historic Uptown Theater in Washington, DC, as a part of their Wall of Sound concert series. So my best friend at the time, Larry Hinkle, and I made a night of it—chaperoned downtown by his father in their burgundy Datsun 280ZX, the poor man's Porsche.

As Larry and I were dropped off at the ticket booth, I nervously expected a theater overflowing with denim-and-leather-clad hoodlums. But when we stepped inside I found that there were only a few hard-core AC/DC fans there, scattered in small groups throughout the rows and rows of empty seats, waiting for the film to begin while unsuccessfully trying to hide the flickering lighters that were sparking their pinner joints and homemade pipes. Like two awkward kids in a socially suffocating lunchroom, we tried to decide where to sit, as the place was practically empty and we were afraid of getting a contact high from the sweet-smelling weed wafting throughout the theater. Knowing that it was the Wall of Sound concert series, we were tempted to sit near the sound system down front but opted for something toward the back so that we wouldn't have to crane our skinny necks to see the giant screen. Thank god we did, because little did we know, there was a concert-sized PA hidden behind those curtains, and as the house lights went down it was soon apparent that this was no regular matinee showing of *Star Wars*.

The movie opened with a rogue road crew of burly, long-haired hooligans like modern pirates disassembling a rock and roll stage before loading it onto a fleet of trucks to be taken to the next city for another night of carnage. This was something I had never seen or considered before. After a concert's last note has been played and the audience are on their way home to the comfort of their warm beds, it's these brave souls who go to work coiling miles of cables and packing up tons of equipment into battered road cases as they wade through your littered beer cups and cigarette butts before passing out in bunks the size of coffins, getting in just enough sleep to set it all back up the next morning. This set the tone perfectly for what Larry and I were about to witness. This was not the glamour that we had been conditioned to associate with the larger-than-life rock stars in the posters on our bedroom walls; this was the real deal, and suddenly all those years of imagining rock and roll to be life's most colorful theater faded into ripped T-shirts and bloody knuckles.

As the trucks barreled down the highway and blasted their air horns, it was immediately apparent that the PA system in the theater was on "stun." I mean, this shit was DEAFENING. And we hadn't even gotten to the music yet. It was, without question, the loudest thing I had ever heard in my eleven short years on the planet. Having not yet been to a rock concert, I didn't realize the ultimate power of that level of volume and had no idea that sound could shake your rib cage with earthquake intensity. Needless to say, I liked it. A lot. By the time the band hit the stage with their first number, "Live Wire," my ears were already ringing and I was on the edge of my seat.

I WANTED TO FUCKING TEAR THAT THEATER TO SHREDS.

The adrenaline that was running through my body caused what can only be described as the transformation that Bruce Banner would experience when turning into the Hulk on the TV series from the late seventies. I felt so overwhelmed and empowered by the sheer intensity of the music, I could hardly contain myself. If my skinny little arms had had the strength to rip the seat out of the floor and smash it in the aisle, I would have, but instead I just sat there shaking in my sneakers as AC/DC did what they have always done best: give every ounce of themselves to the audience and leave nothing behind.

Within a few songs, the drummer is seen replacing his snare because he broke it from rocking too hard. *Whoa.* Guitarist Angus Young, drenched in sweat, is seen on the side of the stage with an oxygen mask in between songs because he just ran at least three marathons from one side of the stage to the next over the course of thirteen songs and his body could barely withstand the rock. *Holy shit.* This was superhuman, I thought. Forget those bands that just stood there and fiddled with their instruments like medieval minstrels; these guys attacked them like it was their last day on earth. By the time the credits rolled, I was a changed boy. IF I AM GOING TO PLAY MUSIC IN A BAND, I THOUGHT, I'M GOING TO DO IT LIKE THAT.

I replied to Jordyn's text with a gigantic "DUH" and pinched myself at the opportunity to finally meet the band that inspired me to kick fucking ass and take fucking names. If you have ever seen a

Scream, Nirvana, or Foo Fighters show, you now know where this energy comes from. I owe it all to AC/DC's *Let There Be Rock*.

It just so happened that AC/DC was in town to perform their new song "Rock or Bust" at the fifty-seventh annual Grammy Awards in 2015. I was not performing that night, only presenting an award, but as a lifelong AC/DC fan I was certainly more excited to see them than any of the other relatively tedious pop performers and their ridiculous, Vegas-like productions. A strong injection of true-blue rock and roll was exactly what the show needed. I would be there, front and center, undoubtedly feeling that same overwhelming rush of adrenaline that had made me want to tear the Uptown Theater to shreds thirty-five years before (except now I would be shoulder to shoulder with Katy Perry and Tony Bennett, feeling like I was hiding my flickering lighter at the end of a homemade pipe).

Seeing as how I was to be there on my own without my trusty Foo Fighters, I called Taylor and Pat to invite them to a post-show dinner with our wives, opting out of the usual after-parties, which are generally just orgies of selfies and industry small talk. We reserved a table at a restaurant called Faith and Flower just a few blocks from the venue and planned to meet for dinner and drinks away from the hubbub after the show. Paul McCartney was in town as well and inquired what we were planning on doing afterward, so we gladly invited him and his wife Nancy along, adding two more chairs to our growing table. Take it from me, any night with Paul is a good night, so this was shaping up to be an epic evening. Apparently, Paul bumped into the AC/DC folks at the hotel, and when asked what was going on afterward, he said he was having dinner with us, which led to my life's most surreal text.

Pause. Reflect.

NOT A DAY GOES BY WHERE I DON'T STOP AND THANK THE UNIVERSE FOR THESE OTHERWORLDLY BLESSINGS, AND I MAKE IT A POINT TO TAKE NOTHING FOR GRANTED. It will never feel "normal" to me to be included in such a waking dream; it will always feel like I'm watching life happen from above, looking down at someone else's fantasy playing out before me. But it is mine, and it's these moments when I try to be present, reminding myself that I am perhaps the luckiest person on earth to breathe the next breath that will lead me to the next adventure.

A few days before the show, I received another text, from my good friend Ben Jaffe of New Orleans's legendary Preservation Hall Jazz Band, notifying me that he was also in town for the Grammys and looking for a party. Believe me, nobody parties like a New Orleans native, and nothing says New Orleans like the Preservation

Hall Jazz Band. Founded in the early 1960s by Ben's father, Allan, they have embodied the sound, spirit, and joy of their great city, keeping traditional New Orleans jazz alive, playing three shows a night three hundred sixty-five days a year, for over sixty years. So, when they put the instruments down (which they rarely do), the party always turns up. While filming our documentary series *Sonic Highways* in 2014, Foo Fighters had the honor of spending a week filming in Preservation Hall itself, a tavern that dates back to 1803. We all became fast friends. By the end of that week, I had decided that New Orleans is an American treasure, and that we all indeed need to preserve its rich culture steeped in European, Caribbean, and Cajun history. There is nowhere on earth filled with the pure magic that New Orleans has to offer. It is, without a doubt, my favorite city in the world.

"Dude . . . we're having dinner with Paul McCartney AND AC/DC!" I exclaimed to Ben. "You wanna come along?" I knew Ben would most definitely appreciate the enormity of such an incredible chance encounter. "Can I bring all the guys with me?" he asked. I paused and did the math. The Preservation Hall Jazz Band consisted of seven musicians, which realistically meant at least ten more people. Of course I would have loved to have them all, but we were on our way to moving from that table of eight to taking over the whole fucking restaurant, so I replied with a tentative "Uh, let me check," afraid that the restaurant would decline our request for another ten chairs. But then Ben sealed the deal:

"How about we all come marching down the street playing in a second line, into the restaurant, straight to the table, and perform a set for you right there?"

There was absolutely no refusing this incredibly generous offer. For anyone unfamiliar with a second-line parade, it is considered a quintessential New Orleans art form, a tradition dating back to the nineteenth century, where a brass band marches down the street playing behind a funeral procession to celebrate the life of a lost loved one. Today, more casual versions of these parades can be found all over the streets of New Orleans at any given moment, and if you hear the sound of syncopated funked-up jazz-swing coming, grab a drink and join in. You never know where it may lead you.

I assured Ben that, come hell or high water, I would make this happen and said that we should keep it a secret so as to surprise all of our honored guests with a night they would never forget (not to mention the entire restaurant, whispering over plates of high cuisine, who would surely be taken aback by the sheer volume of the howling horns, crashing cymbals, and thundering tubas played by New Orleans's most beloved band).

Our quiet little table was now moved to a private room in the back, large enough to comfortably accommodate our ever-growing guest list in a space that would allow us all to grab a partner and swing them around the floor in a night of drunken celebration. I couldn't wait to see the looks on everyone's faces as the band marched into the room, hoping that it would inspire that same feeling I'd experienced the first time I joined in on a second line in New Orleans. A feeling of community and love, shared with people from all walks of life, joined in rhythm and joy as we followed the music wherever it led us. I remember dancing down the street on my first day in New Orleans, side by side with strangers smiling at each other and skipping to the beat, when I saw a familiar face, Ben Jaffe, standing on top of a car in the distance. We had only met recently, but he jumped down, gave me the warmest hug, turned to a man selling beer and minibar bottles of wine out of a rolling cooler, and bought us drinks for our afternoon journey.

Sutter Home rosé never tasted so good at eleven A.M. He instantly became my brother for life.

Once the Grammys were over, Jordyn and I raced over to the restaurant to beat the crowd before our epic evening began. Our secret was mostly safe, though Paul somehow knew, because, well, he is the all-knowing, all-seeing, omniscient and omnipotent Paul McCartney. It turns out Paul actually had his own history with Preservation Hall that dated back to his time in Wings, when he recorded at local hero Allen Toussaint's studio and would go by Preservation Hall to hang. "He was sort of a regular for a while," Ben told me.

Brimming with excitement, I kept my phone close to coordinate the timing of the band's entrance, making sure all was ready for the big reveal.

The room started filling up with the familiar faces of the people I love the most. My mother, my friends, Paul . . . and then, there they were . . . AC/DC in the flesh.

To be fair, I had met singer Brian Johnson once before, albeit very briefly, in a hotel bar in Valencia, Spain, on a day off from our Foo Fighters tour in 1996. Upon pulling up to the hotel after a long drive on a day off, we spilled out of the bus and noticed a few denim-clad autograph seekers standing out front with stacks of photos and magazines to be signed. Standard practice for any touring band, but as we approached, we noticed that they were covered head to toe in AC/DC gear and hadn't the slightest fucking clue who we were. "You guys must love AC/DC!" I joked as we walked past, and in their thick Spanish accents they explained that AC/DC was actually staying in our hotel because they were performing at the local Plaza de Toros de las Ventas bullfighting arena that night, which just so happened to be a rare night off for us. Overcome with excitement, I raced to my room and called our tour manager, demanding that we all get tickets for this show, which would be my first time witnessing an actual AC/DC concert. A few phone calls were made, and we managed to score enough passes for everyone. We called room to room and made a plan to meet in the hotel bar for a few pre-show cocktails before heading down to the gig.

As we stood around the hotel bar devouring our drinks, a man in black jeans, a black T-shirt, and a flat cap nonchalantly walked into the classy room and ordered himself a drink as he sat down on a barstool by himself. Stunned, we fell silent, as this was none other than THE Brian Johnson, the man who sang AC/DC's "Have a Drink on Me" from their most beloved album, *Back in Black*. As the bartender delivered his glass, Brian turned to us, and with a

wink and a smile, he raised his glass in a simple toast, only saying, "Lads!" We all raised our glasses right back at him, realizing the poetry of this beautiful moment. I'm pretty sure he thought we were his road crew, but whatever, I was on cloud nine.

That night, I finally got to see the AC/DC that I fell in love with as a nerdy, rock-and-roll-worshipping eleven-year-old boy. The amount of energy they displayed onstage was exactly what I had expected, with Angus Young running full speed from one end to the other of the giant stage adorned with pyrotechnics and exploding cannons. The full-capacity audience only added to the spectacle, singing not only every lyric at the top of their lungs but the guitar parts as well as they bounced in a rolling human wave to the rhythm of every song. It was transcendent.

To see all of these hugely influential faces file into our own ragtag after-Grammys party would have been enough for me to die a happy man, but knowing what was to come made it so much sweeter. There was no way that I could possibly repay this roomful of icons for the years of inspiration that they had given me, but if I could make them smile, dance, and feel the joy of music, as they had done for me my entire life, I was making a small dent in my debt.

As our back room grew louder with celebration, I checked my phone and saw a text from Ben: "We're down the block in our van, dressed and ready to go!" It was time. "Bring it," I replied with shaky hands as I took my place by the window that looked onto the street, waiting to see the band in their trademark black suits and ties dancing down the sidewalk toward the restaurant. Moments later, I heard the faint sound of that familiar New Orleans swing in the distance, and as they rounded the corner, the hair on my arms stood up at the sight of their shuffling toward the front door in time. Within seconds the restaurant was flooded with the thunderous sound of brass as they wound through the tables of astonished patrons. Conversation in our little group ground to a halt as everyone tried to figure out what the hell was happening in the other room, and then . . . they appeared. Filing into our party in their second-line formation, the Preservation Hall Jazz Band burst into the room and took its place in the center of the floor, surrounded by the bewildered faces of our guests, as they blew their horns with rapturous fervor, only feet from our trembling eardrums. Once the initial shock subsided, the small floor became a ballroom, and everyone dropped their drinks to take their partners for a good swing around the room. In that moment, all of the rock and roll pretense and royalty disappeared, and there was only pure joy. At one point, as we danced along, Brian Johnson turned to me, and with a giant smile he screamed, "I'M ACTUALLY FUCKING HAPPY!!"

My job here was done.

The night continued with more music, more drinks, more joy. It was also a reunion of sorts, with Paul and Ben reminiscing about Paul's time in New Orleans years ago and his friendship with Ben's late father, something that undoubtedly meant so much to Ben. At one point, Paul grabbed a trumpet and began to play "When the Saints Go Marching In," and of course the band joined in and played along. Paul turned to Ben and said, "My first instrument was the trumpet! Then my mum bought me a guitar and, well . . . you know how the rest of that story goes . . ."

Yes, we all certainly do.

The night went on into the wee hours, and no matter how much we wished it would never end, the houselights came up and it was time to wander back to reality, a place that seemed so far away after such a magical evening. I WAS EXHAUSTED—NOT

PHYSICALLY, BUT MY SOUL HAD JUST RUN A TRIATHLON OF EMOTION, NOSTALGIA, AND UNDYING LOVE OF MUSIC. It's hard to put into words the belief that I have in music. To me, it is god. A divine mystery in whose power I will forever hold an unconditional trust. And it is moments like these that cement my faith.

So, when you hear that parade coming down the street, spreading joy and love with every note, don't just listen; join in the march. You never know where it may lead you.

INSPIRED, YET AGAIN

"Excuse me, are you Dave Grohl?"

Standing at the curb outside of the LAX departure terminal waiting to jump on my flight to Seattle, I took a long drag off my cigarette and nodded. "Yep." The young man smiled and said, "I read in an interview that the only person you ever really wanted to meet was Little Richard. Is that true?"

"Absolutely," I replied. "He's the originator."

"Well, he's my dad," he said.

I jumped back, immediately threw my cigarette to the ground, and vigorously shook the man's hand with a crushing grip, honored and amazed to meet the son of rock and roll's great pioneer.

"Would you like to meet him? He's right here in the car . . ."

I could barely speak. This was the moment I had been waiting for. Of all the people on god's green earth that I had met or have yet to meet, there has never been anyone more important to me than Little Richard. There would be no rock and roll without Little Richard. And without rock and roll, there would be no me.

We walked a few steps to the limousine parked on the curb

beside us and the young man tapped the tinted window. It lowered just a few inches, and he leaned in, whispering quietly to the person behind the glass. Suddenly, the window began to roll down . . . and there he was, in all his glory! The hair, the smile, the eyeliner . . . and the voice that screamed, "Well, God bless you, David! It's so nice to meet you!" I was at a complete and total loss for words. I stood there like a blathering idiot as he asked if I was a musician, the name of my band, where I was from, all while signing a postcard-sized black-and-white photo of himself, writing, *To David, God cares.* We shook hands, the window went up, and my life was complete.

I cannot overstate the importance of these moments to me. I walk through this crazy life of a musician like a little boy in a museum, surrounded by the exhibits I've spent a lifetime studying. And when I finally come face-to-face with someone who has inspired me along the way, I am thankful. I am grateful. And I take none of it for granted. I am a firm believer in the shared humanity of music, something that I find more rewarding than any other aspect of what I do. When the one-dimensional image becomes a living, breathing, three-dimensional human being, it fills your soul with reassurance that even our most cherished heroes are flesh and bone. I believe that people are inspired by people. That is why I feel the need to connect with my fans when they approach me. I'm a fan too.

When I was seven years old, my older stoner cousin gave me his copy of Rush's magnum opus, *2112,* to take back with me to Virginia after our yearly vacation in Chicago. At this point, I was pretty much sticking to my Beatles and KISS records, so Rush's prog rock musicianship and mastery was a whole new world to my virgin ears. I was intrigued. But the thing that stood out to me the most about that album was the drums. This was the first time I had ever heard them in the forefront of a song, equally as lyrical and melodic as the vocals or guitar. Although I couldn't play what Neil Peart was playing, I could FEEL it.

Decades later, Taylor Hawkins and I were asked to induct Rush into the Rock and Roll Hall of Fame and to perform the first track on *2112,* an instrumental titled "Overture" (no simple task). I had met bassist Geddy Lee and guitarist Alex Lifeson over the years, both perfectly down-to-earth and outrageously funny, but never the master himself, Neil Peart. Neil was a bit more elusive, understandable considering he was one of the greatest drummers of all time (not just in rock). When Taylor and I showed up for rehearsal the day before the ceremony, we were greeted by Geddy and Alex, but Neil was nowhere to be seen. And then in a flash, he appeared and introduced himself in his deep baritone voice: "Hey, Dave, I'm Neil." All I could think was *He said my name. He said MY name.* I nervously said hello, and he asked, "Want a coffee?" "Sure!" I said, and we walked over to the catering table, where he, Neil Peart, drummer of Rush, the man who made me hear the drums in a whole new way at the age of seven, who inspired me to become a drummer myself, proceeded to make me a cup of coffee, handing it over with a smile.

INSPIRED, YET AGAIN.

It's one thing to see your idols in a musical setting or context; it's another to see them far away from the spotlight, in their natural habitat, like an animal in the wild. Once, while I was pushing Violet in a stroller down a busy London shopping street with my wife and our good friend Dave Koz, Elton John walked out of a boutique directly in front of us and jumped in a waiting car. We all stopped and asked each other, "HOLY SHIT! DID YOU JUST

SEE THAT?!??!" It was Elton. Fucking. John. And he was sitting in a parked car only feet from where we were standing, starstruck. "Go say hi, Dave!" my friend said, nudging me. I laughed and said, "I don't fucking know Elton John! And he sure as fuck doesn't know who I am!" The car started up, pulled away, drove about twenty meters up the road, and stopped. The door opened, and out jumped Elton John, who walked back to us, still frozen in place. He approached me with that big, toothy grin and said, "Hello, Dave, nice to meet you." My smile almost fell off my face, it was so wide. I introduced him to Jordyn and Dave, and he leaned down and gave Violet a kiss before running back and speeding away. *Now, THAT'S how you do it,* I thought. (And yes, his giant sapphire earrings matched his shoes perfectly.)

Years later, I had the opportunity to play drums on a track with Elton for the Queens of the Stone Age album . . . *Like Clockwork*. The song, "Fairweather Friends," was a blistering, unconventional multipart arrangement that we had carefully rehearsed before his arrival, because when Queens recorded, it was always full band live to tape, meaning you had to have your shit together and get it right. Elton arrived, straight from an Engelbert Humperdinck session (not kidding), and said, "Okay, boys, what? . . . Have you got a ballad for me?" We all laughed and said, "No . . . come listen." For anyone to just stroll in and learn such a complicated song straightaway was a huge ask, but Elton sat at the piano and WORKED on it until he got it right, take after take, ever the perfectionist, proving why he is the queen bitch of rock and roll.

INSPIRED, YET AGAIN.

It's the moments with no safety net that keep your spirits at their highest, and if you're an adventurer like me, those moments can always be found. And usually in the most unexpected places.

One night in Osaka, we were informed by our tour manager, Gus, that Huey Lewis was coming to the gig. "HUEY LEWIS!!!" Pat exclaimed. I had never seen him so excited in all the years I had known him. Once again, Pat turned my world upside down by telling me that the album *Sports* by Huey Lewis and the News was one of his favorite records of all time (along with *Butterfly* by Mariah Carey), completely destroying my image of him as the punkest motherfucker on the face of the planet. Taylor then told me that Huey actually played harmonica on Thin Lizzy's *Live and Dangerous* album, which I had no idea about but made a little more sense.

Huey appeared, and before long the backstage was alive with our usual beer and whiskey pre-show ritual. Take it from me, Huey is a most excellent hang. We drank, smoked, and laughed, and I eventually asked about his connection with Phil Lynott and Thin Lizzy (such an amazing band). He told me the story of his harmonica solo on that record and how he too loved Thin Lizzy. And then I had an idea: what if Huey jumped up and did a harmonica solo with us??? He checked his pockets for a harp but unfortunately was not strapped, though he did say, "If you can find one in time, I'll do it!" I looked at the clock; we were on in twenty minutes, so I turned to Gus, asked him to do whatever he could to find one, did one more shot with Huey, and hit the stage. By the seventh song, I looked over, and there was Huey, smiling and waving his harmonica in the air. He jumped out next to me and, with a plastic harmonica bought from a Japanese toy store on a Sunday night, proceeded to rip a solo that would make the guy from Blues Traveler throw down his bandoliers and run to his mama. I was totally blown away. This dude is a grade A, 100 percent badass motherfucker, and I will never question the validity of *Sports* ever again. Shame on me. For one night and one night only, we were "Huey Lewis and the Foos," and I liked it.

ANOTHER TWIST IN AN ALREADY WINDING PATH.

You never know who may appear on the side of the stage, but in those moments, you strike while the iron is hot. Years ago, we were asked by the BBC to record a cover song, something we enjoy and do quite often, amassing an arsenal of songs you never thought you'd hear the Foo Fighters do (or attempt to do). At the time, we were on tour, but we were scheduled to record it immediately upon returning home, so we had to pick a song and have it ready to go within a few days. In our tiny warm-up room backstage at Tokyo's Summer Sonic music festival, Taylor and I sat and played around with a few ideas, and then I noticed that Rick Astley was on the festival bill, as well. "Dude, we should do 'Never Gonna Give You Up' for the BBC thing!" We started jamming around on it, and I quickly realized that the chord progression and arrangement bore an uncanny resemblance to "Smells Like Teen Spirit." Pat, Chris, Rami our keyboardist, and Nate joined in, and before long the two songs were practically indistinguishable, like a mash-up from hell. It was so terrifically funny and absurd that we did it again, and again, and again, until finally Gus came in and told us it was time for the show. We headed out to the massive stadium stage and tore into our usual barn burner set, but after a few songs I looked over and saw a familiar face by the monitor board stage right. It was Rick fucking Astley, rocking out to the band, his unmistakable boyish face bobbing up and down in the distance. During one of Rami's keyboard solos, I walked over to him and extended my hand. Over the crushing volume of the show happening behind me, I said, "We just learned 'Never Gonna Give You Up' half an hour ago. Wanna do it with us?" He seemed shocked but without hesitation answered, "Fuck yes," and within seconds he was onstage singing with a bunch of strangers in front of fifty thousand confused Japanese Foo Fighters fans, flying by the seat of his pants.

God bless you, Rick Astley. That took gigantic balls.

The flip side to meeting a musician who has inspired you is meeting a musician who has had no personal relevance in your life. That juxtaposition is an interesting one. Whereas I have turned into a withering puddle upon meeting the most obscure, unknown, underground hardcore rockers, I have also been cool as a cucumber around legends whose music never became a part of my vernacular. Not to say Neil Diamond isn't a god among men, but the "Sweet Caroline" single did not reside between my Venom and Dead Kennedys records when I was a kid, so when we met at the 2009 MusiCares tribute, where he was being honored, I just found him to be a really sweet dude. But there was one person who I knew would become a withering puddle upon meeting him, and that was my late friend Jimmy Swanson's mom. And she was why we were there.

Mary Jane was a lifelong Neil Diamond fan, and his was perhaps the only music I ever heard in her house besides the screeching satanic death metal Jimmy and I listened to. After Jimmy passed, she was left completely heartbroken, having lost her only son much too soon. She had always been family to me, another mother, so when we were asked to perform a Neil Diamond song at his tribute, I said, "Let me make one call before saying yes." I called Mary Jane and told her that I would only play the show if she flew out to California, her first trip out west, so that she could meet Neil. She tearfully agreed, I called my manager and told him it was a go, and I began searching for a Neil Diamond song to learn, my first foray into his incredible catalog.

I was on double duty that weekend, also playing drums for Paul McCartney at the Grammys, where we blasted through a wonderfully raw version of "I Saw Her Standing There," so Mary Jane flew out and attended the Grammys with us too, going from sitting on the couch in her TV room to sitting in an arena with Kid Rock, U2, and Stevie Wonder. That night we had an after-party at a restaurant with Paul and the band, and when Mary Jane walked into the room, Paul handed her a glass of champagne, kissed her on the cheek, and said, "Hello, luv." I thought she was going to faint. But it was the moment when Paul stood up at the end of the table to make a toast that still makes me shed a tear today. After raising his glass to everyone in the room and toasting the wonderful night of music we had just experienced, Paul turned to Mary Jane and said, "And . . . to Jimmy."

The next night was Mary Jane's big chance to meet her beloved Neil Diamond. I had met him backstage earlier in the day, and he was a vision of seventies cool with his red silk shirt with diamonds embroidered on the collar (which we all complimented him on), his perfect hair, and a voice so smooth it would make anyone weak in the knees. I explained the emotional relevance of the evening, and being the true mensch that he is, he graciously agreed to come say hello to Mary Jane after the show.

I still remember the look on her face when he entered our dressing room later that night. It was the same face that I must have made when I met Little Richard, or Paul, or any of the obscure, unknown, underground artists I loved. The moment where the one-dimensional becomes three-dimensional and you are reminded that these sounds that have given you a life of happiness, escape, and relief all began with flesh and bone. As Mary Jane cried tears of joy, I could only think that Jimmy would have too.

And the next day, Mary Jane flew home to Virginia with that red silk shirt with diamonds embroidered on the collar carefully packed away in her suitcase. Yes, Neil Diamond had literally given her the shirt off his back.

Why do these people mean so much to me? Because people inspire people, and over the years they have all become a part of my DNA. In some way, I have been shaped by each and every note I have heard them play. Memories have been painted in my mind with their voices as the frame. I can still vividly remember when my uncle Tom took me sailing when I was a little boy, and we spent the day listening to—you guessed it—"Sailing" by Christopher Cross. Had this not been such a formative memory, I might not have tackled a terrified Christopher Cross one day at the Austin, Texas, airport baggage claim, just to get a glimpse of the man in person. Or there was the time I approached Ace Frehley of KISS on a Hollywood street corner at night, just for a simple handshake, or nervously confessed my love to Bonnie Raitt as we sat on a dressing room floor at the Rock and Roll Hall of Fame. BECAUSE I STILL WALK THROUGH THIS LIFE LIKE A LITTLE BOY IN A MUSEUM, SURROUNDED BY THE EXHIBITS I'VE SPENT A LIFETIME STUDYING, AND WHEN I FINALLY COME FACE-TO-FACE WITH SOMETHING OR SOMEONE THAT HAS INSPIRED ME ALONG THE WAY, I AM THANKFUL. I AM GRATEFUL.

But it's one thing to meet a hero in passing. It's another thing when they become your friend.

On a drunken night out with my crew years ago in Los Angeles, I was walking toward the restroom of the seedy bar we were currently destroying and noticed the one and only Lemmy sitting in the corner, drinking alone in front of a video poker machine

(I won't say his last name or band affiliation, because if you don't know already, then I have to break up with you). I couldn't resist. This man was the living, breathing embodiment of rock and roll, and I had looked up to him ever since I first heard his gravelly voice roaring through my speakers. I walked up to him and said, "Excuse me, Lemmy? I just had to say thank you for all the years of inspiration you've given me." He looked up from under his black cowboy hat, and in a thick cloud of Marlboro smoke he growled, "Cheers." I was about to turn and walk away when he said, "Sorry 'bout your friend Kurt."

From that moment on, Lemmy was no longer a worldwide-worshipped god of rock and roll; he was a fellow human being. And through the years we became friends, sharing lurid tales of life on the road and a mutual love of Little Richard over thousands of

cigarettes and bottles of Jack Daniel's every time we met. I looked up to his honesty, truth, and strength, but also his vulnerability. Whether bellying up to the bar at the Rainbow Bar and Grill on the Sunset Strip (his home away from home, so much so that once while I was drinking with him there, the waitress came up and gave him his mail) or in his cluttered apartment down the street, I valued every minute in his presence. Because I looked up to him, not only as a musician, but as a friend.

News of his passing came as a shock to me. It was just days after his seventieth birthday and only a matter of weeks since his last show. I had thought he would outlive us all. He walked a hard road that most would never survive, and though that way of living took its toll on him later in life, he had the energy and spirit of a warrior. Lemmy would never surrender, until he finally had to give in and rest.

I went straight to a tattoo shop and branded my left wrist with an ace of spades and the words "SHAKE YOUR BLOOD," a lyric from a song we had written together years before. He was a true lover of rock and roll and lived life to the fullest, two things that we most certainly had in common.

At his memorial service a week or so later, I was asked to speak, and holding back tears, I shared a few stories of our time together with the little church full of his oldest friends. This was a bitter-sweet celebration of his life, for he had brought us all so much joy but was leaving us behind to continue life without his irreplaceable friendship.

Pulling the small black-and-white picture that Little Richard had signed for me years ago from my jacket pocket, I stood and read the words to an old gospel song that Little Richard once per-formed, "Precious Lord, Take My Hand."

Precious Lord, take my hand
Lead me on, let me stand
I am tired, I am weak, I am worn
Through the storm, through the night
Lead me on to the light
Take my hand, precious Lord
Lead me home

I turned and placed the picture on Lemmy's altar to thank him.

Forever grateful for the inspiration.

PART FIVE

LIVING

BEDTIME STORIES WITH JOAN JETT

"Hey, Harper . . . hey, Violet . . . what's goin' on?"

My two daughters sat in stunned silence as the one and only Queen of Rock and Roll, Joan Jett, stood before them at the foot of the couch. With her spiky black hair, weathered Converse Chucks, and tight jean jacket, she cast a long shadow over their cherubic faces like a warrior statue, her trademark gravelly voice bellowing above the sound of the afternoon cartoons in the background. "Guys! This is JOAN JETT!" I excitedly proclaimed, praying for some sort of response. I could see their little minds whirring, desperately trying to process this strange encounter, but they were rendered speechless. I had already warned Joan on the ride over to the house that this would happen, explaining that my girls were certainly familiar with her . . . they had just never met a superhero in real life.

A few months before, on a European tour, I had decided to take my daughters to the gigantic London department store Harrods on a rainy day off for a bit of rug-rat retail therapy. It was too cold for the park and too wet for a walk, so I figured I'd treat them to a tour of its legendary toy department, which dwarfed most American toy stores, in order to get out of the hotel for a bit and have some fun. Not as culturally rewarding as one of the city's many spectacular museums, I admit, but sometimes you just have to say "Fuck it" and give the people what they want. Especially when the people are under four feet tall. As fun as traveling the world with your family can be, keeping kids from going stir-crazy from one hotel room to the next becomes something of a mission over time, and you find yourself constantly researching activities days in advance so as not to fall into a vicious cycle of room service chicken fingers and subtitled cartoons. Even after a night of thrashing my body, drowned in blistering volume, I have always tried to fill these windows of opportunity with adventure, turning an otherwise exhausting tour into a whirlwind rock and roll family trip. Over the years, I have been blessed to show them the world, from the canals of Venice, Italy, to Sydney Harbour, from the glaciers of Iceland to the Eiffel Tower, and everything in between. Along the way, I have proudly watched my children go from car seats strapped into airplanes and bassinets next to the hotel bed, to waving down flight attendants for more ginger ale and ordering room service ice-cream sundaes by themselves at midnight. They are now seasoned travelers, and I love it because it means that we get to stay together.

Upon walking into the massive toy department, I decided to lay down a few fatherly rules. "Okay . . . you have one hour to find a toy, and it has to be small enough to fit in your suitcase. Ready . . . GO!" I set my watch, and the kids frantically shot off like two rabid *Supermarket Sweep* contestants, desperately challenged by the impossible task of choosing a toy that would meet my cruelly unreasonable requirements. One hour? Yeah, right! And . . . define "suitcase." Are we talking YOUR suitcase? MY suitcase? Or, perhaps, a NEW suitcase altogether that would comfortably transport an entire Victorian dollhouse back to California? Mission: Impossible. Nevertheless, it delighted me to watch them scatter, their little shoes pattering aisle to aisle, their heads spinning from the infinite options on display. Admittedly, I soon found myself trapped in the LEGO section, fawning over the giant selection they had to offer, trying to decide whether I should join in on the challenge or remain a conscientious objector. I have always had a weakness for LEGOs, I confess. Ever since I was a child, they have always been my favorite toy. With their intricate little pieces and the gratifying *snap* of two tiny blocks fitting perfectly together, I could spend hours upon hours building castles, cars, and other geometric structures, just for the simple reward of knowing that I had done it myself. I was borderline obsessed in my youth, so much so that part of my "seeing" music is seeing individual parts of songs as blocks of LEGOs, a playful form of synesthesia that still to this day helps me memorize arrangements and compositions.

As the deadline loomed, I gave the girls a five-minute warning in my best game-show-host voice. Predictably, both had yet to find a toy, and both were still darting back and forth across the show-room floor, searching for the perfect prize. How could they possibly choose? I gave them "the look" (head lowered with one raised eye-brow) and repeated myself: "Five. Minutes." At this point, they had narrowed the search down to the Barbie section, which was roughly the size of a large commercial airplane hangar. They circled, eye-ing their prey. This wasn't going to be easy. Hundreds of different Barbies lined the shelves, different styles, different themes, some with accessories, some with additional wardrobe . . . It was enough to make any kid's head explode. I watched as they picked up box after box, carefully examining each one, undoubtedly trying to get the most bang for their buck while pushing the boundaries of the required luggage capacity. The clock was ticking, and the tension rose heavy in the air, until . . .

"TIME'S UP!" I yelled like a Little League referee (if only I'd had a whistle). "But, DAAAAAAD!!!!" they both cried in frustration. "We can't decide what to get!" Laughing, I said, "Come on! Just pick one, any one, and let's head back to the hotel!" Just then, I looked down at the table next to me that was stacked with Barbies and grabbed the first one I could find. "Look! I got a Barbie!" I said as I waved it high in the air. "No fair! You can't get a Barbie!!" they shot back, and as I looked at the box, I noticed that I had unknowingly picked up an official Joan Jett Barbie, complete with red Converse Chucks, leather pants, a sleeveless black T-shirt, and a white Gibson Les Paul Junior guitar slung around her shoulder. *Holy shit*, I thought. *I'm definitely buying this!*

Within minutes we were all standing at the checkout counter comparing our Barbies (Rocker Joan and two super-tricked-out glam gals with accessories galore), anxious to race back to the hotel and play.

Later that night, as I sat at the desk in the living room of our suite, Violet and Harper came into the room and politely asked if they could play with my Barbie. "Of course!" I said with a smile, and I began to carefully open the colorful box, surgically removing the doll from its ridiculously complicated packaging (since when do toys require a degree in engineering to get them out of their fucking packages?). While the girls patiently watched me struggle with each tiny zip tie, I realized that they had no idea Joan Jett was an actual person. They thought that she was just another plastic figurine, one of hundreds that lined the shelves at their new favorite toy store. I stopped what I was doing, put down the doll, and explained that Joan was not only an actual human being but a most important one. A FEMINIST ICON WHO PROVED TO THE WORLD THAT WOMEN CAN ROCK EVEN HARDER THAN MEN. An innovator, an architect, a punk rock pioneer so powerful, she inspired generations of young women to pick up guitars and do the same. They seemed a bit confused, so I opened up my laptop, turned the volume to ten, and played them the "I Love Rock 'n Roll" video. They stood in amazement, transfixed by Joan's swagger and sneer, and were singing along word for word by the final chorus. I closed my computer and said, "See? She's real!" Then they quickly grabbed the doll and skipped back to their room, humming the classic tune along the way, and deep in my heart I could tell that they had just discovered their new superhero.

As the tour continued, we eventually made our way to New York City for a show at Madison Square Garden, one of my favorite venues in the world. The drive into the building always reminded me of that scene from Led Zeppelin's live concert film *The Song Remains the Same,* a movie that I practically studied as a teenager, hopelessly trying to dissect John Bonham's superhuman drumming. On our way to the city, our tour manager, Gus, asked if we wanted to invite any special guests to perform with us at the show. After all, it was Madison Square Garden, and we had to make it a special occasion. Names were thrown around the van, mostly friends that we had jammed with before, and then someone mentioned Joan Jett, who had been living in the city since the late seventies. Having never met her before, I asked if we knew how to contact her. Gus fired back with "Pat knows her!"

Pat Smear, our founding guitarist and reigning minister of cool, knew Joan from his days playing in the legendary band the Germs. L.A. born and bred, Pat was a punk rock kid in the midseventies and a huge fan of Joan's first band, the Runaways, an all-girl group reared on the sounds of Bowie and T-Rex. He had seen all of their shows and eventually became friends with Joan, running in a pack of Hollywood punks who unknowingly would change the course of music forever.

Roughly the same age as Joan, Pat was inspired by the Runaways, as they were all just teenagers at the time, so much that he and his best friend, Darby Crash, decided to start a band as well. And when it came time to make their first full-length studio album, *GI,* in 1979, they asked Joan Jett to produce. So there was a deep history there, not only in the annals of rock and roll, but personally.

A few phone calls were made, and we were told that Joan would be thrilled to make an appearance, so we quickly arranged for her to come down and run through her classic song "Bad Reputation" with us before the show. It was the perfect selection for our audience, as Joan was one of the most celebrated voices of our generation and would undoubtedly cap off the momentous evening with a bang. As we pulled into the venue in our motorcade of vehicles, just as Led Zeppelin had done thirty-eight years before, I bristled with anticipation, pinching myself once again at the opportunity to meet another hero, a badass woman who made her own rules.

As Joan walked through the dressing room door, I stood up in nervous excitement and rushed over to greet her. I was now face-to-face with the real Joan Jett. That black, spiky hair, those weathered Converse Chucks, and that tight jacket were no longer just part of an image on a TV screen, and that gravelly voice was no longer just a sound from an old speaker. She was a strong presence, still badass and punk rock as ever. And . . . my god, she smelled good.

We ran through the song a few times on practice instruments in our dressing rooms and placed it toward the end of the set list, knowing that it would surely be the highlight of the show. Joan was such a pleasure to be around, her killer sneer replaced with a smile that could have illuminated Madison Square Garden all on its own, and it warmed my heart to see her and Pat together after all these years. Without these two, who knows where we would be? I felt like I was an extra in a documentary I would surely pay money to see.

You cannot underestimate the power of Joan's presence, by the way. Before the show, I was standing in a long corridor full of people, catching up with old friends over cocktails, when Joan quietly emerged from our dressing room. As she slowly walked down the hallway alone like a postapocalyptic James Dean, I watched every last person hug the walls, men and women both, positively stunned in her wake. Inspiring a collective swoon that perhaps only Elvis could rival, she cut a swath through the crowd one step at a time. This was fucking rock and roll. Joan was indeed a superhero.

When I introduced her onstage that night, I saw that she seemed to have this effect on most everyone. The roar of the crowd as she walked into the spotlight was a thunderous welcome, the kind that only legends receive, and our performance was tight, fast, and spot-on. Afterward, we celebrated over a bottle of champagne, and Joan and I talked about collaborating someday. "We should write some songs together!" she said in her thick New York accent. I enthusiastically agreed, and we compared schedules right then and there, successfully finding a window of time when both of us were off the road to meet up and record. We set a date and hugged each other tightly, grateful for this chance encounter and looking forward to the next.

I couldn't wait to tell my daughters that their favorite superhero was not only coming to Los Angeles to write with me but also staying with us for the weekend! Their minds would be blown!

It's asking a lot of a child to fully comprehend breaking the fourth wall in life, when the fantasy of toys and videos on YouTube becomes reality. For chrissakes, Violet was only five years old and Harper was two. Nevertheless, I did my best to prepare them for Joan's arrival, hoping that it wouldn't send them into an existential tailspin. I mean, if SpongeBob SquarePants showed up at your front door, I'm sure you'd be a bit gobsmacked, too.

Judging by their reaction on the couch that day, our little pre-game pep talk hadn't really moved the needle.

"Okay, guys . . . remember that Barbie that I bought in London? She's coming to stay with us this weekend."

Crickets.

"So, when she gets here . . . don't freak out . . . she's real."

More crickets.

After settling in, Joan and I made our way to the Foo Fighters' studio, where we began working on a song idea she had kicking around called "Any Weather," an up-tempo number with one of her trademark melodies. It was instantly recognizable as Joan Jett, filled with attitude and heart. Watching her work, I could only imagine the incredible life she had lived, and I could sense her undying love of rock and roll, which was as contagious as it was inspiring, to say the least. After all these years, she still sang from the heart.

We can stay together
Through any weather
We can stay together
Through anything
If we love

That night, we returned home after a wonderfully productive day, and I began my usual ritual of getting my daughters ready for bed while Joan retreated to the guesthouse to change into her pajamas (just when I thought she couldn't be any more adorable, yes, she wore pajamas). I gave Harper her bath, got her into her PJs, read her a few stories, and put her in her crib without so much as a peep. One down, one to go. Violet was next. Bath, PJs, but before putting her to bed, I carried her down to the living room to say good night to Joan.

Standing before the couch where Joan was sitting comfortably in her own jammies, I said, "Hey, Joan, Violet wanted to say good night to you." Joan smiled and said, "Awwwwww, good night, Violet. I'll see you tomorrow!" Violet turned to me and whispered in my ear, "Dad, will you ask Joan if she'll read me bedtime stories tonight?" My heart stopped a moment as I looked in Violet's eyes, and I turned to Joan. "Hey . . . ummmm . . . she wants you to read her bedtime stories tonight . . ." I felt Violet's grip begin to tighten in suspense. Joan smiled and happily obliged. "Come on, Violet . . . let's go!"

As I watched the two walk hand in hand upstairs, I prayed that Violet would never forget this moment, that she'd look back on this night someday and know that some superheroes are indeed real. That maybe someday she would become her own type of innovator, an architect, a pioneer, inspiring generations of young women to pick up a guitar or do whatever she chooses to do to make her mark.

FOR, IN A WORLD FULL OF BARBIES, EVERY GIRL NEEDS A JOAN JETT.

THE DADDY-DAUGHTER DANCE

"Oh, by the way . . . the daddy-daughter dance is March sixth this year. Make sure you put it in your calendar."

My heart froze as my wife's voice echoed over the exaggerated delay of a long-distance call from Los Angeles to my hotel room in Cape Town, South Africa. *March sixth?* I thought to myself. *Oh god, please let that be a day off at home . . .*

I instantly knew that this was going to be a problem, but doing my best to conceal the sinking feeling in my chest, I causally told Jordyn that I'd make note of it, hung up the phone, and broke out in a nervous sweat, praying that this most important date (an event that I had promised I would never miss) fell within one of the short breaks in our never-ending world tour that year. Fearing the worst, I jumped across the room to my laptop and quickly opened my calendar to March 6.

It was a show day, all right . . . in Perth, Australia.

The daddy-daughter dance was a tradition at Violet's school that was practically mandatory for any father trying to raise a girl in the silicone valley (no, I'm not referring to software) of Los Angeles. An opportunity to strengthen the familial bond, share qual-

ity time, and show them that no matter what, a girl can always rely on her dear old dad. From kindergarten to sixth grade, it was an annual parade of middle-aged men doing their best to politely socialize with each other in their starched business suits while their little girls, dressed in miniature ball gowns with corsages carefully pinned, ate candy hand over fist from long tables that would make Willy Wonka blush. All to a Kidz Bop, Top 40 soundtrack being DJ'd by a Nickelodeon-esque dance instructor screaming instructions to the "cha-cha slide" at ear-shattering volume. Usually held in one of the dingy banquet rooms of the infamous Sportsmen's Lodge in Sherman Oaks (house of a thousand Bar Mitzvahs), it was the highlight of most every little girl's year. And a few fathers', as well.

Violet and I never failed to make an event of it. Though I have always had an aversion to formal wear (as I tend to look like a stoner in court to pay a misdemeanor marijuana fine), I would do my darnedest to clean up and look the part. Of course, Violet would also do her Disney best, usually wearing something princesslike in a tricky pair of tiny heels, brimming with excitement and filled with nerves at the terrifying prospect of such an awkward social experiment. Deep down I knew that these formative functions would surely be the foundation of many high school dances to come, so it was imperative that they go smoothly for my girl, otherwise she might be faced with an adolescence of proms resembling the bucket-of-blood scene from *Carrie*.

This year was different, though. For years, Harper, who is three years younger than Violet, would always stand crying at the door when Violet and I would head out to the dance, begging to be included, though she wasn't yet a student at the school. It broke my heart to see her wave goodbye, holding back the tears through her pacifier, unable to understand her ineligibility. I would always try to reassure her, "We'll all go together someday!" Nevertheless, the sight of her standing at the doorway with tears streaming down her face as she held her favorite blanket always hit me right where it hurts. And now that she was finally old enough and I had the chance to make good on my promise to take them both to the dance, something Harper had been looking forward to almost half of her life, I had a fucking show the same night—9,330 miles away.

I immediately called my manager of thirty years, John Silva, and said, "John, we have a problem. Like, a serious problem." I calmly explained the situation in my best measured tone while making it very clear that missing this dance was not an option. He apologetically replied, "I'm sorry, David, but the show's already sold out." DEFCON 1 kicked in as I imagined the horror of my two little girls being stood up at the dance by THEIR OWN FA-THER and I instantly went from zero to sixty, screaming, "Cancel it! Move it! Postpone it! Do whatever you have to do, but I cannot and will not miss this fucking dance!"

Realizing the magnitude of this potential disaster, we put our thinking caps on and started shuffling dates. I mean, if they could put a man on the moon, we could surely get me to the Sportsmen's Lodge on time in my pair of Levi's and dirty Clarks shoes, right? The tour, which was to begin in Christchurch, New Zealand, was a relatively short eight shows, all stadiums in the sweltering summer heat. It was to be our biggest trip Down Under yet, and tickets had disappeared quickly. We have always had a spicy love affair with our friends in New Zealand and Australia, making it a point at least once every album cycle to suffer the fifteen-hour flight and pay a visit. And it's always more than worth it. From the black pebble beaches of Piha, New Zealand, just outside of the cosmopolitan wonderland of Auckland, to the wineries surrounding the hills of Adelaide, Australia, we had spent a decade exploring this heavenly territory, making lifelong friends and rocking the fuck out of every venue we set foot in. So it pained me to even consider postponing, much less canceling, a show. Plus, disappointing fans is just not in my DNA. But, as much as I love a nice, cold Victoria Bitter beer and a meat pie at midnight, I do have priorities. After a bit of brainstorming/shuffling and a few phone calls, we came up with a plan:

The Perth show, which was already sold out, could potentially be moved from the sixth to the eighth, giving me just enough of a window of time to run offstage in Adelaide, board a chartered plane to Sydney, immediately jump on a Qantas flight back to L.A., land at LAX, sleep a few hours, take my girls to the dance, then leave straight from the Sportsmen's Lodge for the airport and fly back to Perth just in time to run onstage and kick their fucking asses.

CRAZY? PERHAPS. DOABLE? BARELY. MANDATORY? INDISPUTABLY.

Our scheme was set in motion, and the kind people of Perth thankfully rearranged their calendars so we could meet on March 8. Crisis averted. I could now rest easy knowing that I would be there for my girls, escorting in my best Levi's and Clarks shoes, reminding them that they can always rely on their father, even if it means forty hours of travel over two days and sixteen time zones. Fortunately, all of those years I spent packed in smelly, crowded vans for months on end, sleeping on floors and living off corn dogs, had prepared me for this exact moment. You do what you have to do to get to the gig. Always.

By the time we got to Adelaide, our intercontinental operation had been planned down to the minute with military precision. Leaving no room for error or delay, my tour manager, Gus, and I were prepared to jump from the stage like soldiers from a Black Hawk helicopter and race to a private plane awaiting us on a nearby tarmac, in which we would be flown to Sydney to connect for the arduous fifteen-hour flight home. Daunting, to say the least, but a ridiculous challenge that we both strangely looked forward to, laughing at the absurdity of it all. The show that night was a ripper, a twenty-four-song blitz that had the stadium going berserk as I closely watched the clock on the side of the stage, making sure that I gave the audience every last second of my time before I had to flee. And as the final notes of "Everlong" still hung in the air, Gus and I jumped into a car and sped off to the nearby regional airport, ready to circle the planet together.

As we boarded our first plane, I was greeted by the familiar smell of a hot bucket of KFC emanating throughout the cabin. This was no accident, mind you. The Foo Fighters have one very peculiar indulgence that we request every now and then for special occasions (and there are many special occasions): KFC and champagne. This tasty combination is something that we inadvertently discovered on a tour of Australia years before. One night, as we were driving to soundcheck, I saw a KFC out of the corner of my eye and said to Gus, "Hey, Goose, can you get a couple buckets of chicken for after the show?" I hadn't had Kentucky Fried Chicken in years, and I was overcome with the need for that secret blend of herbs and spices. He obliged, ordering enough food for an army to be waiting for us in our dressing room. I'll never forget walking offstage that night, soaking wet with a towel draped over me, the aroma of fried chicken wafting down the hall from our dressing room fifty yards away. I collapsed in a chair and tore into that bucket like a raccoon in a dumpster, devouring piece after piece, ravenous from the hundreds of calories I had just spent onstage. After a few pieces, I was parched, and the only liquid within reach was a bottle of champagne in a bucket of ice. I popped it, took a sip, took a bite of chicken, took another sip, took another bite of chicken, and screamed, "OH MY GOD, YOU GUYS, YOU HAVE TO TRY THIS!" Before long, every band member had a glass of champagne in one hand and a chicken leg in the other, marveling at this new discovery, convinced that we were the first to find this most perfect pairing. That night, it became an artery-clogging tradition, one that we still indulge in to this day. Laugh all you want. I could go into a detailed culinary lecture about the juxtaposition of taste and mouthfeel that comes with KFC and bubbly. But just take it from me, it's fucking delicious.

The short two-hour flight to Sydney was a breeze, giving us a few hours' layover before the long haul, just enough time to call home and tell the girls I was coming. I could feel their excitement over the phone, and now it would only be a matter of hours before I could see them again.

The anticipation and adrenaline made the next flight a never-ending affair, but my heart was full of fatherly pride as I imagined walking into the Sportsmen's Lodge with my two amazing daughters, one on each arm.

Upon arrival in L.A., I looked like I had been hit by a garbage truck but was immediately greeted by two screeching little girls as I walked through the front door, a feeling that supersedes even the most ferocious jet lag. Knowing that I only had a few precious hours with them, I staved off any physical exhaustion and "dad mode" kicked in. Full disclosure: I am what some people might consider a silly dad (*shocker*, I know); I often resemble one of those terribly annoying kids' television show hosts who make you want to put your head in an oven. I am not opposed or averse to embarrassing myself for even the slightest giggle from my little ones, from the moment they wake to bedtime stories at night. Example: I have always found that dancing like a fool to Earth, Wind and Fire while serving pancakes in the morning not only elicits the first

2015

URENCE →

EACH BALL

Coachie's Cafe →

★ Stern Point →

Jacobson Lighthouse

← LIGHTNING BEACH ✳

Wolke Surf Shop

smile of the day but gets them out the front door with a skip in their step, even if just to escape my insanity.

The rest of the day was spent drinking an ocean of coffee and trying to keep my eyelids from slamming shut while organizing the evening's festivities. Stretch limo? Check. Fake champagne? Check. Failed attempt at trying to look formal after an almost ten-thousand-mile commute? Double check. This was their big night, so the pageantry and preparation can only be described as Oscar worthy, replete with a glam squad that could very well double as a NASCAR pit crew. At this point, Violet was a seasoned veteran of the daddy-daughter dance routine, but I could see in Harper's eyes that this was indeed something very special. A moment she had been awaiting for so very long. And that was worth every mile I had traveled.

I was never one for school dances. To me, they were painfully awkward affairs that reinforced my crippling insecurities as a nerdy kid and never failed to remind me of the simple fact that I JUST CAN'T DANCE. The terrifying ritual of standing in a circle with friends trying to summon the funk as Rick James's "Super Freak" blasted over the PA has left me with irreparable trauma, deathly afraid of any dance floor outside of the privacy of my own kitchen. Not to mention that one homecoming dance on a boat where I was dumped halfway down the Potomac River with no life jacket. So a wallflower I became. Perhaps a bit ironic considering I devoted my life to rhythm. I've seen many drummers dance, though, and believe me, it ain't pretty.

Soon we were standing in line at the Sportsmen's Lodge with all of the other fathers and daughters, and my grueling fatigue began to kick in, waves of exhaustion that practically made my knees buckle; I was going down fast. *Snap out of it!* I told myself. *This is a night the girls will remember for the rest of their lives, and you only have two hours to share it with them before racing back to the air-port for another ten-thousand-mile trip.* All it took was one look at their wondrous expressions and my strength came right back. I WAS ONCE AGAIN FILLED WITH PRIDE KNOWING THAT, NO MATTER WHAT, THEY COULD DEPEND ON ME. I'VE GOT THIS.

As we entered the main room, we were met with the standard affair of balloons, tables neatly set with beautiful dishes, a grand buffet of plain pasta and chicken nuggets, and a dance floor full of screaming children. Our eyes lit up like Dorothy's as she entered the wonderful world of Oz, and we shared a group hug as we surveyed the scene. What to do first? Eat? Dance? Attack the cotton candy machine? Expecting Violet and Harper to be a bit nervous, I said, "How about we find a table and put our stuff down?" I turned to find an empty seat, and . . . they were gone, racing toward their friends to dance in little packs of squealing glee. I could only smile as I watched them share the joy with all of the other girls. My job here was done, and I was now left to socialize with a roomful of similarly abandoned fathers, biding their time with stiff-as-starch conversations that typically revolved around sports, something I know absolutely nothing about. If fatherhood has taught me any-thing, it's that I couldn't pick a Hall of Fame athlete out of a lineup if my life depended on it, though to be honest, I actually relish be-ing the one dude at the party who is always more interested in the Super Bowl halftime show than the game itself.

I have always felt like a bit of an alien, which obviously I learned to embrace over time. When diagnosed with a crooked spine at the age of seven, I had to begin wearing a small lift on my left shoe to slowly correct the problem. I remember feeling a sense of shame and embarrassment at first, as I wasn't allowed to wear the cool sneakers that all the other kids wore, but at some point that shame and embarrassment turned into a sort of empowerment. I was different from them, even if just because of the shoes that I wore, and I liked it. I didn't want to be like the other kids. As crooked as I was, I liked the feeling of being strange. Still do. So, here I was once again, doing my best to fit in, forever the kid with the weird sneakers.

I kept an eye on the time, knowing that there was little margin for error in my diabolical itinerary. Counting down the minutes until I had to say goodbye again (something I always dread), I decided to hit the buffet line for a little Caesar salad, knowing that the food on the flight was probably going to be a bit more my speed. I figured that I'd get to the airport lounge, have a meal and a few glasses of wine, then pass out in my seat and sleep the majority of the fifteen-hour trip. After all, I had been awake for what seemed like days at this point, and my body would surely surrender to exhaustion, leaving me in a deep hibernation until the wheels touched down in Sydney.

It was time. I scanned the room to find my little ones and held back tears as I saw them having the night of their lives, bouncing and screaming with their buddies, doing their best to nail the cha-cha slide. I pulled them to the side and, in my best *Courtship of Eddie's Father* tone, explained that it was time for me to go, expecting an explosion of tears and suffocating hugs. Instead, they chirped, "Okay! Bye, Dad! Have a good trip!" and without hesitation raced back to the dance floor, leaving me alone in my chair with a half-eaten Caesar salad beneath my dropped jaw. But I could only smile. MY PRIDE WAS NOW THAT OF A FATHER WATCHING HIS DAUGHTERS DISCOVERING INDEPENDENCE, NO LONGER CLINGING TO THEIR DOTING PARENT, BUT RATHER FINDING THEIR OWN WORLD OUTSIDE OF THE ONE WE HAD CREATED TOGETHER. The separation anxiety was all mine. I grabbed my jacket and headed to the airport, leaving them with their mother to close out this most important night.

As I sat in the airport lounge blasting through a bottle of Shiraz, I replayed the previous twenty-four hours in my head, picking out moments that will undoubtedly stay with me forever. The walk through my front door, the meticulous preparation, the sweaty palms, the pinning of tiny corsages to their elegant dresses, their faces in the dance floor lights, the mountains of butter noodles and steamed broccoli . . . now I only had to make it to the gate and this impossible task would be nothing but a memory. One that Violet and Harper would hopefully never forget.

Gus and I boarded the plane, and I poured my weary bones into the spacious seat, passing out in a perfect red-wine haze before we even left the ground. Mission fucking accomplished.

Turbulence. Not the kind that feels like a massage chair at the mall. No. The kind that feels like a 9.0 earthquake, throwing you in every direction like a feather in the wind (thank you, Robert Plant), simultaneously rattling your organs and scaring you to death all at the same time. *It'll pass,* I told myself. *I've got this.* After a good twenty minutes, I felt a sharp pain in my stomach that can only be described as someone taking a knife and carving their initials into my intestines like lovers do on park benches and old oak trees. This was not normal. This was not motion sickness. *This* was food poisoning. As the plane violently lurched back and forth, I realized that I was now trapped in this aluminum tube with thirteen hours to go, and every sudden movement made me want to, well, explode. I broke out in a cold sweat, staring at the seat belt light, praying for it to go off so that I could run to the bathroom and rid myself of these toxins, but the turbulence continued for what seemed like an eternity.

Food poisoning is a touring musician's worst nightmare. If you have a cold, you drink hot tea. If you have a flu, you take medicine. If you have food poisoning, you are absolutely 100 percent fucked. There is no way to keep your body from doing the thing that it's genetically designed to do: puke and shit the poison out of you. Only, I have a bigger problem. I am physically incapable of vomiting. I have maybe thrown up three times since the age of twelve: once at the age of fourteen while listening to David Bowie's "Space Oddity" outside of a keg party (nothing worse than heaving up still-cold Meister Brau), once in 1997 after a bad piece of street pizza in Hollywood (seemed like a good idea at the time), and once after seeing Soundgarden at the Los Angeles Forum in 2011 (it wasn't the music, I assure you). So any bout with nausea is usually a long process of trying to convince myself that I've got this. Basically, it's my hell.

The seat belt light finally went off, and I made it to the bathroom in seconds flat, locking the door and hovering over the sink as I tried to relax and let nature take its course. As the minutes went by, I became more and more aware that not only was this attempt to expel my inner demons entirely in vain, but I was probably raising the suspicions of every passenger and flight attendant in the cabin by "overstaying my welcome" in this tiny toilet. After a good college try, I limped back to my seat and broke out in chills. I looked at the clock . . . twelve hours to go.

The ensuing flight was a nightmare. Multiple trips to the loo, all failed attempts, and back to my seat for another round of spasmodic chills and fever. No sleep. No rest. Just an endless worst-case scenario that couldn't have happened at a more inappropriate time, considering that I had to go straight to the gig for soundcheck upon landing in Perth. This was a test, I thought. A test of will, dedication, and the age-old adage "You do what you have to do to get to the gig."

Now, at the time, Ebola was making headlines. The terrible disease was sending shock waves of fear around the globe, and international travel was full of precautionary measures that required all passengers to be screened in one way or another. As we neared Sydney, I was handed the usual customs and immigration cards to fill out, but now there was also a mandatory Ebola questionnaire that everyone had to sign. A simple yes-or-no form with a list of symptoms that were signs that you might be infected with Ebola. I read the list in horror. Nausea. Diarrhea. Fever. Chills . . . I was exhibiting each and every one of them. My mind fast-forwarded to being thrown in a room full of people with actual Ebola at the airport, where I would then contract the disease and ultimately die alone in the land Down Under. I sat up in my chair, put on my best game face, and tried to will my sickness away.

Drained of all energy, I stood up as we disembarked the plane and whispered to Gus, "Dude, I have food poisoning." His eyes widened, and we held our stare as the airplane door opened. We still had another five-hour flight to Perth. This was not over; it had only just begun. His phone came out, and just as he had always done, he began scrambling to find a way to remedy this most disastrous situation as we walked to baggage claim. Our master plan had been derailed, all bets were off, and it now became a rock and roll version of *The Amazing Race*. What had seemed like a ridiculous adventure at first was now a challenge of basic survival. All in the name of the father.

By the time we boarded our next flight, Gus had arranged for a doctor to meet me at the hotel in Perth. Fortunately, it seemed that the worst of it was over, and it was now just a matter of trying to keep down some tea and toast, hoping that it would provide even the slightest bit of the energy that I would need to pull off another two-and-a-half-hour screaming rock show. That felt like an impossible task, I thought, but there was no turning back now. The stage was set, gear was ready to go, and thousands of hard-core Foos fans were preparing for the night of their lives.

The doctor arrived at my room, and looking at his watch, he explained exactly what I had to do in the short period of time before the houselights went up. "Take this pill right now, I'll give you a liter of fluid, and I want you to lie down for one hour." I popped the anti-diarrheal pill into my mouth, I watched the bag of fluid empty through the IV into my vein (where does it go?), and my head hit the pillow like a ton of bricks. *I've got this,* I thought once again.

I was welcomed backstage by my fellow bandmates with a sense of amazement. They had been warned that I might be a bit under the weather, so there were discussions of altering the set list with emergency plans in the event I pulled a GG Allin and covered the stage in a puddle of filth. My usual pre-show routine of bouncing in place while laughing over cocktails with the guys was reduced to sitting on the couch with a half-eaten banana in my hand, trying to summon the power to belt out twenty-five songs in the summer heat. *This ain't gonna do it for me,* I thought. I looked over at the mini-fridge and noticed a Guinness tucked behind the Gatorade and coconut water. "Well, hello . . . ," I said as I cracked that bad boy, downed it, and hit the stage running. Hey, if it is good enough for nursing mothers in Ireland . . .

What could have been a career-defining train wreck of epic proportions turned out to be a triumphant night of deafening sing-alongs and joyous end-of-tour celebration. The thirty-six hours that preceded this performance ultimately fueled not only my body but my soul, reminding me of all the things I am thankful for in my life. My family. My friends. My music. I was cured by life and retreated back to the hotel after the show, no longer broken but stronger, with one more incredible Australian tour under my belt.

The next morning, I woke, ate a meal, and turned right back around toward the airport for the twenty-two-hour trip home. Mission fucking accomplished. I had this.

As I circled the planet one last time, I took stock of this wild gesture of love for my children, reflecting on my relationship with my own father and wondering if he would he have done the same for me. Would he have moved heaven and earth to be with me on such an important day? Doubtful, I thought. Perhaps I love so fiercely as a father because mine could not.

I firmly believe that your understanding or "version" of love is learned by example from day one, and it becomes your divining rod in life, for better or worse. A foundation for all meaningful relationships to stand upon. I surely have my mother to thank for mine. I LOVE MY CHILDREN AS I WAS LOVED AS A CHILD, AND I PRAY THAT THEY WILL DO THE SAME WHEN THEIR TIME COMES. SOME CYCLES ARE MEANT TO BE BROKEN. SOME ARE MEANT TO BE REINFORCED.

Years later, I was driving Harper to school and she asked, "Dad, what's the longest flight you've ever been on?" I smiled and said, "Well . . . remember that time I came home for one night to take you to your first daddy-daughter dance?" She nodded. "That was about twenty hours in the air," I said. She looked at me like I was crazy. "Twenty hours??? You didn't have to do that!!!"

We smiled at each other, and after a long pause, she turned to me and said, "Actually . . . yes you did."

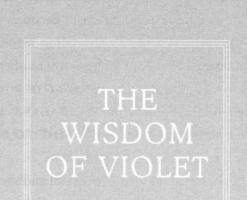

THE
WISDOM
OF VIOLET

"Are you sitting down?"

John Silva's voice, terminally hoarse from decades of screaming orders from his cluttered Hollywood office, couldn't have been more crystal clear in this moment. After all, these are four words that no one wants to hear at the start of any phone call, especially from the man in charge of their career. "Yes . . . why, what is it???" I quickly blurted back, anticipating some devastating news as shock waves of fear and anxiety began to pulse through every vein in my body.

"The Academy Awards called. They want you to perform 'Blackbird' by yourself on the show this year."

I stopped in my tracks and my mind instantly went to the moment when all eyes and cameras would turn to me, alone with only an acoustic guitar, live on television in front of thirty-four million people. Even though I was currently wearing sweatpants in my living room and the show was weeks away, the crippling stage fright immediately hit me. I couldn't imagine a more terrifying prospect. A quiet "Holy shit!" was all that I could muster in response.

I was no stranger to the song, of course. The arrangement had been burned into my memory since I was a child, and eventually I'd learned Paul McCartney's intricate fingerpicking guitar technique while singing along to his timeless melody. Though, it's one thing to gracefully execute such a difficult song from the comfort of your couch at home. It's another to pull it off while the ENTIRE FUCKING PLANET IS WATCHING (not to mention Jennifer Lawrence and Sylvester Stallone).

With the phone practically slipping from my already sweaty palm, I croaked back, "Wait . . . why?" It made little sense to me.

The band was on hiatus (or, as we call it, "I hate us") for the moment, and I surely wasn't nominated for an Oscar, so why on earth would they call me? "They would like you to be the musical accompaniment for the 'In Memoriam' segment," Silva answered. *Not the cheeriest opportunity,* I thought, but having never been one to easily back down from any challenge, I said, "Let me sleep on it, and I'll call you tomorrow."

I hung up the phone and sat in silence as my mind bounced back and forth from every reason to accept this unprecedented opportunity to every reason to politely decline. The idea of being invited to pay tribute to those the movie industry had lost that year was an immeasurable honor, but . . . I questioned whether I could pull it off. Deep down, I was scared. "Blackbird" is no walk in the park, after all, and playing the Oscars is very different from playing to an arena full of Foo fans.

Luckily, I had performed the song before, but to a very different audience.

That would be at Violet's third-grade Student Entertainment Day the year before.

No longer referred to as a talent show for fear of the lifelong psychological impact that any sort of competition might incur on our next generation of children (cue exaggerated eye roll), Student Entertainment Day was usually a cavalcade of children performing piano recitals or lip-syncing along to Katy Perry songs with intricately choreographed dance routines for a gymnasium full of helicopter parents in Lululemon active wear.

Upon its announcement that year, Violet had raced home and excitedly asked if she could perform "Sgt. Pepper's Lonely Hearts Club Band" with a group of her closest friends. Not an unusual request by her standards, as I had made it a point to brainwash her with the Beatles' entire catalog from an early age, hoping to lay some sort of substantive musical foundation before she moved on to the likes of Cardi B and Iggy Azalea. I could sense in her enthusiasm that she felt this was finally her chance to share her undeniable talent with others, something I had been anticipating since the first time I heard her beautiful voice singing along to Amy Winehouse songs from her little car seat on long drives through the San Fernando Valley. A few phone calls were made to chum the waters, but to our dismay the general consensus from her group of besties was "Sgt. who?"

Violet was devastated by the news that her friends would not join her for the show. As we sat on the couch together and I watched the tears roll down her cherubic little face, the protective father in me kicked in. "Hey, what if you and I perform 'Blackbird' together? I'll play guitar and you sing!" She looked up and wiped her face, and her expression instantly changed as she nodded excitedly with a relieved smile. I ran to fetch my guitar, sat down before her, and began to play the song. Without even a moment of rehearsal or lyric sheet to refer to, she came in on time, in tune, and we played it together perfectly, first try. It was beautiful. I would say that I was surprised, but I wasn't. I knew that she could do it. But . . . could I? We high-fived and made a plan: we would rehearse every morning before school and every night before bed until the gig, ensuring that we'd be more than ready by the time we hit the stage.

Saturday Night Live, Wembley Stadium, the White House— each of these monumental performances was a highlight of my career, but my anxiety about all of them paled in comparison to how nervous I was for this event. The fact that it was just a gymnasium full of parents sipping iced nonfat lattes while fingering their cell phones made no difference to me. I was there for Violet, and it was crucial that this performance go smoothly. So, every spare moment I had from that day forward was spent preparing to be her flawless musical accompaniment, trying to perfect that beautiful guitar arrangement until I had blisters on every finger. THIS IS THE MOST IMPORTANT GIG OF MY LIFE, I THOUGHT.

We arrived for soundcheck the morning of the show, smartly dressed and well rehearsed. I requested a stool to sit upon while I played. Violet requested a music stand for her lyrics in the unlikely event that she needed them. We tested the guitar and microphone levels and then nervously waited for the room to fill up. Having been at this school since kindergarten, Violet knew most everyone, and most everyone knew Violet, but her amazing singing voice had been a well-kept secret, and it was about to be unleashed upon this most unsuspecting audience.

After a few adorable performances, our names were called, and we climbed the stage to a smattering of supportive applause. We took our places and got settled, and in the horrifying pin-drop silence I looked at Violet and said, "Ready, Boo?" Petrified with nerves, she nodded, and I began the delicate guitar intro, reminding myself that this was, without question, the most important performance of my life, and hers as well. As usual, she came in perfectly on time, perfectly in tune, and I looked out at the audience's faces as their collective jaws began to drop. Her innocent, crystalline voice filled the PA, and the room was stunned. I could only smile, knowing that they were finally meeting the Violet that I knew so well. As the last chord rang out, we were met with thunderous applause and a standing ovation. We took a bow, high-fived, and left the stage to the next performer. "You nailed it, Boo!" I said, giving her a hug.

My heart was filled with pride. Not just pride in Violet's musical ability, but pride in her courage.

Courage is a defining factor in the life of any artist. The courage to bare your innermost feelings, to reveal your true voice, or to stand in front of an audience and lay it out there for the world to see. The emotional vulnerability that is often necessary to summon a great song can also work against you when sharing your song for the world to hear. This is the paralyzing conflict of any sensitive artist. A feeling I've experienced with every lyric I've sung to someone other than myself. *Will they like it? Am I good enough?* It is the courage to be yourself that bridges those opposing emotions, and when it does, magic can happen.

Still on the fence about the Academy Awards, I waited for Violet to get home from school to tell her the news. After much back-and-forth, I had finally made the decision to decline, convincing myself that I didn't *need* to play the Oscars and that I'd probably screw the whole thing up anyway, but I thought I'd share the absurdity of the offer with my daughter. As she came bounding through the door with her backpack full of books, I excitedly said, "Guess what I got asked to do today!" "What?" she asked. "To play 'Blackbird' on the Academy Awards!" She looked me dead in the eyes and said, "Well? You're gonna do it, right? I mean . . . you did it at the Student Entertainment Day!"

The gauntlet was thrown. In a flash, I realized that I *had* to play the Oscars. As her father, I now had to show her that I had the same courage that she had summoned in the gymnasium that day, no matter how terrified I was. OF COURSE, I HAD TO PROVE TO HER THAT I COULD DO THIS, BUT DEEP DOWN, I ALSO HAD TO PROVE IT TO MYSELF.

I called John Silva, accepted the offer, and began preparations for the biggest performance of my life.

It was decided that I would be playing the song with an accompanying orchestra as a montage of photographs was displayed above me. But there was a twist: the song was entirely rearranged to fit with the sequence of photos, and the orchestra was to be piped in from a studio down the street, leaving me alone on the stage with no conductor to refer to in the event that I needed help following the wildly fluctuating tempo. Therefore, I was to play to a "click track" through an ear monitor, which would serve as a sort of metronome reference. Easily done, right? Fun fact: I do not and have not ever played with in-ear monitors (earbud-like gadgets that are used to help you hear yourself and have become industry standard over the years). I still prefer old-school floor monitors, the kind that look like dirty old speakers and blow your hair back with every kick drum hit. So this posed a serious problem. With no conductor to watch or click track to follow, how was I going to pull this off?

I finally relented and reluctantly agreed to use an in-ear monitor for the first time in my life while thirty-four million people looked on. *What have I gotten myself into?* I thought. I decided that in the event of a train-wreck-level emergency, I would just find Jennifer Lawrence in the front row and serenade her the best that I could. Or Sylvester Stallone would do in a pinch.

Of all award ceremonies, the Academy Awards is some next-level shit. You practically have to get Pentagon-entry clearance just to plug in your instrument, and the process of getting "dressed" is something straight out of *Cinderella*. Not my vibe. I'm used to wandering into an event after a few cocktails wearing a jacket that's perfectly acceptable at both funerals and court appearances. But this was different. I was soon given an appointment at a boutique in Beverly Hills to be fitted for the perfect suit. I was a fish out of water, to say the least.

Standing before the racks of clothes, I had no idea where to begin. Anyone who knows me knows that I am the least fashionable person on earth and basically still dress the same way I did in ninth grade (Vans, jeans, band T-shirt), so I was assigned a stylist to assist me in finding and fitting the perfect suit. I was soon introduced to a stylish young blond woman with huge blue eyes named Kelsey. "We've actually met before," she said. I looked at her face, and though it did seem familiar, I couldn't place the memory. "I was the little girl in Nirvana's 'Heart-Shaped Box' video . . ." Silence. Then I instantly saw it in those big, blue eyes. It was her.

Mind. Fucking. Blown. THE UNIVERSE WAS HARD AT WORK.

That video, filmed twenty-three years before and directed by legendary photographer Anton Corbijn, was a surrealist collage of birth, death, anatomy, and chaos all set in a fantasy world with an elderly man hanging on a cross in a Jesus Christ pose. Standing in the middle of it all was a little girl in a white hood and robe, her giant eyes full of sadness, perhaps a representation of the innocence Nirvana had lost with our traumatizing rise to fame. And now, here we were, reunited in a fitting room, pinning the cuffs of the pants that I'd be wearing while playing a Beatles song to a room full of movie stars. Irony much?

As the date drew nearer, I grew more and more nervous. When I had dinner with Paul McCartney a week before the awards, I told him that I would be performing on the show. "What song will you be playing?" Paul asked me. "'Blackbird,'" I nervously replied. "Cheeky," he said, smiling and waving his finger at me. Funny, but it did further amp up the pressure, as now I had one more reason to not fuck this up.

I would constantly revisit the image of Violet onstage, proving to herself that she had the courage to bare her innermost feelings, reveal her true voice, and stand in front of an audience and lay it out there for the world to see. I was inspired by her bravery, therefore finding my own and dedicating this performance to her in my heart.

For anyone wishing to attend the Oscars, take it from me, it's much more enjoyable from your living room with some spinach dip and a nice cold Coors Light. I applaud anyone who devotes their life to the arts, but good god, it felt like the longest Catholic Mass you could possibly imagine, just without the crackers and thimbles of cabernet. And my performance was well toward the end of the program, leaving me to my rising anxiety. Hours passed. Days. Weeks. After what seemed like an eternity, I was finally called backstage to prepare.

As I walked out to my chair in the middle of the stage during a commercial break, I looked down at the front row, where Jennifer Lawrence and Sylvester Stallone had been sitting all night, searching for their faces to rescue me in the event that I choked up and my performance derailed into disaster. They were nowhere to be found, replaced by seat fillers who all stared at me with confused expressions, clearly expecting Lady Gaga. "One minute!" a director shouted over the PA. I pushed in my tiny ear monitor, adjusted the microphone, took a deep breath, and closed my eyes.

I saw Violet. I saw her first steps as a baby. I saw her first day of school, waving goodbye to me in the distance. I saw her pedaling away on a bicycle for the first time, no longer needing the assistance of her doting father. And I saw her onstage, singing "Blackbird" in the school gymnasium. I FELT HER COURAGE AND FOUND MY OWN.

Too bad Jennifer and Sly missed it.

CONCLUSION

ANOTHER STEP IN THE CROSSWALK

"You okay, buddy?"

Slumped over in my chair, I gave a silent, reassuring nod to Chris as I hid my face in a dirty backstage towel and wept, my muffled cries echoing in the awkward silence of our dressing room as the other guys quietly opened their wardrobe cases and changed their clothes behind me, still sweating from the three-hour show we had just played. After twenty years of being a band, this was the first time Pat, Nate, Taylor, Chris, and Rami had ever seen me, their fearless leader, completely break down in front of them. But I couldn't hold it all in any longer. I had to let go. In a moment of catharsis, it was as if every emotion that I had suppressed in the last forty years came to the surface and finally breached the levee inside of me, spilling onto the concrete floor below.

It wasn't that I was unable to walk and yet had continued on an exhausting tour of sixty-five shows where I had to be lifted onto a chair each night to perform, only to be carted away afterward like a broken theater prop. It wasn't that I still felt the searing pain from the sharp titanium screws drilled deep into my bones that will forever remain as a humbling reminder of my vulnerability and fragility. And it wasn't that I was filled with the devastating longing for my family that breaks my heart when we are apart for weeks on end, preying on my fear of absence and the separation anxiety left behind by my father.

No, this was something else.

It was the fact that I had just finished playing a sold-out show at Chicago's Wrigley Field to forty thousand people, directly across the street from the Cubby Bear, that tiny club where I saw my first concert at the age of thirteen and was inspired to devote my life to rock and roll.

I had played stadiums twice this size before, conducting a sea of fans in chorus after chorus, all of us joining together in rapturous harmony for hours, but it wasn't the sheer capacity of the room that brought me to tears on this night. It was the fact that Wrigley Field was just a crosswalk away from that dimly lit corner bar once filled with bodies writhing and dancing to the deafening shriek of feedback and crashing drums that served as my dawn. That summer night in 1982 when my cousin Tracey took me to see Naked Raygun was my baptism; I was bathed in the distorted glory of the music. From that day forward, I was changed, empowered by the revelation that I felt as my skinny little chest was crushed against the tiny stage and I came face-to-face with the raw power of rock and roll. I had finally found my niche, my tribe, my calling. But most important, I had found myself.

This was my great awakening, and dreams were no longer dreams; they became my divining rod. I was an idealistic misfit, empowered by the audacity of faith and a reckless determination to do it my way. Punk rock became my professor in a school with no rules, only teaching the lesson that you need no lessons and that every person has a voice to be heard, no matter the sound. I have built a life on this notion and blindly followed it with undying conviction.

It was that night that I had stepped out onto that crosswalk, and there was no turning back.

As the band quietly filed out of the dressing room, I was left alone in my chair to reflect and slowly put the jagged pieces of this lifelong puzzle back together. I thought of the long drives that my mother and I would take in our old 1976 Ford Maverick sedan, singing along to AM radio, where I first heard the sound of two voices in harmony forming a chord. This was the spark that ignited my fascination with music. I thought of the glorious instrumental fury of Edgar Winter's "Frankenstein," my first record, purchased at the drugstore and played on the record player that my mother brought home from school until its old needle wore out. I thought of the Silvertone guitar with the amp built into the case that I played every day after school, strumming along to my Beatles song-book, learning the beauty of composition and arrangement. And I thought of the old pillows that I substituted for drums on my bedroom floor, thrashing away to my favorite punk rock records until my hands were bloody.

Each tear another memory. Each memory another step in the crosswalk.

Maybe my séance had worked after all. It had been thirty years since I begged the universe for this blessing as I knelt before the flickering candlelight of the altar that I'd constructed in my car-port. Maybe this was all just a matter of manifesting desire, believing that anything is possible if you devote yourself to it entirely. Maybe it was the audacity of faith in oneself. Maybe I *had* sold my soul. These things could all be true, but I knew that if it weren't for the epiphany that I had that night at the Cubby Bear, I never would have dared to try.

I surely never would have taken the chance and made that phone call to audition for my favorite local band, Scream, setting off a chain of events that would change my life forever. Had I never seen that flyer on the bulletin board at my local music shop, I undoubtedly would have followed an entirely different path, but I saw a door open before me, and rather than stay within the comfort of my tiny bedroom, I decided to dive through it, leaving a life of stability and security behind. Though still bound to my youth, I was ready to be free. I was ready to bet everything on this burning passion that raged inside of me, and I made a commitment to honor it. When I was seventeen years old, music had become my counselor when I needed guidance, my friend when I felt alone, my father when I needed love, my preacher when I needed hope, and my partner when I needed to belong. That night when I saw the B-52s dance their mess around on *Saturday Night Live* in a quirky, hyperactive blur, I connected to something and knew that I would never live a life of conventionality. I was not destined to fade into the sleepy suburban streets of Springfield, Virginia, just another trench coat at the bus stop. I was born to let my freak flag fly and celebrate all of life's beautiful eccentricities. I had to break away from the norm.

Another memory, another step in the crosswalk.

With my mother's blessing, I was let go. Through her limitless empathy and understanding, she recognized my purpose and granted me the freedom to wander, no matter how far. Life soon became a lesson in survival, and home was a hard floor, but I was LIVING, and music was my food when there was none to eat. With my feet up on the dashboard, I watched the world fly by through a dirty windshield and learned to surrender to the unpredictability of a life without design, to rely on a road map with no destination, letting it take me wherever it might lead, never knowing what was around the next corner but faithfully relying on the music to keep me alive in the event that everything fell apart and I had to start over.

And start over I did.

It seemed like only yesterday that I'd spent those long nights on that dirty couch in Olympia, Washington, tucked away in my sleeping bag thousands of miles from home, waiting on my next dream. I was a stranger in a stranger's house yet again, but the ringing in my ears from the sound we made together in that little barn outside of town lulled me to sleep each night and kept my fire raging. My faithful divining rod had led me to yet another well, one so deep that it eventually overflowed and drowned us all. I was lost without a lifeboat.

I could have sunk. I could have given up. I could have gone home. But surrender was never in my DNA.

As I heard the room next door begin to fill with the usual parade of after-show guests, I gathered myself and prepared to join them. I could hear their voices, and I recognized them all. These were the voices of the people who had carried me through these years. An extended family that has become my new tribe.

I entered the room and saw Gus Brandt, handing out drinks and passes, always doing his best to make sure that everyone felt welcome in our chaotic little world. From broken guitars to broken limbs, Gus had taken care of me for decades, part therapist, part big brother, part bodyguard. He had become my beacon when I felt lost in a sea of strangers, my shelter when I needed protection, and I could always confide to him my innermost turmoil. Though not a musician, his love of music was equal to, if not more intense than, my own, and without his shoulder to rest upon, I would never make it to the next song, the next city, the next stage. He is always there, and I am grateful for his protection.

I saw Rami Jaffee, my faithful confidant, gliding around the room with the grace and nonchalance of a gypsy maître d', spreading his vibe as the true "good times" ambassador of the Foo Fighters. Though he was tucked away in the corner of the stage every night, his addition to the band over the years had proved invaluable, and he had introduced an element of musicality that had taken us to another level album after album. But beyond his proficiency as a musician, his friendship had become a joy every day, a welcome break in the *Groundhog Day* monotony of life on the road. And each night after the curtains are closed and the audience has wandered home, Rami and I will climb aboard our shared tour bus and drink, smoke, and dance as we race down the highway to our next destination. Though he joined the band a decade after its inception, deep down he was one of us from the beginning, and I am grateful for his comfort.

There was Chris Shiflett, the man who saved our band in our most desperate time of need when we were without a guitarist and required dire musical rescue. Though our paths had coincidentally crossed at a Scream gig in Santa Barbara ten years before his fateful audition (the only time we ever attempted such a thing), we had lived parallel lives up until that point, playing in punk rock bands with friends and living out of vans on pennies, with the music and adventure being the only real rewards. Before he had even played a note, I knew that he would fit in perfectly because he would appreciate every moment of being in this band, and I am grateful for his gratefulness.

Tearing through the room like an F5 tornado of hyperactive joy was Taylor Hawkins, my brother from another mother, my best friend, a man for whom I would take a bullet. Upon first meeting, our bond was immediate, and we grew closer with every day, every song, every note that we ever played together. I am not afraid to say that our chance meeting was a kind of love at first sight, igniting a musical "twin flame" that still burns to this day. Together, we have become an unstoppable duo, onstage and off, in pursuit of any and all adventure we can find. We are absolutely meant to be, and I am grateful that we found each other in this lifetime.

There was Nate Mendel, my voice of reason, my barometer, the one who I could always turn to when I needed grounding. If it weren't for that chance meeting at my Thanksgiving dinner in 1994, huddled around a Ouija board to contact the spirits of my haunted house in Seattle, the world would have never known the Foo Fighters of today. We had built this thing together from the ground up, cleared countless obstacles, and somehow remained relatively intact. Though I rarely communicate it, his role in my life is indispensable, and I don't know what I would do without him. I am grateful for his dedication and loyalty.

Then there was Pat Smear. The man who once was my punk rock hero and who became not only a bandmate, twice, but a trusted anchor in my life. From the minute he strolled into Nirvana's rehearsal space in 1993 and gave the band another year of life, Pat was always there to walk through the fire with me, no matter the highs or lows. He was always present for my life's greatest challenges, and with his wisdom and wit, he gave me reassurance that I could make it through anything. That WE could make it through anything. I hoped that we would be shoulder to shoulder from the day we met, and I have stood happily in his shadow ever since. Every night onstage when I look to my left and see the thick plumes of smoke wafting from his smile, I feel safe, eternally grateful for his loving and sagacious spirit.

As a band, we had each become a whirring wheel in a thunderous clock, only ticking because the spinning teeth of one gear met with those of another, locking us into synchronized movement.

Without this, our pendulum would stop. The revolving door that had once plagued our early years had now been locked, and we had become a forever thing. Once you're in, you're in for life. The stability and security that we had all longed for as children of divorce and teenage rebellion were now found in a barrage of distorted guitars and laser-lit stages. We had become a family.

Holding court in the far corner of the room with a glass of champagne in her delicate hand was my beautiful wife, Jordyn, the mother of my children, the queen of my world, the weight in my scale that keeps the arm from tipping. Our paths had crossed at a time when I thought I was doomed to live forever in the past, but through her strength and clarity, she showed me a future. Together, we created my life's greatest achievement, my family. And, as our family grew, my appreciation for life did as well. With each child born, I was born again, and with each step that they took, I retraced my own. Violet, Harper, and Ophelia gave me life in return, and words cannot express my gratitude to them. Fatherhood eclipsed any dream, any wish, any song I had ever written, and as the years went by I discovered the true meaning of love. I no longer just live for myself; I live for them.

But it was the voices that could not be heard that were perhaps the loudest in the room.

Jimmy should have been here, I thought. He was the first person I played my Naked Raygun record for in 1982 upon returning home from my trip to Chicago, and the moment we dropped the needle on that primitive slab of vinyl, we embarked on a new musical journey together as allies in the unorthodox world of punk rock. We were two misfits in a sea of conformity who created our own world, our own language, our own universe, through our obsession with music. No matter how far out I was, he always understood me and embraced my weirdness, just as I embraced his. I looked up to him as the older brother I never had, and so much of who I am came from who he was. We were inseparable, sharing everything together our entire lives, and it broke my heart that I couldn't share this moment with him. But deep down I knew he would have appreciated this victory, because it belonged to both of us.

"This will never last," my father had once told me, and it very well may have been this challenge that drove me to ensure that it did. We had struggled our entire lives to connect, but even in his absence I was shaped by his presence, for better or worse. I had let go of any resentment toward him long ago and had forgiven him for his shortcomings as a parent, ultimately lightening the burden of our relationship, leaving us to become good friends. As his child, I had inherited more than just basic physical attributes from him: we had the same hands, the same knees, the same arms. I have to believe that my ability to decipher sound and play music by ear was handed down from his blessed genetic code, and it was he whom I had to thank for this most precious gift. Something that he surely recognized as I became a man.

I know that he would have been proud, and I wished that he were alive to close this circle beside me.

And Kurt.

If only he could have seen the joy that his music brought to the world, maybe he could have found his own. My life was forever changed by Kurt, something I never had the chance to say while he was still with us, and not thanking him for that is a regret I will have to live with until we are somehow reunited. Not a day goes by when I don't think of our time together, and when we meet in my dreams there's always a feeling of happiness and calm, almost as if he's just been hiding, waiting to return.

Though they're no longer with us, I still carry these people in my heart everywhere I go, just as they once carried me, and it is their faces that I see every night just before the houselights go out and I am hit with the roar of applause. It belongs to them as much as it does to me. Had they just hung on a little longer, I thought, maybe they would have joined in this celebration, another reunion of lifelong friends bound by years of deep connection.

But standing in the middle of it all was the irrefutable matriarch of this extended family, the person who every one of those forty thousand screaming fans had just sung "Happy Birthday" to earlier that night: my mother. As she stood on the stage beside me while the entire stadium rang out in thundering chorus, I was overcome with emotion, knowing that this woman who had worked tirelessly to raise two children on her own—struggling to make ends meet, working multiple jobs, living paycheck to paycheck—and devoted her entire life to the benefit of others as a public school teacher was finally getting the appreciation she deserved. It goes without saying that none of us would have been there if it weren't for her. She had given me life not once but twice, by allowing me the freedom to become who I wanted to be, ultimately releasing me to my own destiny. Through her faith in me, she gave me the courage and the confidence to have faith in myself. Through her passion and conviction, she taught me to live with passion and conviction of my own. And through her unconditional love for me, she showed me how to love others unconditionally. She could have given up. She could have gone home. But surrender was never in her DNA either.

She was forever my hero and greatest inspiration; I owed all of this to her.

That crosswalk had taken a lifetime to travel, but I was grateful for every step, still that same little boy with a guitar and a dream. Because I still forget that I've aged. My head and my heart still seem to play this cruel trick on me, deceiving me with the illusion of youth as I greet the world every day through the idealistic, mischievous eyes of a rebellious child who constantly seeks adventure and magic. I still find happiness and appreciation in the most basic, simple things. And as I collect more little lines and scars, I still wear them with a certain pride, as they almost serve as a trail of bread crumbs, strewn across a path that someday I will rely upon to find my way back to where I started.

My tears had now dried, and I carefully entered the room on my two battered crutches to a giant communal embrace. The circle was now complete, and we had all made it to the other side of the crosswalk together, everyone grateful for life, music, and the people we love.

AND SURVIVAL.

ACKNOWLEDGMENTS

When the world closed its doors in March 2020, I was faced with my life's greatest fear:

Nothing to do.

As a restless, creative spirit, the thought of sitting on a couch watching bad soap operas while waiting for the stadiums to reopen sent me into an existential tailspin. Who was I without my music? What was my purpose in life without an instrument in my hands? Did life have a greater meaning outside of preparing spaghetti and meatballs twice a week for the world's most captious food critics, my children? I had to think of something fast, not just to bide my time, but to take advantage of this break from my never-ending, exhausting schedule.

So I decided to write a book.

Having never had the time (or courage) to attempt such a gargantuan undertaking, I wandered into the process with the attitude that I've taken with most things in my life: "You fake it till you make it." After all, I am the child of two brilliant writers. How hard could it be? *I can do this all by myself!* I thought.

Boy, was I wrong.

Without the amazing people at Dey Street/HarperCollins, this almost-four-hundred-page beast never would have made it into your hands. Who on earth would trust a high school dropout turned punk rock drummer to write a book about corn dogs and Motörhead? I'll tell you who. Publisher Liate Stehlik, who allowed me the honor of telling my story (or at least a tenth of it) to the world. Thank you. Someday I'll have to tell you the rest. Jeanne Reina for designing the cover and making my hangover look so regal. (Next time catch me before the party.) Ben Steinberg for being in my corner between rounds, along with Heidi Richter, Kendra Newton, Christine Edwards, Renata De Oliveira, Angela Boutin, Rachel Meyers, and Pam Barricklow. Perfect grammar courtesy of Peter Kispert.

But if there is one person who made this experience a joy, it is the most amazing Carrie Thornton. From the moment we met, I knew she was the person to guide me through this process, and she did, every step of the way. Our mutual love of music, Virginia, and ridiculous eighties goth culture was a match made in heaven, and I could not have asked for a more perfect chaperone to walk me through the best and worst days of my life. I could share this with only you, and I am forever indebted. We made a great team, but we also made great friends, and once that happens it's no longer work, it's pleasure. Thank you, Carrie. For your patience, your wisdom, and your care. You're stuck with me now. (Insert standing ovation here.)

Because once you're in, you're in. My manager, John Silva, can attest to this. After thirty-one years together, I cannot imagine life without his ravaged vocal cords screaming through my phone receiver every morning. I wouldn't have it any other way. John Cutcliffe (who I have never heard scream) has also been there from day one, and I feel blessed to have shared the last three decades of adventure with his ultimate badass cool. But without the wicked genius of Kristen Welsh, the loving introspection of Gaby Skolnek, and the lifelong devotion of Michael Meisel, I would surely not be here today. The entire SAM team should be knighted. Go tell the queen.

Steve Martin (not the funny one) should be thanked for his twenty-six years of service in the publicity room of our Death Star, and there is no one more qualified in this galaxy. Look in the front pocket of your airplane seat. If there's a band feature in the complimentary magazine, it's probably his doing.

Eve Atterman at WME, thank you for leading me into this new territory. I'm so happy with the result.

I always credit our band's success to starting our own label, Roswell Records, twenty-six years ago and doing everything our way. But if there is one person to credit for that lifesaving decision, it's my lawyer of twenty-seven years, Jill Berliner. She built this city on rock and roll.

Without all of the musicians and bands I had the pleasure to play with over the years, I never would have become the musician that I am today. From my early punk rock bands Freak Baby, Mission Impossible, and Dain Bramage, to discovering the world with my brothers in Scream, to turning the world of music on its head with Nirvana, each and every one of these people shaped my playing and tuned my ear. Without them, I wouldn't have had the wherewithal to jam with such musical titans as Queens of the Stone Age and Them Crooked Vultures, two bands that restored my love of music, for whom I am forever grateful. To every band I've loved before . . .

But if it weren't for my faithful Foo Fighters, none of this would matter. You have made music more than just music, you have made it my life. And what a life we've made together! Thank you, fellas.

And to the brave men who captured all of this on tape, Barrett Jones, Butch Vig, Gil Norton, Nick Raskulinecz, Adam Kasper, and Greg Kurstin, there would be no soundtrack to accompany this book without you. You have given us all a gift by sharing your brilliance, encouragement, and creative input when I needed a friendly boost over the wall. Thanks for the lift!

Over the years I have found inspiration in the strangest places, but having been blessed with so many brilliant friends, all I have to do is turn to them to spark a fire within me. Preston Hall for building my Virginia basement studio, Jim Rota and John Ramsay for being my partners in the world of TV and film, the entire crew of Studio 606, and our tireless roadies who devote their lives to making sure the rock rocks. Not to mention Russell Warby, Anton Brooks, Jeff Goldberg, Virginia Rand, Bryan Brown, Paola Kudacki, the Varlays, Katherine Dore, Joe Zymblosky, Magda Wozinska, Ian Mackaye, Judy McGrath, Larry Hinkle, everyone at Sony/RCA, my extended family from DC to the San Fernando Valley . . . the list is so long, we could be here for another four hundred pages.

For Jimmy. I miss you, man.

Without my beautiful family, I would not have made it past go. Jordyn, Violet, Harper, Ophelia, you remind me each day that I am not a "rock star," I am just a father to this most amazing family, and there is nothing on earth that I love more. You inspire me.

And, yes, there is a yin to my musical yang, and her name is Lisa Grohl. If it weren't for my sister's record collection (Neil Young, Bowie, Tears for Fears, Squeeze, etc.), I may have followed a life of only death metal and corpse paint. She should be thanked for saving you all from that happening.

Oh, and . . . hey, Mom.

Thanks. For everything.

- ANYONE SEEN SKEETER?
  - STRANDED.
- BUT NOT FIRST TIME....
- BACK TO OLD TOURS — THEN PRESENT.
  - SUBSTITUTES
    - CONTRACT (THEN SUED)
  - L.A.
  - MUDWRESTLERS / HOUSE
    - MOTORCYCLE DREAMS.
    - PHONE CALL.
    - MOM ADVICE.
    - FLY TO SEATTLE.... ↓

SANDI —

Springfield / Childhood —
New School / New People —
Love At First Sight —
Going Steady / Heartbreak —
(! DREAM)
Reunion / Hometown Gig —
Show / Same As Dream

- HARPER "I WANNA LEARN DRUMS"
  - FIRST LESSON
  - ONE STEP DOWN ⟩ (LENNY)
  - MY FIRST LESSON
- BACK TO HARPER / SITTING IMAGE
  - VIOLET / EAR
  - PERFORMANCE / GENERATION
    - MOM (DNA)

END QUOTE

"WE WERE SURROUNDED"
↓
TREES NIGHTCLUB / DALLAS
↓
SMALL VENUES
↓
GUITARS
↓
BUILDING / AUDIENCE SIZE
(TEEN SPIRIT)
MTV
SHOW / RIOT / FEAR
HOME - GOLD RECORD

END QUOTE
"SURROUNDED"

"HOW OLD ARE YOU?"
DOCTORS / CHEST PAIN...
LIFE PICKING UP SPEED
2009 — 40th
VULTURES / FOOS — QUEENS SIDE PROJECT

[COFFEE] — (HARPER)
4th OF JULY D.C.

"PHONE CALL"
PETTY — HISTORY
WILDFLOWERS / SNL
IN STUDIO RECORDING FOOS
POST NIRVANA?
↓
RECORDING ALONE — BARNETT HOME
↓
ROBERT LANG SESSION
↓
DOWN TO LA REHEARSAL
JAMMING - HEARTBREAKERS
(SHOW)
JOIN T.P.?
CROSSROADS
FOOS · BEGIN

"DO YOU MIND IF AC/DC COMES..."
AC/DC HISTORY
"LET THERE BE ROCK" — NONE INSPIRED
DUH!
PAUL / DINNER / ARIES HALL
NEW ORLEANS — SECOND LINE
GETAWAYS.
AC/DC - SPAIN - FOOS
DINNER

HAPPY.

"HAVING A GIRL"
FATHERHOOD / BRIDGE SCHOOL
NEIL HOUSE / REVELATION
CRASH COURSE... (FACULTY)
BIRTH - BEATLES
(GUITARS)
LOVE / VIOLET
NEW LIFE / OLD LIFE
#2 HARPER
TRAVEL — LIFE ON ROAD
PAUL - PIANO
FIFI — #3
HOME — FAMILY — DAD